C000186675

A Brilliant Foundation for Life

A Portrait of Wells Cathedral School

A BRILLIANT FOUNDATION FOR LIFE

A Portrait of Wells Cathedral School

PATRON: HRH THE PRINCE OF WALES

EDITED BY VAL HORSLER AND DIANA DAVIES

THIRD MILLENNIUM
PUBLISHING, LONDON

HRH The Prince of Wales, Patron, hosting an event for Wells Cathedral School at Highgrove. (See page 71)

© Authors, Wells Cathedral School, and Third Millennium Publishing Limited

First published in 2008 by
Third Millennium Publishing Limited, a subsidiary of Third Millennium Information Limited.

2–5 Benjamin Street
London
United Kingdom
EC1M 5QL
www.tmiltd.com

ISBN 978 1 903942 72 7

All rights reserved. No part of this publication may be reproduced or transmitted in any form or by any means, electronic or mechanical, including photocopying, recording, or any storage or retrieval system, without permission in writing from the publisher.

British Library Cataloguing in Publication Data
A CIP catalogue record for this book is available from the British Library.

Edited by Val Horsler and Diana Davies
Designed by Simon Borrough
Production by Bonnie Murray

Reprographics by Studio Fasoli, Italy
Printed by 1010 Printing International Ltd

Acknowledgements and picture acknowledgements

The editors would first like to offer heartfelt thanks for all their unstinting effort and support to the members of the editorial board, Tony Bretherton, Charles Cain, Elizabeth Cairncross, and Alwyn Gillen. Many other staff, former staff, governors, alumni, and pupils were hugely helpful and supportive; their names appear in the text as contributors or interviewees. Grateful thanks go to Sylvie Barham, Katy Chantrey, Christine Edwards, Molly Porter, Sarah Tew, and Jean Windridge for their help and patience; and particular thanks to Anastasia Page for giving so much of her time, professionalism, and support in the choice and provision of the images.

The archive office has benefited from a great deal of material sent in for the book. Every effort has been made to credit copyright holders; if we have unwittingly omitted this information we will be happy to make corrections in a future edition. Thanks to Jon Cannon for permission to use material from his book *Cathedral. The great English cathedrals and the world that made them* (Constable & Robinson, 2007) and to Marion Meek, whose book *The Wells Liberty and Bishop's Palace* (with drawings by Anna Cowern) was invaluable on the buildings. Grateful thanks also to the staff at Third Millennium – Neil Burkey, Christopher Fagg, Michael Jackson, Susan Pugsley, and Bonnie Murray – as well as to Simon Borrough, who provided an elegant design and unstinting commitment, and Julian Andrews and Will Pryce for their splendid photographs.

The Wells Cathedral archivist, Anne Crawford, kindly arranged for photographs to be taken of material held by the cathedral: the documents on pp 16 and 22 are © the chapter of Wells Cathedral; photographer, Michael Blandford. The image on p 7/8 is © Commission Air 2007; p 14 © James Hughes/Alamy; p 27 © Mary Evans Picture Library/Alamy; the drawing by Hablot Browne, engraved by B Winkles, on p 28 (right) is © ZEVART Collection/Alamy. The photograph of Linzee Colchester on p 44 was taken by Geoffrey Hall and is © A Parslow. The school photograph which forms the back endpaper is © H Tempest Ltd. Photographs © Julian Andrews appear on the front and back covers and on pp 4 (middle), 8, 10, 17 (middle), 20, 22 (middle left), 25 (top right), 26, 31, 50, 66, 67 (top), 74 (top right), 75, 78, 80, 81, 97, 100, 105, 108, 112 (top), 116 (middle), 121, 126 (middle), 129, 132 (right), 134, 140, 148 (middle), 150, 151 (bottom), 158 (middle), 161, 166, 168 (top), 182. Photographs taken by Will Pryce © Wells Cathedral School appear on pp 2, 4 (left and right), 11, 29 (bottom right), 32/3, 37, 39, 56, 63, 64, 68, 76 (top), 101, 114, 128, 130, 133 (top), 147, 151 (top), 176. Photographs taken by Bill Bradshaw © Wells Cathedral School appears on pp 180 and 181.

Thanks are owed to Rose Fay for the drawings on p 143; and to Tony Smith for the photographs on pp 38, 46; Anne Brierley pp 43, 49, 110; Melanie Edwards p 54; Giles Thorman p 61; John Baxter pp 70, 71; David Rowley p 72; John Fennell pp 17, 84; Philip Peabody p 85; Andrew Parker pp 86, 93; Nick Wilson pp 96 (top), 99; Jane Graham p 107 (bottom); Tony Bretherton pp 154, 179 (bottom); Duncan Gowen p 172; Elizabeth Tudway Quilter p 175. All other photographs and images are copyright © Wells Cathedral School.

CONTENTS

FOREWORD BY LORD ARMSTRONG OF ILMINSTER

Eleven hundred years is a very long time in the life of any institution, and Wells Cathedral School can look back with pride on its origins and on the way in which it has evolved and developed over the centuries. But this is not just an exercise in self-indulgent retrospection. It is an opportunity to learn, from the changes and developments that have enabled the school to survive and flourish through eleven centuries, how best it can now be further improved and developed so as to meet the needs of coming generations.

There are two abiding factors which have shaped the character of the school and which provide a strong foundation for its future development: its place and its music.

As to its place, it is deeply and securely rooted in the cathedral city of Wells and the surrounding district. Many of its pupils, and especially pupils seeking to develop a talent for music, come to the school from further afield and even nowadays from far distant countries. These pupils are very welcome: they broaden the horizons of the school; and enlarge its national and international reputation. But the school remains faithful to its roots in Somerset and its commitment to the local community: it continues to provide, as it has done for many years, an independent general education, with an increasingly broad and flexible curriculum and high academic standards, for the sons and more recently also for the daughters of local families. The majestic beauty of the cathedral and the close, the sturdy elegance of the Cedars, the varied charms of the old houses which have been incorporated into the life and fabric of the school, and the strength of the Mendip hills all make their marks, often perhaps unconsciously at the time, on the minds and sensibilities of the pupils who pass through the school.

As to its music, it was originally founded as a means of providing an education for the choristers who sang the services in Wells Cathedral, and it continues to this day to provide the cathedral with its choristers – nowadays girls as well as boys. So for more than a thousand years music has been an integral element in the life of the school.

Music is one of the areas in which the school has especially developed its expertise (mathematics is another, but that is another story). In recent times it has adapted its curriculum so as to enable it to provide for the special needs of pupils who wish to concentrate on developing their talent for music. Wells Cathedral School is now officially recognised and enjoys government funding as one of the four specialist music schools in England. The musical tuition of the specialist musicians is embedded in the general curriculum of the school. Many of them go on to achieve success in the musical profession, benefiting greatly from the general education with which the school has furnished them.

The musicians benefit from the school; but the school benefits from the integral role of music in its activities. Not all the pupils are specialist musicians; but the pupils who are not specialist musicians learn to appreciate the value and importance of music as an enrichment of life, and are stimulated to show comparable commitment in developing their talents with focus and discipline to achieve similarly high standards in their own chosen fields of activity.

These two factors – the school's location in Wells and its place in the wider community in Somerset, and the importance of music in its life and activities – give the school its own distinctive qualities and are fundamental to its success. They will be respected in its development to meet the needs of the twelfth century of its life.

All the main aspects of the life of the school will benefit from improvements already in train. The academic curriculum is being supported by the provision of new classrooms. Sporting activities will benefit from the provision of a new and well-equipped sports pavilion. A new Cedars Hall, serving the needs not only of the school but also of the wider community, will provide a much-needed venue for recitals and chamber music concerts and better facilities for orchestral and choral rehearsals, to the benefit not only of the musicians themselves but also of others who have opportunities to come and listen to and learn from them and their teachers.

The school is fortunate in being able to find room for these exciting new developments in and around its existing grounds.

So, as we look forward, we can be confident that Wells Cathedral School will be able to rise to the challenges of meeting the changing educational requirements of the future as it continues to develop in the spirit and tradition which it inherits from its evolution in its first eleven hundred years.

Robert Armstrong
August 2008

Perhaps the special quality of Wells was something in the air: the histories of all those who had lived out their lives in the utopia of this tiny city oozing out of the ancient buildings and echoing on the cobbles of Vicars' Close. But despite spending five years in this protective, nurturing environment, I left Wells with my feet on the ground. I had shared my world with people from all walks of life: those from 'old public school' families, children of parents in the forces, overseas students from Asia, inner city children on DFE scholarships, some of the finest musicians in the world. I can say with certainty that I was privileged to rub shoulders with some of the kindest, most genuine people I have ever met. And what better preparation is there than to start the next chapter of one's life with a strong sense of self and the quiet confidence that comes from understanding the foundation that Wells was built on: *Esto quod es!*

Caroline Hamilton (née Cowan, 1993–8)

Editors' note

THE LIFE OF A CATHEDRAL CHORISTER in England in the centuries before the Norman conquest is excellently described in Aelfric's *Colloquy*, written about AD 1000. It was after discussing this work with the Wells Cathedral choristers in the Deanery garden in the summer of 1883 that Dean Plumptre chose as a motto for the boys and their school the words of the counsellor, written, as was the *Colloquy* itself, in both Latin and Anglo-Saxon: *Esto quod es; Beo Iþæt Iþu eart*. Like many school mottos it lends itself to a number of interpretations: 'Be what thou art' can be rendered as 'Be yourself' or 'Be the best you can' – in whatever sense, an encouraging and all-embracing exhortation.

The dean was showing the choristers of the time how their predecessors had lived 900 years before and what sort of school they had attended. At that point Wells had few pupils beyond its choristers, and as a grammar school had rather fallen into the doldrums. Yet even so, both elements of the school could undoubtedly lay claim to a long and glorious tradition of education in Wells for over a thousand years.

It may be true, as is stated in the first two sentences of *A History of Wells Cathedral School*, published in 1985 towards the end of Alan Quilter's headship, that 'Wells Cathedral School cannot be counted among the oldest schools in the country. Probably it dates only from 909, when the church of Wells was made a cathedral.' But that splendidly throw-away remark by Linzee Colchester, author of the first part of the history, does little to conceal a justified pride in the school's great age. As a review of the *History* in *The Wellensian* says, 'Obviously, one doesn't boast openly about a mere thousand years and more', even though evidence for those very early years mostly has to be deduced from what was the norm for the time in cathedral cities.

As with all such venerable institutions, there have been many vicissitudes in its progress down the centuries, and many periods about which little is known. But despite the silences, the survival of Wells Cathedral School means that it now takes its place among modern educational institutions supported by both its impressive history and its thoroughly up-to-date approach to the needs and wishes of today's young people.

The modern history of the school really starts with Dean Plumptre and other members of the Wells Cathedral chapter in the 1880s when, according to the minute book that received its first entry on February 5 1884, they decided 'to restore their ancient grammar school which has been suspended for some seven years past'. But the minute book records no special notice of the year 1909, when a school first established in 909 might have been expected to celebrate its millennium. Therefore the milestone reached in 2009, when not just a millennium but a millennium plus a century will be reached, is well worth commemorating – and not just with an updated history of a school that is in itself part of the history of England, but also with a true celebration of a flourishing and remarkable place.

Esto quod es; Beo Þæt Þu eart

The Wells Cathedral School motto is unlike many other school mottos of venerable age in having a strong resonance even in the twenty-first century, and even though both the original languages in which it was rendered have long become unfamiliar. Phillip-Luke Simmons-Hedges, who suffered some racism at school but who glories in the nickname 'Chokky' conferred on him when he first arrived, is just one of the school's alumni who uses the motto to sum up the supportive and benign way in which the issue was dealt with and the respect which he himself received from teachers and classmates. Others cite it to underpin the freedom they felt while at the school to be themselves, and the encouragement they received to stretch and develop. From its origins as a sonorous Victorian maxim to its central role in the lyrics of a 2007 pop song, 'Be what you are' means as much to the Wells pupils today as it did to their predecessors.

A BEAUTIFUL ENVIRONMENT

NIKOLAUS PEVSNER, the eminent architectural historian, wrote that Wells can boast the most beautiful square mile, architecturally, in the whole of the British Isles. No one who lives in or visits this small city would dispute that statement. The buildings that surround the cathedral and its green form a haven of medieval beauty and calm that echoes with the footsteps of history. The water from St Andrew's wells behind the cathedral still cascades down the High Street in gullies on either side of the road, just as it did when Bishop Bekynton constructed a water system for the people of Wells in the fifteenth century. And those who study and teach at Wells Cathedral School are lucky enough to live and work at the centre of all this splendour.

It is a striking fact that the school in the twenty-first century still occupies a building on the site on the north-east corner of The Liberty where its first known home was in the early thirteenth century, in the house bequeathed to the cathedral by master mason Adam Lock. The school moved around a great deal during the intervening centuries, occupying a number of premises owned or rented for it by the cathedral authorities, but when it first leased, and later bought, the Cedars, it landed back precisely where it was nearly 800 years ago.

In Wells, The Liberty is what at other English cathedrals is known as the Close – an area around the cathedral with offices and accommodation for the cathedral clergy, who live and carry on its business there. Here, as elsewhere, the green provides a peaceful open space as a fine setting for the grandeur of the cathedral west front and as a place of meeting and entertainment. The young men of the past who played football here – 'a common, undignified, and worthless game' in the eyes of a medieval writer – are echoed today by the youth of Wells who gather and kick balls around here after the end of the school day. But The Liberty is not simply an enclave round the cathedral; in the early thirteenth century it was established by Bishop Jocelyn as a separate jurisdiction from the city from the taxes levied by the city and the bishop.

Right: Vicars' Close with the cathedral tower and Shrewsbury House

Below: Cedars field and the Quilter Memorial Garden

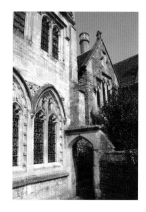

Above: The north end of Vicars' Close with the chapel to the left

Below: Claver Morris House on the north-east corner of The Liberty

The crenellated wall that can still be seen in some places was built later in the thirteenth century by Bishop Burnell to underline The Liberty's separateness. The approach to the cathedral from the city still today involves passing through one of the fifteenth-century gates through the wall – either Penniless Porch, which leads through from the Market Square and was where beggars were (and are) allowed to sit, or Brown's Gate further up Sadler Street.

The grand houses that line the north side of Cathedral Green were once the residences of the main cathedral dignitaries. The chancellor's house – now Wells Museum – became the main school house when the dean and chapter refounded Wells Cathedral School in the 1880s, with classrooms and a gymnasium very shortly afterwards provided in the Bernard Building on the North Liberty (now Ritchie Hall). It was when the chancellor's house became too small in the 1920s that the lease on the Cedars was taken, and the centre of the school moved to the other end of Vicars' Close. And it was when music became a new focus under Alan Quilter that the school regained a foothold on Cathedral Green, when the Theological College vacated what had been the Archdeaconry, opposite the north door of the cathedral, and it became the new music school.

Vicars' Close has been a major artery between the school and the cathedral ever since the move to the Cedars. John Dennis, who was a chorister between 1935 and 1944, calculated that he must have participated in at least 3500 cathedral services during his nine years at the school, which meant that he must have walked up and down Vicars' Close at least 7000 times. The school has been based there at

several points in its history; today one of the boys' houses, Shrewsbury, occupies number 16, and music can often be heard drifting out of the windows of number 26, which is part of the music department. In addition, the chapel at the top is used by the school for house services.

Bishop Bekynton noted in the fifteenth century that learned inhabitants of Wells would be ideal teachers at the school – if only they could find it. Visitors to the cathedral enclave today might be forgiven for asking where the school is not to be found. Almost all the buildings on the north and north-east stretches of The Liberty are now in school use. The same is true along New Street, from Ritchie House, once the home of the junior school and now one of the three senior boys' boarding houses, up to the head's house. Most of the buildings bear the names of Wells notabilities, ancient and

> In 1908 Virginia Woolf, the novelist, spent a week at number 16 Vicars' Close finishing her book *The Voyage Out*. She wrote, 'I am in the midst of ecclesiasticism here, bells tolling for prayer, clerics scantering past, ladies with wreaths, choir boys… It's a lovely place and the country round is as good as it can be.'

modern. Cedars itself is named for the magnificent trees that stand in front of it on the inside corner of The Liberty, each one planted on his twenty-first birthday by successive Tudway elder sons. There is another at the back of the house in the middle of the lawn, which was planted by the Prince of Wales and is covered with Christmas lights every year. The lawn itself is not just a lovely vista from the back of the main school house: it provided valuable playing fields when the school first moved there, and is still used for hockey and cricket, and for croquet in summer; the cricket square is one of the finest in the county. There are playgrounds and gardens behind the other school buildings along the North Liberty too, stretching across to the backs of the New Street

> When I visited Wells with my wife in September 2006, from our home in America, Alwyn Gillen kindly arranged for us to be taken round by a sixth former. Some of the school looked unchanged, notably the playing fields with their fine trees at the back of Cedars, and the Bernard Building, now Ritchie Hall, of which my persistent memory is of how cold it was. But much was different: the dining hall on the College Road side of the garden; the stable yard on the other side of College Road which was not accessible in my time, and indeed was a bit of a mystery, but is now bustling with school activities; and several houses along The Liberty and New Street which in my day were private residences but are now part of the school. It was nice to see the name 'Mullins' retained for the house where, in my day, the school doctor lived.
>
> Our guide told us that the basement rooms in the Cedars are now staff common rooms; when I was at school one of them was the chapel, and the rest were store rooms and also used as air raid shelters during the war. I couldn't help wincing to hear that Mundy's Meadows, which we used for cricket in the summer and hockey in the spring, had been cut in half by a new road, and that there was now only enough room for one pitch, now surfaced with Astroturf. Then we went to the music school, which used to be the library of the Theological College, a handsome building opposite the cathedral. Inside, there was a huge bustle: in the main room, a symphonic rehearsal; in one corner, a solo performer practising a different piece without any apparent distraction; in the adjacent room, more activity. We left after only a brief look, so as to avoid disturbing this delicate equilibrium, and walked into Vicars' Close, which of course I remembered well. And then it was time to cross The Liberty (using the new light-protected crossing) and return to the Cedars. It was a most entertaining tour, which brought home to me the huge changes that have occurred in the school over the last sixty years. To the normal person, eyeing the exterior of these handsome buildings, nothing has changed. We know that it has!
>
> Brian Taylor (1940–8)

houses. And what used to be stables, outhouses, and yards on the other side of College Road, next to De Salis, is now a complex of sports facilities, classrooms, and offices – including the school clothing shop in what was once a storehouse set on staddle stones to deter rats.

Wells Cathedral School is trebly fortunate in its environment: despite being in the middle of a bustling (albeit small) city, it enjoys open spaces and splendid views; despite being spread along several public roads, it offers security to those who study and work there; and most of all its buildings and its surroundings resonate with both history and beauty.

A window in the music school

The first thousand years

Although there are no extant documents to record the presence of a school in Wells in AD 909, when the church of Wells became a cathedral, it is certain that one existed. Cathedrals and great churches needed to train, educate, and house the boy choristers who were an essential part of the music for the services, so at the very least a school had to be provided for them. Moreover, in those centuries before the establishment of universities, the church, through its cathedrals and monasteries, was the centre for the education of young men destined for a clerical career, and also provided a wider liberal arts education for the sons (and sometimes the daughters) of the nobility. It can safely be assumed that Wells was no different from other church institutions of the time in this respect.

The first specific mention of the school occurs in the twelfth-century Cathedral Statutes, which survive in a fifteenth-century copy. This document names

A remarkable letter concerning Wells Cathedral Grammar School survives from the early thirteenth century. Written by Pope Innocent III to Bishop Jocelyn and dated March 28 1213, it sheds light not only on the teaching methods employed in those far-off days but also on some reprehensible behaviour by 'a poor scholar' of the diocese and how the authorities dealt with it.

This was a young man who had been appointed by the master of the school to teach his younger fellow pupils. He owned up to the pope that while doing so he 'did severely beat them, not so much for the desire to teach them as for the purpose of obtaining something from them'. He had also 'laid rash hands upon other clerks' and had not obtained absolution for these offences before proceeding to take minor orders. He now asked for the pope's intervention in the hope that he would be pardoned for this behaviour and be allowed to go on to take major orders.

At that time, when the church was one of the twin pillars of the state and an important career path for those aiming at both high office and personal prosperity, it was clearly incumbent on this young bully to confess his sins and beg those in authority to overlook his past and allow him to continue his career. That the pope would deign to intervene indicates how interlinked were the various Catholic countries of Europe under his authority, and how even minor matters could be brought to the man who was then the supreme arbiter of justice and morals.

Left: Wells Cathedral in evening light with Glastonbury Tor in the background

Above: The thirteenth-century document naming Richard Nortcuri as 'master of the school of liberal arts at Wells'

As a coda, it is perhaps equally remarkable that this document – now in poor condition but safely conserved within the cathedral's archives – could be so disregarded as a historical artefact that on May 1 1884 Chancellor Bernard could be allowed to produce it casually from his pocket on the occasion of the opening of the building which he had endowed.

two officials, the chancellor (*cancellarius*) of the cathedral and the master (*archiscola*) of the school, whose duties tallied so closely that they were almost certainly the same person combining a teaching and an administrative role in the business of the cathedral generally. The school over which the chancellor presided was the 'grammar school', for older boys. Existing alongside it was the school for the young choristers with their unbroken voices, a quite separate establishment which came under the direction of the precentor and the master of the choristers. The two schools were to remain separate for the first six centuries of their history, becoming a single institution sometime in the middle of the sixteenth century.

The first named master of the school (*magister scolar*) was Peter de Winton, whose name appears as a witness in a document of about 1188. At this time there would have been only one teacher, though it was usual for senior pupils to help by teaching their juniors. The name of another schoolmaster is known from the seal attached to a document of the later thirteenth century, where Richard Nortcuri, chaplain, was described as 'master of the school of liberal arts at Wells'. All schoolmasters at this time were in holy orders and all at Wells were vicars choral, so at least in minor orders if not deacons or priests.

Numbers of those attending the school at this time are conjectural, but there is one solid piece of evidence dating to 1377, when it is recorded that there were thirty-four scholars at Wells, all tonsured and over the age of fourteen, who were required to contribute 4d each towards the cost of Edward III's wars in Scotland. Nor is it known where the first school buildings were. It is however likely that the school started roughly where the west front of the cathedral now stands, since it is recorded that it was moved to new premises when the cathedral was realigned and building began on the present west front. And in 1235, it was located precisely where it is now: Adam Lock, the master mason who oversaw much of the work on the cathedral in the early thirteenth century, bequeathed his house – the middle one of three on the site where Cedars now stands – to Canon Roger de Chyuton, and this house, together with the one next door, was in 1235 made over to the chancellor for the use of the school. Here it stayed until 1399.

Peter de Winton, 'magister scolar' of Wells, witnessed this twelfth-century document.

The grammar school

Wells Cathedral Grammar School was the seedbed which produced many distinguished members of the clergy throughout the centuries of its existence. In Wells, as elsewhere, all those intending to embark on holy orders, major or minor, were required to attend the grammar school, as is recorded in about 1680 by Nathaniel Chyle, then the bishop's secretary: '…the vicars such as be not to study by themselves, shall dayly at all times vacant, forenoone and afternoone, the service time excepted, resort unto the gramer schoole, and learne such things whereby they may afterward be the more able to serve God in the commonwealth'.

Choristers in the 1950s

After a temporary move elsewhere, its next home from the early years of the fifteenth century was in an outhouse of the building now known as De Salis – though it appears to have been at a rather low ebb at this point in its history if a curious document probably dating to 1460 is to be believed. This statute, drawn up by Bishop Thomas Bekynton, recorded the comment that there were plenty of people in Wells with a good knowledge of Latin and therefore ideal as teachers within the school 'if only they knew where it was'. He therefore laid down that it should remain in perpetuity where it was currently situated; though this edict was not to persist for long, as he soon began to build a new schoolroom over the west cloister which continued to be used, on and off, by the school until the second half of the twentieth century.

This apparent low profile did not last, and Wells Cathedral Grammar School was in the fifteenth century nationally and internationally famed for its learning, and regarded as at the forefront of the so-called English Renaissance fostered by Henry VI. Meanwhile, alongside the grammar school, the choristers' school too had flourished.

The choristers' school

Early medieval liturgy required the clear, unbroken voices of young boys as a counterpoint to the deeper voices of the men. Under the tutelage of the precentor, the choristers had to attend most of the services: 'They must attend evensong, compline, prime, mass, vigils for the dead when the corpse is present… on all double feasts and Sundays, and on festivals of nine lessons all boys must be present, and the boys on duty for the week must attend daily at all times to sing the responses…'.

The choristers were well looked after: as Aelfric's *Colloquy* records, a boy who was being questioned about his daily routine by the master told him that he ate meat, as well as 'herbs and eggs, fish and cheese, butter and beans, and everything wholesome, for which the Lord be thanked'. Drink was 'ale, if I have any; or water, if I have not any ale'. At Wells, they lived in what was known as 'the choristers' house' – one gable of which still stands in the cathedral precincts, and now forms the northern end of the new restaurant

Schoolmaster's salary

In medieval times, the master of the grammar school received a salary of two marks a year (26s 8d – of which the equivalent in today's money is £1.33) taken from manorial rents and dues owed to the Prebend of Biddisham. In addition he received an allowance (known as commons) of a penny a day – though all the monies paid to him were contingent on him carrying out certain cathedral duties on top of his schoolmaster's work. If he failed to do so he could be penalised, as the incumbent was in 1408–9: for that year he received no commons payment at all 'because he did not wear his habit in quire', and his salary was halved to 13s 4d for the same reason. These payments remained the same until the reign of Edward VI in the sixteenth century, when the combined wages were increased from their total of just under £3 a year to £13 6s 8d. But after that there were no further increases for the next 200 years.

and shop. It was small; but it needed to accommodate only six choristers and their master, in addition to six older boys whose voices had broken and who stayed on to carry out duties within the cathedral during the remainder of their time at the school. The master had his own room, and the boys slept in four beds in the dormitory, three to a bed top to toe – two lying one way and one, in the middle, the other.

Apart from singing, they were taught Latin and received religious instruction, and lived according to a detailed set of rules codified by Robert Cator, master of the choristers in the first half of the fifteenth century. These rules laid down how the master was to teach the boys: he should be 'short and concise for if the teacher is too long-winded, the pupil tends to become bored and so becomes nauseated and loses confidence'. Appropriate clothing was prescribed: cassocks reaching to the ankle, long tunics, and short stockings 'with the purpose and intent that the boys being so clothed should be made more humble, and consequently less inclined to be led astray'. And if they should take to 'following the fashions of the present wanton age' and wearing 'pointed slippers, long hose, strait doublets, and short cassocks barely covering their buttocks', such clothing would be confiscated.

They had to be polite at table, and though they were allowed playtimes they were expressly forbidden from larking around or throwing stones in the cathedral, cemetery, or cloister in case harm was done to themselves or the buildings. It is also known that they played football. And – in common with most of the other cathedral schools, until the practice was banned as unseemly in the time of Henry VIII – they enjoyed the annual series of ceremonies and jollity centred on the election of the Boy Bishop and marking the feast of the Holy Innocents in late December. This was when one of their number was chosen to officiate as the 'bishop' at services (though not at mass), wearing a bishop's regalia and served by the other boys as canons.

There are a number of distinguished medieval musicians associated with Wells, including Henry Abyndon, the first to receive the MusB degree at Cambridge, and Robert Wydowe, the earliest known BMus at Oxford, who died at Wells in 1505. They were contemporaries of Richard Hygons, who became master of the choristers on December 7 1479; the cathedral still possesses his indenture of appointment, which laid down that his quarterly stipend was to be £4 13s 4d, augmented by £3 6s 8d for the maintenance of the choristers and their house, plus other small payments and allowances. In return he was to instruct the choristers in music and in virtuous behaviour, and was himself to take part in a stipulated number of cathedral services 'wearing a proper and decent surplice'.

Cathedral music now involved polyphonic singing, and music for full chorus instead of just

for teams of soloists. One of Hygons' compositions survives in the Eton choir-book of around 1510; a recent thesis describes it as 'an elaborate composition of a high standard… Its demanding nature implies that the choir contained very accomplished singers…'. Indeed, it is on record that Hygons' successor as master of the choristers, Richard Bramston, poached one of the singers after he left Wells for another post in Bristol; in

February 1510, it seems that he returned '… in privye and disguised apparel to have hadd away one of our best queresters, that is to say, Farre, and therwit takyn'.

Presumably this 'kidnap' was with the aim of improving the singing at Bristol; but Bramston

An engraving of the north-west corner of Vicars' Close with number 14 and the chapel

Vicars' Close

Reputed to be the oldest continuously inhabited street in Europe, Vicars' Close was built by Bishop Ralph of Shrewsbury in the 1340s in order to keep the cathedral's vicars under close supervision. The vicars, who were usually in minor orders, were there to substitute at cathedral services for the canons whose duties often took them away from Wells. They had previously lived wherever they wished in the city, but this left them open to the temptations offered by the outside world so they were provided with their own residential community. Even this did not keep them totally away from the pleasures of the city, so Bishop Bekynton later added the Chain Gate at the cathedral end of the close, which provided a bridge across the road so that the vicars could pass from close to cathedral without stepping outside and being faced with the temptations of secular life.

For its first sixty or so years the close would have been more like a quadrangle than a street, because there were no front gardens and the central part was grassed. Bishop Bubwith added the gardens in the early fifteenth century, as well as the chapel at the north end, and later that century the fireplaces in all the houses were improved and the tall chimneys added. There was a communal hall where the vicars dined while being read to from the Bible, and where they drew their daily rations of bread and beer; and administrative chambers, built on to the hall in the early fifteenth century, still boast many rare and original features.

The houses initially consisted of one room on each floor with a winding stair at the back and a latrine in the yard at the rear. When, after the Reformation, the number of vicars declined, they were allowed to have two houses each, and both comfort and privacy improved. Today there are fourteen double and twelve single houses. There have been many changes over the centuries, but Vicars' Close retains its integrated plan and, with its excellent state of preservation, still exudes an overwhelming feeling of the Middle Ages.

Wells Cathedral School was housed in number 14 during the late eighteenth and early nineteenth centuries, and today occupies two properties in the close. Number 26, at the cathedral end, is part of the music department and is frequently responsible for adding to the atmosphere of the place through the music that wafts through its windows. And at the other end, those boys who are fortunate enough to be boarders in Shrewsbury House at number 16 must be all too aware that they are living in a street which has been inhabited for over 600 years. It is a place very familiar to the choristers too, who process up and down it daily, sometimes several times, while marching in their crocodile between cathedral and school. The chapel in the close is also used by the school for almost daily house services.

Vicars' Close witnesses lighter moments, for example when it is used as a film location. One such occasion involved the heartthrob American actor, Johnny Depp, whose appearance on the scene was too much for several girls from the school who had been allowed to watch provided they maintained strict silence. They could not suppress their squeals, and were promptly evicted. There may be some truth in the rumour that there were some staff present as well.

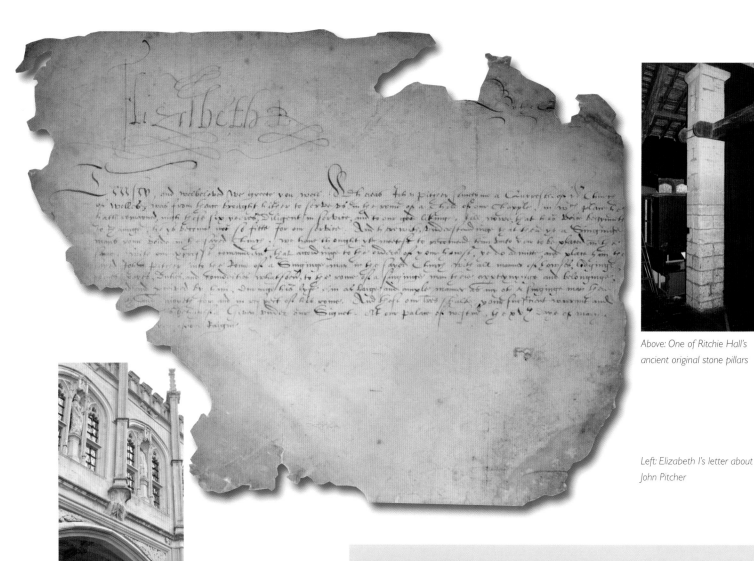

Above: One of Ritchie Hall's
ancient original stone pillars

Left: Elizabeth I's letter about
John Pitcher

must have been an excellent musician, because despite what was described at the time as his 'unkynde trespas', it was not to be long before he was reinstated at Wells, where he continued as master of the choristers until 1531.

This was by no means the only episode recorded of a good singer being lured away; the cathedral financial documents include several instances of bribes offered to royal servants to turn a blind eye to good choristers whom they might otherwise have abducted for service in the royal chapels. And the cathedral still has a letter (above) personally signed by Elizabeth I, expressing her indignation at the refusal of the cathedral authorities to reinstate as a vicar choral one John Pitcher, whom she had poached but whom she now wished to send back as his voice had broken.

Medieval football

The choristers and scholars at Wells Cathedral Grammar School in the Middle Ages would certainly have played football. A contemporary chronicler described the game as '…called by some the foot-ball-game. It is one in which young men, in country sport, propel a huge ball not by throwing it into the air, but by striking it and rolling it along the ground, and that not with their hands but with their feet. A game, I say, abominable enough, and, in my judgment at least, more common, undignified, and worthless than any other kind of game, rarely ending but with some loss, accident, or disadvantage to the players themselves.'

Injuries are indeed recorded. Footballers everywhere and from all ages will suffer alongside one William Bartram who was 'struck in his most sensitive parts by the foot of one who played with him, sustaining long and intolerable pains'. And Canon William of Spalding, while kicking the ball, inadvertently caused the death of a fellow player who 'ran against him and wounded himself on a sheathed knife, carried by the canon, so severely that he died within six days'. The canon asked for, and received, papal dispensation for this involuntary manslaughter.

The two schools become one

In 1547, during the reign of Edward VI, all cathedrals were ordered to establish a free grammar school if none existed already, and the stipend paid to the master was decreed to be £13 6s 8d a year, plus a house. In addition, there was to be an usher, or under-master, with a salary half that of the master's, along with a free room. Choristers whose voices had broken were in future to be given exhibitions of £3 6s 8d so that they could continue to attend the grammar school. This effort to enable choristers to continue at Wells after they have left the choir and no longer receive the choral scholarships available through the cathedral and the school continues to resonate for contemporary heads of the school.

Boys of the city and Liberty are forbidden to let off 'squibbs'; this document is in the handwriting of Benjamin Andrews, clerk of the ecclesiastical courts

This massive salary increase for the master (up from just under £3 a year), combined with the need to appoint an under-master and the other new financial requirements attached to the choristers' school – all of which had to be funded from cathedral revenues – may have been the incentive behind the obviously financially prudent decision to unite the two schools. In any event, it is known that

Money then and now

Decimal currency was established in this country only in 1971, so older readers will remember the imperial system of pounds, shillings, and pence, as it appears in this book. Twelve pence – a penny was written as 'd' for *denarius* – made up one shilling (or 'solidus'), and twenty shillings made up one pound, the symbol for which remains the familiar £ (derived from L for Libra). An additional unit of currency was the guinea, £1 1s or 21s; the gold guinea coin is long obsolete, but the name lives on, notably attached to famous horse races. The noble was the term used for a third of a pound, 6s 8d, and the mark was two-thirds of a pound, 13s 4d.

The modern equivalents, although meaningless in terms of actual buying power, are:

1d = roughly two-fifths of a modern penny (p)
1s = 5p
6s 8d = 33p
13s 4d = 67p

at some point during the sixteenth century Wells Cathedral's two schools became one – and this was certainly the case by 1583, when records indicate that the headmaster had authority over both choristers and grammar school pupils.

The headmaster appointed in 1592, William Evans, remained in post for thirty years, and in 1609 bought the old college building at the junction of the East and North Liberty on the site of the house where the school had been quartered in the thirteenth century. This house remained in the Evans family until 1755, when Charles Tudway bought it, demolished it, and built the house later known as the Cedars. The name Tudway had already appeared in school records, in the form of an earlier Charles, a chorister in 1679 when clothes were bought for him; a bill for them still exists (opposite). He does not appear to have been a success as a vicar

Above: The steps at the north end of Vicars' Close, well trodden by the pupils

Left: The bill for Charles Tudway's clothes; he was a chorister in 1679

Unclerical behaviour in the seventeenth century

Sometime in the 1680s Robert Hodge, who had been cathedral organist for only three months, was censured for having been in the company of a disorderly group of people who broke a window at night in The Liberty; he was warned about his behaviour, and only three years later had apparently 'gone off' elsewhere. At the same time, Gabriel Greene, the master of the choristers no less, had to confess before the bishop in the chapter house that he and another vicar choral had riotously assaulted William Peirs, the archdeacon's son, in the Mitre Tavern in Sadler Street. Greene was later dismissed from his position, but his successor, Thomas Webb, was little better. He was charged with 'having carried himself very indecently to Dr Creyghton, the president of the chapter'. It seems that tenure of positions at the cathedral and grammar school at this time did not necessarily guarantee decorous behaviour.

choral as he 'in a discontented manner, did throw off his surplice in the body of the cathedral church… and did also bid the receiver of Close-Hall to strike his name out of his book…'.

That the school continued to flourish during the seventeenth and eighteenth centuries is evident from the names of the distinguished scholars who were appointed to lead it. But apart from financial information, few facts and little detail have come down to us from those centuries. The tenure of Aaron Foster, however, headmaster from 1771 to 1782, was marked by some bad behaviour which had one positive and illuminating result. He lived at 14 Vicars' Close where he also housed the school boarders; and he seems either to have had little disciplinary control over the boys or not to have cared very much about the school's or the cathedral's assets, since it was reported that

'Mr Foster's school boys were suffered to throw about [the many old books in the vicars' library] and demolish them since which time the library has been totally neglected and allowed to go to ruin.'

Some valuable old books were destroyed or damaged; but the boys had also used school books as part of the ammunition for their high jinks, and these became mixed in with the vicars' books and came to light again in the 1960s when the library was being conserved. The boys' vandalism two centuries previously now therefore results in today's cathedral owning a collection of rare eighteenth-century school books, which not only shed light on what was taught then but also give us names and insights into some of the pupils themselves. One of the books had belonged to Francis Taylor of Winscombe, whose brother John was also at the school; Francis's certificate of matriculation, dated March 19 1723, was found stuck into the back of his copy of *Excerpts from the Oxford University Statutes*. Both brothers went on to become clergymen, and might be expected to have disapproved of the cavalier use made of their books by their successors at the school later in the century. But an unnamed owner of a translation of Cicero's *De Oratore* seems anyway to have had his mind on less exalted matters, since he had written on the flyleaf:

> Phoebus is a bright god
> Mars is a monkey
> Juno is better
> But Venus is my honey.

One of the choristers in the first years of the nineteenth century was James Turle, later to become organist at Westminster Abbey. His obituary notice in 1882 included a probably exaggerated account of his memories of his time at Wells, when the nave of the cathedral was the choristers' playground; he himself had claimed responsibility for a well-aimed stone which broke the nose of the statue of St Andrew. And it was at this time, under John Vickery – when it seems that there were few scholars other than choristers at the cathedral school – that there

was a short-lived merger with the Blue School, a foreshadowing of late twentieth- and early twenty-first-century curriculum partnerships.

In 1833, when William Aldrit was appointed headmaster, the response to an official education enquiry revealed that there were twenty-six boys in the school of whom eight were choristers. His prospectus set out what was on offer – a mixture of traditional academic subjects and practical skills, presumably tuned to the likely clientele, which included 'the Latin, Greek, and Hebrew classics, the mathematics, merchants' accounts, ancient and modern history, elocution, English grammar and composition, penmanship, geography, and arithmetic. The French, Italian, German, and other languages, drawing, dancing, military and other exercises, etc, by the respective masters, on the usual terms.'

A couple of decades later, when Henry Harold was headmaster, his prospectus offered fewer subjects but was eloquent on method: 'Every effort will be made to accelerate the mental, moral, and religious improvement of the pupils; [the basis of] his system of tuition… is that the scholar instead of learning a number of words and rules by rote, is obliged to reflect upon and endeavour to discover the reason of what he is doing, and this is effected not by rigid measures, but by combining the advice and undivided attention of a friendly tutor, with that of a strict disciplinarian.'

Harold – described by an ex-pupil as 'a stoutish, well preserved, fresh complexioned man, arrayed in a well brushed and well fitting frock-coat and light summer trousers and glossy tall hat' – clearly had an enlightened approach to teaching, and was to remain in post until the late 1860s. But by that time both he and the school were showing their age: the schoolroom was in a state of disrepair and there were only three boys on the roll beside the choristers. In 1870 Harold was pensioned off and the pupils were all transferred to Wells middle school. There they remained until the revived cathedral school moved into the house on St Andrew's Street which is now the Wells Museum.

The cathedral and St Andrew's wells in 1871

The reconstructed school prospered under its able new headmaster, George Abram, and shortly afterwards was able to expand into its own new building, generously financed out of his own pocket by Thomas Dehany Bernard, Chancellor of Wells. Its renewed status was set out in February 1884 in a new minute book, which detailed the governance and management of the school, laid out the financial arrangements for the headmaster and the choristers, and fixed the scale of fees, which varied between £3 10s a term for day boys under the age of twelve to £17 10s a term for boarders in the headmaster's house.

The Dean of Wells at the time, Edward Hayes Plumptre, took a strong personal interest in the school. In those days before motor traffic, he used to give out the prizes for the pupils' foot races in the North Liberty, and would make a point of watching their football and cricket matches, and offering his help in their studies whenever they needed it. His influence was felt after the boys left school too in the weekly letters he wrote to several of them, and also long after his own death, since he left £2000 to the dean and chapter 'with directions to apply the interest to continuing the education of deserving choristers at the grammar school after they left the choir, and generally to advancing them in life'.

W J Tate, along with his brother, was a pupil at Wells between 1848 and 1856. He later wrote an account of his time at the school, published in 1895 in the *Wells Journal*. His father was the local wine merchant whom the headmaster, Henry Harold, patronised. One year when Mr Tate received the bill for his sons' tuition, he deducted from it what he was owed for a year's supply of liquor; this left the headmaster owing him a shilling. Tate had fond memories of Harold: 'I am sure all of us had at heart a real respect and affection for our old schoolmaster, for he was manly and good-hearted, and could unbend and relax at times, and had the happy knack of getting the best possible out of a boy. Moreover, he encouraged our games, cricket especially, and he had a great fund of humour, as well as a strict sense of justice. He was thoroughly impartial, showed no favouritism, and would not tolerate "splitting" or "tale-bearing". He was most assuredly not cruel, but he sometimes winked at fights, and he was always on the side of the weak.'

He also remembered the punishments that were dished out: writing out lines, or lists of words from a spelling book; being placed on the Victorian equivalent of the 'naughty step' or sometimes sent to 'the dungeons' (little rooms off the schoolroom where, it was falsely believed, refractory monks had been confined); and the inevitable cane, 'though he did not thrash us unless we richly deserved it'. And, as he adds, 'Once I was punished by being put on the battlements outside the sanctum window. It was a glorious day in spring, and I enjoyed myself hugely, for the rooks were busy in the Bishop's Palace rookery.'

A view of Wells from the road to Bath, 1835

During the 1880s and early 1890s, the school was flourishing under its respected headmaster. The *Wells Journal* report on prize day in July 1891 recorded Canon Buckle asking if he might be 'allowed to express the peculiar pleasure he felt in seeing so many of the choristers come up to receive prizes, the more so that they had not the same opportunities as the other boys owing to their being choristers'. One of those choristers receiving prizes

Wells Cathedral Grammar School

ESTO QUOD ES

Certificate awarded to
Awad.
Form *III*
For *Reading.* *H J Green*
Head Master.

31st July 1907

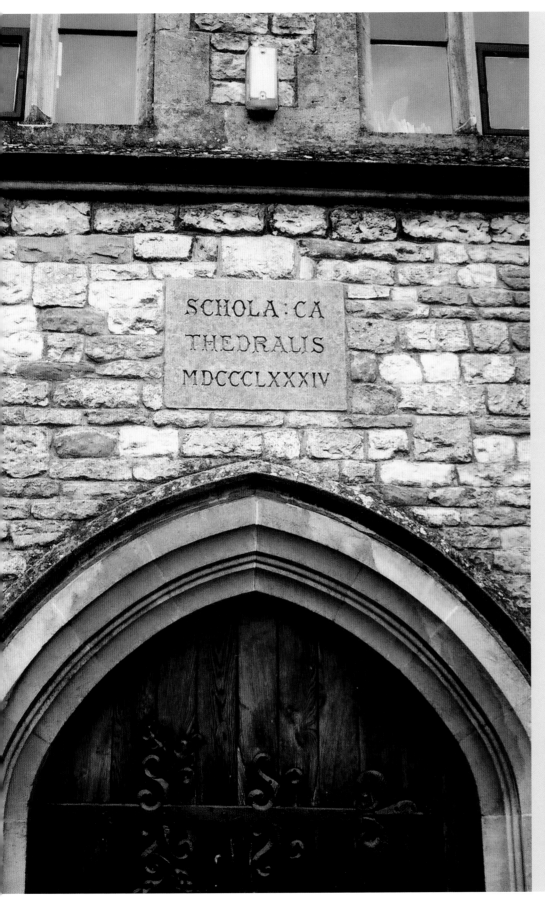

The Bernard Building
(now Ritchie Hall)

In 1883 Chancellor Thomas Bernard was left a legacy which enabled him to fulfil a longstanding dream and give the school its own building. Set back from the North Liberty were the remains of the ancient Canons' Barn, which had probably been erected in the late twelfth century at the same time as the early part of the present cathedral. This building – then being let to a farmer – was granted to the school by the dean and chapter, and Bernard's architect adapted what was left into a gymnasium and added a new section which contained three classrooms and a small tower above the porch which was to house the library. The building still retains six of the tall, square-sectioned stone piers of the original medieval aisled barn, which are unique in Britain and impossible to date exactly (see page 22).

It was renamed Ritchie Hall in the 1950s, and then contained a small hall where the senior school met for assembly and a little room to the side which was the main music room. Behind stood classrooms which had been converted into laboratories and a geography room, and the library was still in the tower. In Alan Quilter's time the hall was enlarged and a permanent stage created by opening out the main wall at one end. Today it is the main assembly hall for the junior school.

A nineteenth-century Wellensian

The school archives contain a fascinating survival – a small collection of material (opposite) relating to chorister and Old Wellensian Reginald Henry Cocks, starting with the end of term report from his first term at the school in the summer of 1888, aged nine, and ending with an undated press cutting reporting his death at the age of eighty-six sometime in 1965 or early 1966.

One of the later press articles about him, at the time when he was headmaster of Glendale County School, Wood Green, London, reports that he was the eldest of the five sons of Mr W J Cocks who was for forty years a postman in Wells. Two of his brothers were also choristers. Reginald had a distinguished school career, and his first report shows him starting as he meant to go on, with several 'very goods' and 'excellents' and the overall comment 'A very good boy – always eager to improve himself.' He was only eleventh in both term and exam placings at that stage, but this soon changed and he was frequently at the top of both lists, ending his time at the school (admittedly when there were very few pupils in his form) consistently coming first. He was also head boy, and press cuttings from the *Wells Journal* show 'Cocks ma' receiving a variety of prizes during his progress up the school, culminating in his final year with the form prize, the captain's prize, and the Plumptre silver medal.

Maths was his best subject, though he did well at most of the others too, apart from writing where early approval gave way to comments such as 'does not improve' and 'legible but peculiar', until he made an effort and managed to become regularly 'neat'. He was also given to being a bit of a chatterbox.

His record is illuminating about the disadvantages in academic terms of being a chorister. By the time he was in form V, his teacher could say 'His general English is excellent. He is one of the best workers we have had in the school for a very long time'; and his general progress in maths was echoed in Latin 'especially in translation in which he is decidedly the best'. But only a term later, when the report on Greek said 'He has little time for this, but has nevertheless made excellent progress', the comments against French and drawing bemoaned the fact that 'He loses here altogether by being in the choir'. And in his penultimate year at the school he was generally lauded, but 'if his work were not so interrupted by his choir duties I should expect him to take a high place in the Cambridge Local Examination'.

Being a chorister did not, however, ultimately disadvantage Reginald Cocks. As the series of press cuttings goes on to record, he went to Lincoln College, Oxford, became a teacher of maths and science, and was appointed a headmaster at the age of thirty-five. His obituary reports a life in retirement in Gloucestershire spent working for local educational and other causes.

that year was Reginald Cocks (see box, left), then in the lower fourth: 'Cocks ma' received the form prize, a copy of Scott's *Poems*. Mr Bisgood, whose sons appeared frequently in the lists of prize-winners, also spoke, and said 'he could bear testimony, as a parent of boys educated at the school, to the efficiency and ability with which they had been taught. He had never known a headmaster who had devoted more attention and care to the pupils placed under his care than had Mr Abram.'

Miss Katharine Lewis, daughter of Rupert Edward Lewis, headmaster from 1910 until 1922, was asked in the early 1990s by her great-niece to write down some of her memories of her time at Wells. She was very young at the time, but remembers that they had fourteen boarders in their house (now Wells Museum). If any were ill her mother nursed them, and stayed away from her own children if any of the boys had something infectious.

'Father was a wonderful disciplinarian… One day a man called at the house saying that he had been up to the school to see him, and found all the boys working away though there was no master there to oversee them. "Yes," was the reply. "They knew where I had gone and I trusted them to get on with their work." We only had August free of boys as that was the only month they were not needed to sing. One solo boy, Conrad Eden [later to be organist at Durham Cathedral] played the piano well, but had dreadful chilblains on his fingers, despite which his mother insisted he practise every day. But during the holiday my mother had other ideas; she covered the piano with a dustsheet and told him he was not to touch it. It must have worked as his chilblains got better. Another time, during auditions for solo boys, one boy started singing "O for the wings of a dove" and stopped, whereupon his mother carried on. He was told to start again and the same thing happened. His mother was sent out of the room, but again he stopped singing. He had made up his mind that he did not wish to go to Wells.'

Abram retired in 1896, and was succeeded by two priest vicars working together, William Henry Creaton and Harry John Green, assisted by another priest vicar, Leigh Lye; but this somewhat strange arrangement did not prove a success. By 1901 there were only six pupils in the school besides the choristers, and the minutes record that there were no applications for scholarships. Even applications for chorister places went down. By 1903 Creaton had resigned through ill health and Green became the sole headmaster; he stayed in post until 1910, when he was replaced by Rupert Edward Lewis who saw the school through to the early 1920s. Wells Cathedral School was tottering along, barely viable but maintained by the dean and chapter not least because of the continuing need to educate and house the choristers. It needed a new dynamism; and this was to be injected into it by the next headmaster, who joined in October 1924: Alistair Ferguson Ritchie.

Wells Cathedral Grammar School.

REPORT for the TERM ending *April 20th* *1894*

NAME *Locks ma.* FORM *V*

Place in Form { in Term *1st* / in Examination *1st* }   Number in Form *4*

Age *15 – 1*   Average Age *15 – 7½*

ENGLISH :—
Bible Knowledge —
History —
Geography
Grammar and Analysis
Spelling and Composition
} *His English word is all good —*

CLASSICS :—
Latin *Grammar v. good. (R.D) — Translation very much improved*
Greek *He has little time for this, but has notwithstanding*

MATHEMATICS :— *Excellent progress — G P A*
Arithmetic — *Very good —*
Algebra *Excellent*
Euclid and Geometry *do —*
Mensuration ~~and Trigonometry~~ *Very Good.*

FRENCH
DRAWING } *He loses these altogether by being in the Choir —* *h.a.*
MAPPING
WRITING *Very neat & clear.*
DRILL *good*

J.W.P.

ATTENDANCE *Regular – punctual*
GENERAL CONDUCT *Very good —*

G. P. Abram
Head Master.

The School will re-assemble on *Tuesday May 8th* at 9 a.m., when every boy is expected to be present.

The new headmaster proved an instant success. Within a year, numbers had risen so quickly that the dormitory accommodation became inadequate. New arrangements had to be made; and it was fortunate that the Cedars now coincidentally became vacant, and Ritchie persuaded the dean and chapter to take it over for the school. An additional benefit was the park at the back which would provide much-needed playing fields.

Cedars

After occupying master mason Adam Lock's house on the north-east corner of The Liberty, together with the one next door, the school had to move at the end of the fourteenth century when the site was commandeered by the bishop for a hall and lodgings for fourteen chantry priests. These were clerics whose particular role was to say mass and pray for the souls of donors who left

money for that purpose, and their college remained there until Edward VI dissolved chantries in 1547; it lives on, however, in the name of the road that still runs through the site. The school's direct connection with the north-east corner of The Liberty therefore ended for 500 years – though it had a link for a while through its headmaster, William Evans, who bought the old chantry college building in 1609 for his own use. The building remained in the possession of his family for nearly 150 years, until in 1755 Charles Tudway bought it for the sum of £3442 4s 3d.

Tudway was a prominent member of the local community whose wealth derived from the family sugar estates in Antigua. He quickly demolished the old building and started to construct a grand new mansion. Contracts with builders and architects as well as detailed costings survive, totalling £4871 16s 8d. Soon afterwards he paid £877 14s 3d for the stables and coach house on the other side of College Road, and in 1761 did a deal with the archdeacon whereby he exchanged six and a half acres of pasture land near Dulcote for the acre and a quarter of land on the corner of The Liberty in front of the house. This arrangement, which had to be sanctioned by an Act of Parliament, seems to have been a bargain for the dean and chapter; but Tudway was content, because his view at the front of the house was protected; and it was not long before the two oldest of the cedar trees that still stand on the corner were planted and gave the house its name.

The Tudways lived at the Cedars until the beginning of the twentieth century, when financial pressures induced them to move to the much smaller Milton Lodge. The Cedars became a military hospital during the First World War, and was then leased to Wells Theological College, but by 1926 it was proving too large for the college and so the dean and chapter leased it for the school. It has been in school use ever since, though it remained the property of the Tudways until 1967 when the cathedral bought it. Now the property of the school after its recent purchase, Cedars today houses offices, staff facilities, and a boys' boarding house; its eighteenth-century dignity creates a calm centre for the school.

The dean and chapter agreed a lease with the Tudway family in 1926 at a rent of £250 a year. It was further agreed to sublet the Cedars to Ritchie at the same rental less £80. This was in line with the arrangements common to many boarding schools at the time, whereby the headmaster personally received boarding and other fees paid by the pupils and was in turn himself responsible for paying the school's costs. The governors' minutes over the next decade or so reflect the financial juggling act that this arrangement involved and the tensions that inevitably arose as a consequence.

The 1930s was a decade of ups and downs. In March 1934 the head was able to report that the previous three years had each shown a profit, with 110 boys in the school. But by 1938 the dean and chapter, as governors, were becoming increasingly gloomy: there were only 100 boys in the school, when 130 was the optimum number to make it pay, and they fretted that this number would never be reached, and that applications had probably peaked. They were wavering in their commitment to the continuation of their school, and were frightened by the need for it to grow because they feared for their own liability if it were to collapse.

I recall being picked up by Gordon Wicks in a rowing boat at the foot of the steps from St Andrew's Street, and rowed across the Cathedral Green following a particularly heavy thunderstorm which resulted in the cathedral being flooded to a depth of about three feet!

Donald Baggs
(left in 1931)

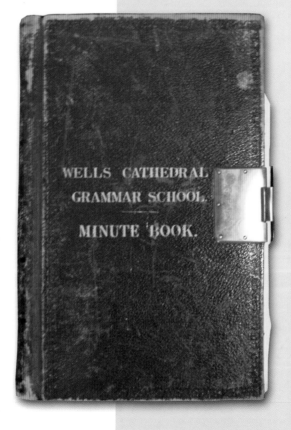

Reports

A series of leather-bound reports books, starting with Ritchie's arrival in 1924 and continuing until 1956, contain class and exam placings for each boy in each form, with a single line appraisal by the form teacher. It seems likely that these appraisals never reached the eyes of those reported on – still less their parents – but were there for the edification of the staff and the headmaster: even in those less politically correct days, some of the comments would undoubtedly have caused consternation if they had become public, though they could also be incisive and positive.

Many of the appraisals were on the standard lines of the predictable 'working well', 'has improved', and 'could do better'; some were rather more pointed: 'vacuous', 'bovine', or even 'about six years mentally retarded'; and bright pupils could be prone to hints of acid, like the boy consistently at the top of his class who was damned with faint praise one term by his teacher: 'Rather a dull boy. I wish he would smile at me once in a while.' To spare any residual blushes, those below are quoted without giving the year or the names of pupil or teacher:

'Still his mother's little boy'

'Nice boy; works quite well. I find him dim'

'I find it impossible to believe he reached third position by fair means'

'I get rather tired of praising him, but he deserves it' (of a boy consistently in first position)

'Makes good use of his limited ability'

'A good boy who has recovered from being misunderstood'

'Poetic, chaotic – he has a contempt for all detail'

'An enigma within an enigma but always seeking to win sympathy'

'Content to get to the top and no higher'

'Lazy – in fact, bone idle'

'Has been described as a genius. I disagree'

'A happy imp with plenty of intelligence'

'Sinking fast, I am afraid'

'He tries. Writing and a sense of hopelessness are against him'

'If merit always won roses, he would win them'

'Man of the world honouring us with his presence for a final term. Amused me'

I think of the 1930s: Prebendary Ritchie, Jimmy Carl, L S Colchester, Jackie Carlton, Alan Tarbat – great characters and brilliant schoolmasters all, who lived their roles – as would be described today – 24/7. Role models of prefects: Rowland, Treen, Jones, Middleton. Contemporaries: Martin, Davies, House, Barrett, Dennis, Clapp, Waudby-Smith. All have done their bit in moulding or influencing a little schoolboy of eight who came to Wells in 1935.

The routine of study and team sport, during the first four years to 1939, was such a great way to grow, mentally and physically. To be seen to be well behaved by those in the 'town' was a special requirement of Mrs Ritchie, the headmaster's wife. And then Alan Tarbat gave us the news, in the junior dining room, that the Second World War had started. The school suffered from then on, because all the young masters had to change their lives to fight the war.

These were very difficult times for everyone. How the head and his wife kept us so fit amazes me now, when I think of the shortages that had to be endured, but growing and fit we were. Experience has taught me to admire the effort that had to be encouraged all round, by both staff and pupils. Wide academic education was difficult to create and manage in a little boarding school; but somehow we, the pupils, were endowed with character and abilities by the staff, motivated by the Ritchie family, that were to be so valuable to our successes in later life.

As a past chairman of the Old Wellensian Association, who restarted the members list that had been lost during the war, I take pleasure and pride in reading about the achievements of pupils recent and in the past. How the school has developed and changed. But I recognise the special ethos that has been and still is created in the school by the staff and pupils and within the environment of its surroundings – the city and the cathedral.

John A B Cook (1935–42)

Being chapel organist, there were several occasions when the headmaster would send for me on a Sunday afternoon, to inform me that he was taking evensong in a neighbouring village church and I should accompany him to play the organ. I had started organ lessons with Denys Pouncey so I knew a little about the various stops and combinations – or I thought I did; but some of the old village instruments were a complete mystery to me. The writing on the stops was usually in Gothic German, which was hard enough to read, and as we generally arrived at the church five minutes before the service was due to begin, and the congregation was already present, it was impossible to practise. All the stops were very loud so I could not hear the singing, even though the head did his best to shout in my direction; so I usually lost count of the verses in the psalms and hymns.

I recall an incident during the summer holidays in about 1937 when the choristers were still 'working'. Linzee Colchester was in charge of us, and one Monday – no matins for the boys – he took us up to Priddy for a picnic. It was a hot sunny day and we had a marvellous time swimming in the ponds and getting very sunburnt. At evensong that afternoon the choir consisted of fourteen choristers, eight with normal complexions and six bright red lobsters. The precentor, Canon Davis, was furious.

Christmas at Wells will always stay in my memory. The choir was on duty until after the carol service on Boxing Day. Christmas Day morning was very busy, with services in the cathedral and carol singing to the bishop and dean. Then it was back to the Cedars for Christmas dinner with the Ritchie family, a most enjoyable occasion which culminated in the 'ceremony of the Terry's Chocolate Orange' when the head dropped one on to the table, and it always opened symmetrically. I still keep this custom going at our family Christmas dinners. At 3pm we staggered back to the cathedral for evensong. Then it was back to the Deanery for the dean's tea-party, which was always very enjoyable. After tea we played 'Murder' all over the house in the dark. I drew the murderer card on one occasion and duly committed my crime in pitch darkness. Someone had a torch and shone it to reveal that I had murdered my victim in the dean's private chapel. I was rather upset!

My final memory is of the last day of term in our upper sixth year when we had nothing particular to do. So the head, who was a renowned crossword compiler with the pseudonym Afrit, was persuaded to show us on the blackboard how to compile a crossword. I owe my love of crosswords to Afrit.

Frank Martin (1934–41)

My father became a vicar choral in 1924, and so I was fortunate enough to live at 5 Vicars' Close until I left school. I remember the tortoises, which appeared in Woolworth's one day in a heap in a glass-surrounded display counter. They were 6d each, and many of them found their way to temporary homes somewhere in the Cedars. A memorable occasion soon afterwards was when Preb Ritchie was taking a class in the Orangery and a queue of tortoises slowly made their way through the door from the small room to the left of the window. In today's vernacular, he merely said 'Get rid'! So, as my mother had a sympathetic ear for the boarders, our front garden became the home of at least half a dozen of them. They had to survive on a diet of grass, the occasional dandelion, and the odd bit of lettuce, and were much admired as the boarders went up and down the close on their ritual walks. But we had little experience of looking after them so only the strongest survived more than a year or so.

Richard Kenney (1937–46)

Chorister stay-ons during the summer holidays were full of warm, long, and pleasant days. We had four weeks or so to fill. Due to the services at the cathedral there was not much that could be done before lunch except on Mondays. Afternoons afforded some opportunity for walks around the moat, to Tor Woods, or in the hills around Wells. The space behind the Cedars gave opportunity to play cops and robbers or cowboys and Indians. Wednesdays offered the greatest spread of time. On many summer Wednesdays the Priddy lead mines beckoned. There were two quite substantial ponds – the most southerly, deep, cold, sinister, was not appealing, but the northern one, quite extensive, shallow, and usually warm was another matter. At one time we built a raft there. No one knew or cared about lead poisoning, nor did we appear to suffer any ill effects. Priddy was a wondrous place. The long, horizontal chimneys stretching out across the land to provide adequate draught offered opportunities for exploration. Even in spring the place was a miracle of nature with squadrons of breeding toads.

There was other excitement as well during the holidays. I remember an outing, I think it was to Burnham. I have a strong impression of seeing the German airship, the Hindenburg – could this have been so? In the summer of 1940 we went to Weston-super-Mare. I very confidently identified a lone aircraft flying over the beach as a Handley Page Hampden, but it turned nasty and dropped its bombs not far away. We ran for safety to the bus station with its flimsy roof and stocks of petrol. One summer just before the war a monumental storm hit the Wells area. Croscombe church was damaged and the roof of the Cedars leaked so badly that water flooded down the main stairway into the basement leaving a high tide mark of a couple of feet. Mr Colchester donned a bathing costume and sallied forth on the roof to see what could be done, but with little success.

John P Dennis (1935–44)

In the event, the Second World War came to the rescue. In October 1939, a month after the declaration of war, the headmaster reported a surge in numbers; and in addition, a small prep school from Bexhill called Normandale, owned and run by a former Wells master, found itself homeless after its premises were requisitioned for military purposes, and its headmaster asked whether he could link up in some way with the cathedral school. As it happened, the house on the eastern corner of the North Liberty (now Claver Morris) had just become vacant, so it was arranged that Ritchie would take over the lease and Normandale would occupy and pay rent for the house where the boys and masters would live. For all other purposes – teaching and games – the Normandale boys would be integrated into the cathedral school classes and the two schools would operate as one entity. The growth in numbers was welcome; by 1941 the head could state that 'the school is in a very satisfactory financial position at the present time'. Increases in fees seemed to bring no difficulty, and the boarding accommodation was practically full.

Claver Morris, Plumptre, and Edwards

These are the three former canons' houses at the top end of what was known as the East Liberty, now numbered 19, 21, and 23 The Liberty.

Number 19 (right) was built by Dr Claver Morris who was a physician in the first quarter of the seventeenth century; he married three times, was passionate about both music and a good argument, and kept copious diaries which offer fascinating insights into the life of a country doctor 300 years ago. He began to build his house in 1699; it took three years and cost £807 14s 6d. The original house had thirty-eight windows, but when the window tax was increased in 1710 he had some of them blocked: a bill dated March 25 1710 has him paying 10s to Richard Simons and partners for stopping up nine windows, bringing the number remaining to twenty-nine. At some point at least one other window was covered up too: in 2005 a window with the date 1751 etched into its lead was found hidden behind an old lath and plaster wall. In 1940, when the school took over the house, it had been occupied by Prebendary Denison and his two sisters, but he had just died and his sisters wished to move away (the younger of them, aged ninety-one, was heard to rejoice in the fact that now, finally, they could do as they liked!). It has ever since been a boarding house of the school, currently housing the younger girls.

Plumptre, number 21, takes its name from Edward Hayes Plumptre, the dean who was in office in the 1880s when the decision was taken to revive the school. He was a formidable benefactor, and left a substantial amount of money in his will to provide bursaries to allow ex-choristers to remain at the school. The house was leased to the school in the 1960s and is now a senior girls' house.

Edwards, number 23, is named for David Edwards, the dean with whom Alan Quilter forged a beneficial relationship when he arrived as head in 1964. It was built in 1819 for William Parfitt, the chapter clerk, and bought in 1933 by the Church Commissioners from the butcher who owned it, amid fears that he might ruin it by turning it into a garage with forecourt petrol pumps. The house was leased to the school in the 1960s and is now a senior girls' boarding house.

The war at Wells

The editorial of *The Wellensian* for the Michaelmas term of 1939 begins: 'Fortunately we have scarcely been affected by the war, and are among those who find it hard to believe that there is a war on. Wells being a "safe" area, many people have found an asylum here, and have brought their offspring with them.' The next term opened with a freezing cold spell which resulted in an epidemic of burst pipes, but offered opportunities for winter sports such as skating and tobogganing, and for trips up to the Mendips to see the winter fairyland. But it was not to be long before the war began to have an impact. There were so many air raid alerts during the summer term that year that the decision was taken to move the dormitories into the basement. As a result, the boarders could report that 'we have suffered from no lack of sleep, and have had the morbid satisfaction of seeing tired day boys arriving at school at all times of the day'.

The first school (and city) casualty was also recorded: Trooper Douglas Chisholm, who died in the Military Hospital at Alexandria. They now followed regularly. *The Wellensian* began to carry a 'Roll of Honour' feature with brief obituuaries of those who had died and anxious mention of those missing, with the hope that they might after all prove to be prisoners in enemy hands. Medals were recorded too: DFCs awarded to three Wellensians in the RAF who died in action, an MC, an MM, several 'Mentioned in Despatches' – plus Wing-Commander Antony Watson who first won the DFC for a hair-raising rescue of a fellow pilot whose plane had been brought down in Libya, and later added the DSO and the Croix de Guerre.

Watson was a true action man, according to the account of his exploits given in *The Wellensian*. After *The Times* of December 4 1942 reported his DSO, at a point when he was still missing after being shot down in north Africa, the magazine could triumphantly proclaim that 'this most distinguished old boy is safely back at his base in Malta'. He and his fellow officer had managed to evade German patrols in Libya for many days while seeking safety, and had adopted all sorts of unlikely stratagems to avoid being noticed and challenged, including lulling the suspicions of a German sergeant-major on a motor cycle by 'walking up to some natives nearby, shaking them warmly by the hand, giving them cigarettes, and "talking" in unintelligible words'. As the report concluded, 'Tony Watson is just twenty-one years of age'. He visited the school while on leave in 1943, and as the Roll of Honour pamphlet published in 1946 recorded, he safely survived the rest of the war. The magazine also followed the fortunes of members of staff who had joined up, including 'Jackie' Carlton, who lost a leg, 'a cruel blow to one so keen on sport'.

Areas of the gardens were dug over and planted with foodstuffs to aid the war effort, and everyone was expected to muck in; Ann Brierley, the Ritchies' daughter, remembers 'Alan Tarbat coming down on Sunday mornings, minus teeth and collar, to help make breakfast for seventy boys'. The railings around the Cedars were taken away to be melted down, and various Ministry of Information instructional films were viewed. The first one, on fighting fire-bombs, proved to be too rapid in pace to be helpful: 'our chief memories are of a confused mass of flames, smoke, and hosepipes'. But one on parachuting was received so enthusiastically by some young members of the school that it was found necessary to stress that parachutists had to be of a certain age.

Although Wells remained relatively peaceful, the west front of the cathedral 'looks nowadays over a hayfield instead of the closely-clipped sward of pre-war days'. And there were reflections on the effect of the war on the boys: 'No one can be entirely unaffected by the news of raids on neighbouring towns and of tragedies… We can take comfort, however, in the thought of the natural resilience of youth and the shortness of childhood's memories, and hope that this younger generation will not suffer unduly because of the prevailing martial atmosphere in which it is growing.'

I was a boy in the Cedars under the late Alan Tarbat whom I regarded as an exemplary master. He was a classics scholar, having been a boy at Lancing College (with Evelyn Waugh, whom he disliked) and Keble College, Oxford. He possessed a remarkable gift as a poet, writing in verse several hymns which we sang in the school chapel on days of festival. As a housemaster, he was firm but compassionate and generous. I was also a chorister under Denys Pouncey and Garth Bawtree-Williams, who took over when Pouncey was called up for active service in 1943. I was happier as a cathedral chorister than I was at the school. The headmaster's wife wielded considerable power, and there were few 'stars in my crown' at her behest. But she and her husband, Prebendary Alistair Ritchie, were very fine individuals, and their care and concern for those of us who were boys at that time, with them in the Second World War, was of the highest order. I also became enormously impressed with the men who made up the dean and chapter of the cathedral, and remained in touch with many of them. So I was richly blessed, and regretted my father's mistaken decision to take me away when my voice broke.

Geoffrey Chick (1942–5)

As the war drew to its close, *Wellensian* editorials began to reflect on its aftermath and the post-war world. But it was not yet over; the Roll of Honour in the autumn edition of 1944 was the longest yet, with two old boys killed during the operations following D-Day, another death in India, and a posthumous DFC awarded to Flight-Lieutenant Selwyn Alcock who died with all his crew on a mission over Belgium. The piece concluded, 'We share in the grief of the parents and close connections of the fallen, as we do also in the honour they have won.'

VE Day was celebrated in the summer term of 1945 with services in the cathedral, sing-songs, and sports – including a staff obstacle race where 'the spectacle of their elderly mentors wriggling under blankets, and leaping over improvised hurdles like young sheep, gave the smaller fry much delight'. There was also a splendid feast, ably catered for by Mrs Ritchie, and a bonfire: 'It was grand to think that black-out regulations had at last gone with the wind!' And later magazines were able to rejoice in the safe return of Old Wellensians who had been prisoners of war. One was J P Barrett, who had survived the rigours of a Japanese camp in Thailand: 'Though thin, he looked surprisingly well. A born philosopher, he said that, once the building of the ill-famed railway was completed, things were "not too bad".'

Throughout it all, of course, school life had gone on. *The Wellensian* recorded cricket, hockey, and rugby seasons, matters concerning the choir, school debates, the activities of the scouts, the cubs, and the various clubs, expeditions to Glastonbury, and much more. Boys left and new boys came, exams were taken and passed, prefects were appointed, and games colours awarded… The war was weathered – and finally, on March 7 1946, the whole school was once again photographed on Cedars lawn, nearly four years after the last photograph had been taken.

I was not a chorister, but was head boy in 1941/2 and captain of games. The danger from bombs was real – I remember an occasion when the other prefects and I were on night duty as wardens and we had to throw burning incendiary bombs off the Cedars roof which had been dumped by a German bomber either going to or returning from a raid on Bristol.

Alan Clements (1934–42)

War was declared on September 3 1939, during the summer holidays, and I returned to school a week or so later, as a boarder, to start in the upper fifth. I was at the school until early in 1942 when I left for the army and the Royal Armoured Corps. Life was quite Spartan – there were cold baths in the morning for the senior boys followed by a good walk before breakfast. The baths were run overnight and so they might have a thin sheet of ice on them in the winter – you jumped in and lay down until the wave reached the taps and came back to your chin, and you could then jump out.

However there were also the excitements. St Brandon's, the Clergy Daughters' School, was evacuated from Bristol to the Bishop's Palace in Wells. We had special joint services in the cathedral on Sundays – the girls on one side and the boys on the other. This may not sound a big deal now but we were then a boys' only school and there was a lot of ogling across the aisle. The senior girls were billeted in Vicars' Close and notes were often left on doorsteps.

When the bombing of Bristol and Bath started the dormitories were moved into the basement – we were all in the Cedars in those days. I was a prefect then and we had a small area to ourselves and one morning when we went upstairs to our common room we realised that one of us was missing. He'd suddenly vanished, together with his set of drumsticks, and strangely the young assistant matron, who also slept in the basement, had disappeared too. No one said anything and we didn't ask and, if we had, we certainly wouldn't have been told anything. I remember his name quite clearly but it would be rather unkind to mention it in print.

Michael James (1934–42)

As a pupil during the war, I can recall that life and tuition carried on quite normally, other than on the sounding of the air raid siren when we all made great haste to the Cedars basement. Any tendency to fool around was soon checked by the threat of the cane from Jimmy Carl, the much-feared senior master. A bonus was a US Army engineer company located nearby, which provided free candy and cigarettes. Membership of the army cadet force became part of life, with shooting on the ranges and annual camps often under canvas in various parts of Somerset. The ACF band took part in many marches through the streets of Wells in conjunction with the Home Guard, Civil Defence, and other organisations to promote wartime fundraising; and as a bugler I remember well standing on the battlements of the Bishop's Palace playing the 'Last Post' to signify the end of a Home Guard camouflage, weapons, and tactics demonstration.

In the lead-up to D-Day many of the roads across the Mendips were closed and utilised as temporary parking for large numbers of military vehicles. As a sergeant I was involved in driving a number of heavy lorries to a point where the rest of the school ACF sprayed their undersides with a protective coating to prevent salt water damage during shipment across the Channel – a small but no doubt useful contribution to D-Day!

Gordon Jacobs (1939–46)

The lighter side of a headmaster's life

An extract from an obituary of Prebendary Ritchie recorded his two hobbies: 'crosswords and bees, in both of which he had made himself expert. The former made him nationally famous when a series was published both in the *Listener* and the *Sphere*, and later in book form under the pseudonym of "Afrit". In his earlier days the headmaster, a really good player, often helped the Wells City Cricket Club.'

He kept bees in what had been the 'laundry garden' where, up until the end of the Second World War, Mrs Coleman and her helpers used a criss-cross of washing lines to hang out to dry all the clothes which they had washed in enormous coppers. When the bees took the garden over, Ritchie persuaded gangs of volunteers to help him take care of them – and it seemed that the volunteers usually emerged from the work unscathed, whereas the headmaster, despite cloaking himself in the beekeeper's traditional hats and veils, always managed to get stung.

In his eulogy at Ritchie's funeral, Alan Tarbat recalled a beekeeping incident: 'A neat package labelled "Italian bees via Frome" was delivered to the school. But at once they swarmed, and were later discovered in the grounds of the Roman Catholic Carmelite convent. "Naturally," said the headmaster's friends, "good Italian bees could not stand the atmosphere of an Anglican cathedral, so they sought sanctuary where they were more at home."'

Many of his pupils recall their headmaster's crossword expertise, including William Whittle (1939–46), to whom Ritchie said one Sunday after lunch, 'Congratulations, you won the *Observer* crossword prize last week. Would you be good enough to let me have it sometime?' Ritchie, who could no longer enter under his own name, had exhausted the names of all the members of staff and was now using those of members of the sixth form.

Croquet, at which he was 'devastatingly accurate' according to his daughter, was one of Ritchie's passions

Linzee Colchester

Affectionately known as 'Horse', Linzee Sparrow Colchester was at the centre of both school and cathedral life during the many years he spent at Wells after joining the school in September 1936.

Tributes to him recall that 'if he saw that something needed doing, he did it'. This included repairing and refurbishing school properties, reorganising and cataloguing the library, putting on plays (including designing and making the sets), and being the driving force behind the scout troop. Typically, when organising the timetable, he taught everything that was left when others had been allocated subjects and slots: an ex-pupil still links Latin with 'Horse's' Capstan cigarettes, and recalls lessons from him up to O-level in French, RE, art, and English. Even when he was away on active service he would turn up to visit and, as *The Wellensian* for Michaelmas term 1942 records, 'as usual, went about the school unobtrusively making improvements and suggestions, and raising all our spirits by his presence'.

He was also senior school housemaster, beginning each day, winter or summer, with a cold bath, after which he would rouse the boys with a handbell while taking the back stairs three at a time clad only in a towel. And he quietly became an expert in medieval cathedral architecture, with an emphasis on his beloved Wells Cathedral, on which he wrote many pamphlets and books.

Peter Henfrey

After Major Henry Fitzhenry 'Peter' Henfrey arrived on a fortnight's trial in February 1949, he remained a part of the school until his death in 1989, even after failing eyesight in 1965 forced his retirement. When he arrived, as the new and the first bursar of the school, he had to start from scratch in bringing a sense of order to the school's financial affairs, and was also faced with the problems caused by the aftermath of a long war for an institution that had never been on a sound financial footing. And his influence was felt not just through his management of the finances and the administration. He commandeered war surplus material to build new laboratories and classrooms, some of them still in use – though considerably refurbished and upgraded – and now known as the Henfrey Block. And he spent his time during the school holidays repainting classrooms and dormitories, often in partnership with Linzee Colchester.

He had to employ enormous resourcefulness to make his limited budget stretch as far as possible. And he imbued those around him with his own sense of mission for the school – woe betide junior staff who left a gas or electric fire on unnecessarily. He always had a clear view of what the school could and could not afford, and would disabuse the headmaster about any over-ambitious project while plying him with copious glasses of sherry in his rooms in the stable yard. But he was always forward-thinking, and was eager to encourage Alan Quilter in the then newish idea within independent education of fundraising. This was just before Henfrey took the decision to retire, but he was there to set the process on its way. And he remained a friendly presence at the school in his retirement, living a contented life in Vicars' Close and welcoming to his house the pupils he called his 'grandchildren', the sons and daughters of those whom he'd known as boys at the school and who now kept him company while doing their homework.

Ritchie started a cadet corps in the autumn of 1941, and by autumn 1942 the boys had been to camp and won proficiency awards. The laboratory which had been set up in the old gymnasium was gradually coming into use, though science teaching was mostly confined to physics with a little chemistry. The staff who had come with Normandale were an asset, and Ritchie was pleased that, despite the exigencies imposed by the war, he had managed to retain the services of a couple of youngish men in their forties. Exam results were generally very good. In short, the school at the end of the war was in a much stronger position than had seemed possible in 1938.

In 1944 Ritchie became a prebendary, an honour he much appreciated. But the strain of keeping the school afloat during the war had taken its toll on his health, and he began to think about retirement. In 1948 he decided to cater for his future by starting a junior school, which he called St Andrew's, in a house he bought for the purpose in New Street. And in the immediate post-war world the school began to think anew about its direction. In accordance

with the 1944 Education Act, the governors decided to address the question of formal recognition by the Ministry of Education, when in 1951 they applied for an assessment by ministry inspectors. The report throws a great deal of light on Wells Cathedral School at this point in its history, both academically (see page 124) and in terms of the extra-curricular life led by staff and pupils. Indeed, despite the

Alan Tarbat

Much respected by generations of the boys he taught, Alan Tarbat was one of the stalwarts of the school during almost all of Ritchie's headship, as well as that of Commings and the early years of Quilter's. He came to Wells in 1927 and, apart from two short periods when he taught elsewhere, he remained at the school until his retirement in 1969. Even then he stayed on, in a small flat in St Andrew's Lodge, where he lived until just a few months before he died in September 1978.

As his obituary in *The Wellensian* recorded, 'It is impossible to give a full assessment of the contribution which Alan Tarbat made to the life of this school. As housemaster of the Cedars he was responsible for the development and welfare of generations of boys. From them he demanded the very highest standards of personal conduct. His boys quickly recognised him as a man of the highest integrity in whom they could place their trust. He could show genuine interest and concern for their smallest problems and he was prepared to give unstintingly of his time and energy to any who needed his help.'

William Whittle remembers him as an inspirational teacher of English (affectionately known as 'Pudge') who also taught Latin and Greek. He was always the first teacher old boys asked for when coming back to the school; even a policeman in Johannesburg was once seen to hold up a restraining hand and say, 'Wait there Mr Tarbat; I will tell you when to cross.' He was known for his aphorisms, called 'Tarbat's twaddles'; Chris Nicholas (1959–68) remembers one in particular: 'If you want to be a star, planet.' He would exhort his charges 'not to try to be a cat while you are still a kitten, because kittens are so much nicer'. And Richard Phillips (1960–2) recalls 'a light-hearted moment during an English lesson, when he asked his class "By what name are the gentry of Calne known?" We were flummoxed, so he gave us a clue: for what was Calne famous? We all knew the answer – for Harris's sausages and little else – but still could not come up with the answer. Then he told us: "they are the Harristocracy of Calne". Groans all round!'

In addition to his work at the school, he was widely respected as a writer and poet. For many years he published a weekly poem in the *Daily Sketch*, and he also had his own column in the *Bristol Evening World*. He loved telling jokes from what seemed like an inexhaustible supply, and was full of memories of his own childhood. As the obituary concludes, 'Alan Tarbat once claimed that if he had taught a single boy to write a decent English sentence he would not have lived in vain. Most would claim that it was an enriching experience simply to have known him.'

inspectors' comments on the starkness of the accommodation – by no means unusual in boarding schools in those days – what comes across both from this report and from the memories of those who were there at the time is that, despite its lack of a strong academic reputation, Wells Cathedral School was a place where the boys flourished under a regime dedicated to their interests and within a community where they were cared for and nurtured. As the report said:

> …an impression was gained of a community with much to offer out of school hours. Several masters are unsparing of their time in organising games and such activities as the cadet corps, the school scout troop, and the wolf cub pack. No less energy seems to be put into more intellectual activities. A debating and two musical societies, lectures, recitals, and excursions to places of interest indicate this. Less formal pursuits, such as gardening, occupy some boys. A background of this sort, with the ever-present influence of the cathedral and its gracious surroundings, must be a large factor in the courteous independence of the sixth form boys.

The generally positive nature of the inspectors' report was both gratifying and encouraging. And a step in the right direction had been the appointment in the late 1940s of the school's first bursar, Major 'Peter' Henfrey, who would be able to take a more professional approach to its finances. His presence at the school now, in the early 1950s, proved doubly fortunate, in that the dean and chapter were once again wavering – still worried about their responsibility for an institution that was apparently flourishing but was (they felt) bound to come a cropper. Henfrey was able to produce authentic financial accounts and projections, which stilled their fears and encouraged them to believe that Wells Cathedral School was a viable entity.

A classroom in Ritchie Hall

By the beginning of 1954 it was clear that Ritchie's tenure was coming to an end. New teachers joining at the time recall that the school was really being run by Mrs Ritchie, and that the head was a shadow of his former self. In February that year, therefore, Dean Harton asked advice from colleagues within the independent schools sector as to how best to move forward. There were two major alternatives: to restructure the school along the lines of a traditional preparatory choir school; or to develop a more academic approach within the senior school and to establish a stronger sixth form. There was disagreement within the chapter as to the best solution, but both bishop and dean were firmly in favour of the sixth form option, and this was the decision ultimately taken.

In addition to the nickname 'Fergie', Prebendary Ritchie was also known as 'Uncle Gren'. This arose from his grace before meals, Benedictus benedicat, which came out like a series of small grunts. He was an intellectual and would certainly have achieved higher office in the church if he had not chosen to see the school as his life's work. He always appeared in his cassock and rarely without a cigarette protruding from an elegant holder.

Great amusement was caused at the end of every Christmas term with the final concert. The cry would go up, 'Simon the Cellarer', and Preb Ritchie would produce the copy from within his cassock. Knowing on one occasion that I would have to accompany him, I had practised assiduously for days before, but was mortified to discover that I had been practising the version in C major whereas I was presented with a version in two sharps. There was the additional difficulty that a piece of music folded many times does not willingly stay on the music rest.

Another person who must not escape mention was Denys Pouncey, the cathedral organist, as well as his wife, Evelyn. Their Sunday evening soirees were greatly enjoyed, especially when the entire Pouncey sweet ration was handed round.

William Whittle (1939–46)

The current head, Elizabeth Cairncross, keeps a photograph of Dean Harton, given to her by Jeffrey Bigny, in her study, as a reminder of his influence and vision for what the school has become. He was a shy and reserved man, in his time a distinguished theologian, who was respected by the school's staff not only for his vision for its future but also because he, with his wife, a former Anglican nun, regularly, warmly, and hospitably entertained them.

Ritchie now felt able to tender his resignation, and informed the dean and chapter in March that he would be leaving at the end of the school year. However, he died suddenly only a few weeks later, on April 8 1954, aged only sixty-six. A governors' meeting in May asked Linzee Colchester to act as headmaster for the summer term, and after the shock of the headmaster's sudden death, they set quickly about recruiting his successor.

The school dining room in the Cedars, now the drawing room

As the youngest of A F Ritchie's four children, I lived at the Cedars from when I was born in 1930 until my marriage in 1954 just after my father died. We lived 'among' the school, without special defined accommodation. This meant dining at the masters' table in the school dining room, turning out of the drawing room when parents were interviewed, helping in the kitchen, and seeing half-clothed boys flicking towels at one another on the 'washing landing' with Alan Tarbat's voice raised in protest as a background. During the war, when space was short, I had to give up my room to a matron during term time. We had advantages, though, in the holidays when we could lay out our Hornby and farm on the green-linoleum-covered tables in the dining room. I well remember the choristers being with us over Christmas; I used to fill their stockings, a tangerine in the toe of each, and we would sit down to Christmas dinner with about thirty people. There were presents for everyone afterwards.

My mother, Violet, was a strong character whom some found formidable; but she was sensible, kind, fair-minded, and often supported the underdog. She also understood boys! Her mission for them (and us) was to make them well-mannered and considerate of others, and to feed them as well as possible. I knew my father as a kind man with a wry sense of humour. As well as his crosswords and his beekeeping – making the winter syrup for the bees was his only cooking skill – he was an accomplished book-binder and a good sportsman, though in later years he confined himself to croquet (played with devastating accuracy). He was also a reluctant camper. He would only agree to come to our pre-war summer camps near the Quantocks – borrowing the scouts' tents and involving family, friends, and sometimes boys who were staying for the holidays – if he could have the relative comfort of an iron bedstead.

I was away at boarding school and then university from 1944 on, so I was not so much involved. But when Major Henfrey arrived, he enlisted my help in trying to sort out the school accounts which were in a mess; I was struck by the number of boys who were on reduced fees. Looking back, it was a privilege to live at the Cedars for twenty-three years, and to have been part of the school. The grounds were and are beautiful – but where is the fountain with the four storks where we used to paddle, and the big cedar tree where we had our swing? I see that the Wellingtonia is still there. When I was a child some of the boys (and I) used to try to climb it, running a few feet up the trunk to clutch at the first slippery, sloping branch. Do boys and girls climb it now, or does 'health and safety' stand in the way?

Ann Brierley, Prebendary Ritchie's daughter

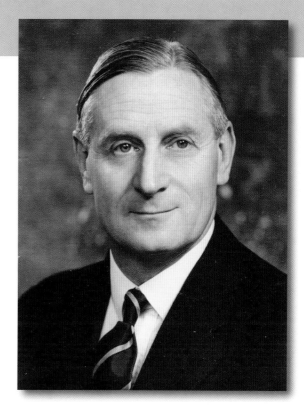

IF, AS THE DEAN AND CHAPTER had decided, Wells Cathedral School was to be transformed into a much more modern institution, fit for purpose under the sweeping provisions of the new educational legislation, it needed a new broom. Ritchie had rescued it from almost certain demise in the 1920s, after several years of gentle decay, but had not sought to turn it into anything other than a place that provided a basic education for choristers and the sons of local farmers and tradesmen. Now, if there was to be a flourishing sixth form and if the school was to make its mark in the bustling post-war world, there would have to be changes.

Frank Commings: new broom

In June 1954 it was announced that the new headmaster was to be Frank Commings, who came from St Paul's School. Almost his first action on taking office in September that year was to raise the salaries of all teaching staff to conform to the Burnham scale. Whereas previously the staff had suffered large deductions from their already low salaries for board and lodging, with no consideration given to all the additional duties they undertook, they were now properly recompensed. One result was that good young staff now stayed at the school, many of them – like Jeffrey Bigny,

---

School rules

The old list of rules was headed by the following injunction:

> Always remember the traditional heading of these rules: 'Any breach of common sense is a breach of school rules'. Remember also that your behaviour shows the kind of person that you are and reflects upon your school…

The old rule about wearing the school cap rather curiously excluded boys over 6ft in height (as well as sixth formers). Day boys were allowed to visit shops in Wells on the way to and from school, but 'all loitering in them whether singly or in groups is forbidden'. And St Thomas Street, including the Cathedral Coffee Tavern, was out of bounds. More recent rules forbade 'the lighting of fires and the climbing of trees'; and a general prohibition of 'behaviour which is considered dangerous to life' was honest about its purpose: 'In practice this is principally a warning about secret smoking in school buildings.'

Geoffrey Williams, and Michael Carter – for years or for their whole teaching lives.

During the first two years of his headship, Commings dealt with issues like the assimilation of Ritchie's junior school in 1955, and the school's incorporation in 1956 as Wells Cathedral School Limited. He also immediately set about raising academic standards, both throughout the school and within the enlarged and improved sixth form. Despite continuing financial stringency, new staff were recruited, new classrooms and laboratories were built, and playing fields purchased – the lower half of Tor Furlong, bought from the Church Commissioners for £1200 in 1957, was the first piece of property actually owned by the school. Other changes were afoot, including the increasingly frequent appointment of married members of staff for whom, if they took on houses, accommodation would have to be provided.

Frank Commings had announced on taking the job that he would stay for ten years and no more, which is what he did, announcing that he would leave at the end of the summer term of 1964 to return to St Paul's as Surmaster. A valedictory article in *The Wellensian* after his retirement recorded the respect, honour, and liking in which he was held:

'The friendly spirit has remained. The happy atmosphere of the place is still one of its most striking characteristics. The headmaster was never too busy to see a boy who needed help or a member of staff who sought his advice. He possessed full knowledge of every activity of school life, yet could never be accused of undue interference. Being a fine rugger player and cricketer, he ran one of the school

Wells Cathedral School.

FEES.

The fees *per annum*, payable termly in advance, are :—
(a) Boys over 12 ... ... £90
(b) Boys under 12 ... ... £84

These fees are inclusive of Board and Education, Laundry, Games, Stationery and ordinary Medical Attendance. Books are not included.

The Fees *per annum*, for Choristers are :—
(c) Major Choral Scholars ... £30
(cd) Intermediate Choral Scholars £45
(d) Minor Choral Scholars ... £60

Exhibitions are granted to Sons of Clergy, reducing fees to :—
(e) Sons of Clergy £75

Other Entrance Scholarships (£50 a year) and Exhibitions (£21 a year) are offered annually in June, and are competitive.

A deposit of £3 is required with the first School Account to stand against personal expenses incurred during the term. This amount is finally credited against the last School Account.

Optional termly charges are :
Piano or Violin Lessons, 2½ guineas.   Woodwork, 10/6.
Elocution (Junior Forms) 1 guinea.
Insurance Premium (see below).

Absence.   If they desire to do so, parents may take advantage of an Insurance Scheme, whereby, on payment of a small premium a *pro rata* remission of fees is made for the full period of absence from School in excess of seven days due to illness, accident or contact with infection. Full particulars will be found on a separate sheet.

Application for Entry should be made on the attached form, accompanied by a Registration Fee of one guinea.

sides whenever time would permit, and was ever present on the touchline in school matches. Often on a summer evening the headmaster could be seen in the cricket nets trying to get one of the junior boys to play a cover drive correctly. And perhaps one of his greatest characteristics was the enthusiasm he brought to all his tasks.' His decade as headmaster had undoubtedly turned the school round, notably in the firmly established academic reputation that Wells could now boast. In 1964 there were around fifty boys in the sixth form and places at university were regularly being won.

He had led the school firmly and decisively into the modern era; and there has been a recent squaring of the circle with the appointment in 2006 of Ben Taylor, the Surmaster of St Paul's, who decided to retire from the London school early and come to Wells to teach French and Italian and to run the higher education advice facility in the school.

Hair and clothes in the 1950s

Schools and head teachers down the centuries have fought a continuous battle against young people determined to follow the fashions of the time in their clothes and their hairstyles; see page 19 for a fifteenth-century proscription of 'the fashions of the present wanton age'. This particular war, it seems, would never be won; in July 1957 Frank Commings wrote to parents as follows:

'Over the whole country there is a big cult among the worst types of teenagers of wearing flashy clothes and adopting eccentric hairstyles. Last term about half a dozen boys (three day boys and three boarders) began to displease me by their exaggerated dress and revolting haircuts. It would aid me greatly if parents would NOT buy their boys clothes other than of strictly school pattern. I hate being ritualistic about school clothes, but once we depart from the norm all sorts of difficulties arise, on the lines of "Oh but so-and-so has one just like this". Please don't let your sons persuade you into buying duffle coats, fancy shoes, narrow trousers, etc for school wear. My advice to boys about haircuts is "not too long, not too short, not too floppy, not too bristly", which is the nearest I can get to a general rule.'

Two years later, an article in the Lent term edition of *The Wellensian* seems to indicate that little notice had been taken of the head's plea: D W Jarrett wrote:

'It has been suggested that the many peculiar heads of hair that can be seen about the school are due to the carelessness of the barber. This scandalous rumour is false – indeed, the barber takes immense pains to execute the latest styles in haircuts… Mr Tarbat has done much to popularise the Yul Brynner or billiard-ball cut; of course, none of the boys have gone the whole hog, but many, by having their heads cropped to an inch or more above their ears, have gone as far as they dare. There is reason to suppose that the film *Jailhouse Rock* has had great influence upon the new hairstyle now sweeping the Cedars, and among the senior boys sideboards cut daringly at different angles are very much in vogue. Then there is the brush or thatched-roof cut; the matrons are constantly gleaning from the heads of boys who sport such a style in order to stuff cushions or pillow cases. Several boys have developed the "Prince of Wales" or shaggy-dog style. But it is hoped that, in the near future, the cream of all will realise that the sure way to fashion is to adopt the style of the prime minister.'

Frank Commings was known as 'the boss' (an epithet which justly reflects the huge respect we all had for him, and more than a little awe). Not only was he headmaster, but he also took us for Latin until he left (and Peter Bishop arrived). Firm and standing for no nonsense whatsoever, he came over as pretty stern. But he was also fair. And if he came in for the first period after break and smelled pear drops, he'd demand the whole bag from the poor unfortunate who was forced to surrender it in fear and trembling – only to have it returned immediately, less one item which was now being sucked happily by the magister, with a smile on his face as if proud of his own audacity. I also remember the occasion when he threatened to cane the whole class out of total frustration that not one of us could remember one simple Latin construction. It wasn't difficult, but I think we were all mesmerised at the fear of his wrath if we spoke up and then got it wrong. So we were all ordered to report to him in his study during break, to be given one more chance, individually, and then caned (two strokes) if we still failed. Well, naturally, the boarders all knew what to expect and so headed the queue outside his study, to get it over with. The day boys in the class – to a man – hung back at the tail end of the queue, no doubt hoping to put off the evil moment. But the break only lasted fifteen or twenty minutes, and by the time it had finished the boss's wrath seemed to have evaporated. So who got caned? And who escaped? I think we (the boarders) held it against the 'day-bugs' for a long time after that.

Mark Brown (1961–8)

Geoffrey Lewis

When Geoffrey Lewis was interviewed in 1949 for a job at Wells, his interviewer was Conrad Eden, ex-Wells chorister and organist at Durham Cathedral. When the job was offered, Eden strongly advised him not to take it because he knew that the school was in dire financial straits and believed that it might not survive for much longer. Lewis decided, however, to accept and started his Wells career as assistant to Linzee Colchester, occupying a tiny bedsit at the top of number 23 – with, as he said, 'limited creature comforts but a lovely view'.

Geoff Lewis was one of the staff members who were crucial to the survival of the school in the 1950s, when the new headmaster, Frank Commings, was putting enormous drive and energy into ensuring that it had a future at all. He ran most of the school games, taught history, and was housemaster of number 2 East Liberty (now Edwards, and where his daughter, Melanie, was a houseparent until 2007). After Commings left, he was acting head for a term and then deputy head under Alan Quilter. He took responsibility for much of the day-to-day running of the school, and was a calming presence during those frenetic months and years in the 1960s when changes arrived thick and fast. And he also had to learn to deflect with tact and care some of what the head himself acknowledged were his wilder ideas. As Alwyn Gillen put it in his address at Geoff Lewis's memorial service, 'he kept the common room steady, as coeducation and the specialist music scheme broke in successive waves on the traditional calm of The Liberty'.

When complex arrangements had to be made for major school occasions, from the organisation of prizegiving to a visit by the Queen Mother, it was Geoff Lewis who handled them – and until he retired in 1986 he remained a teacher dedicated to the highest standards and a housemaster who genuinely cared for his charges. His colleagues also remember with affection his endless supply of amusing stories and anecdotes, both at school occasions and at sports dinners throughout the West Country. His professional broadcasts on Radio Bristol, during which he deployed his encyclopaedic knowledge of rugby and cricket, led to him being regarded as the local answer to Bill McLaren with – Alwyn Gillen again – 'his lovely mixture of Welsh and Geordie accents giving a warm and distinctive colour to his delivery'.

Weekly dance lessons were held in the rarely used and very dusty old gym in the stable yard, which couldn't have been a pleasant environment or experience for the nasal passages of the 'ladies from the town', half a dozen girls who were brave enough to leave the comfort of their homes of an evening to come to dance, only to return somewhat battered and bruised by us boys who, like the gym, must have been a bit whiffy for such close encounters as we were offering. Never mind the fact that many of us had truly uncoordinated extremities for this caper!

So who were some of the more adventurous maidens who attended? Well, first and foremost in my mind will always be the assistant instructress (her name sadly forgotten) for whom I always tried to make a beeline as a partner for every dance. Of those that came as dancing partners there are only three that I recall now. One was Gay Southall, with whom I mostly danced following continual 'interceptions' by Miss Hayden who kept reminding me not to keep monopolising her assistant. I can recall too that I sneaked out of bounds just to be able to sit with Gay in the back row of the Regal cinema – a very bold step for a boarder to take in those tightly controlled school days of the early 1960s.

Then there was Penelope 'Neppy' Wilson who always seemed to dance with Mordaunt. They were both much taller than most of us which, for me, never felt right for comfortable dancing. She and Mordaunt seemed to the rest of us 'a bit of an item', as one would say now, although – who knows – maybe she only looked his way because he was the right height? The last of the three (whose name again escapes me) was a girl with a pleasant but rather plain face, together with a gentle and sweet disposition. But she was much overweight and, to disadvantage her more, she would wear a perfume that was not in her favour. She would always be the last to be selected, if at all sometimes, and I clearly see her now still sitting in the corner window all alone with her head down while there were boys still needing partners. However, for me the most memorable image of the classes indirectly concerned the generous chest of Miss Hayden's assistant. Being, as we were, shy and totally unprepared to approach this new experience of touching body parts with the fairer sex, Miss Hayden had to put a lot of effort into encouraging some of us to dance very close to the girl and not at arm's length, and definitely not with our

bottoms stuck out, which she referred to as the 'toilet seat position'. In order to achieve the desired manoeuvre, she made the offenders among us dance with an old 78 record placed between our chests. In the subsequent fifty years, I have rarely needed to do any ballroom dancing. Sad maybe, but I still thank all those fair maidens for their perseverance and forbearance in helping me to get over shyness around the opposite sex after leaving school, a prerequisite in any boarder's life!

Nick Brown (1956–64)

A footnote from his younger brother:

I still find it amazing that girls were provided as partners back in 1963/4 when my brother attended. Two years later when I was senior enough – not a chance! Banned after earlier misdemeanours? Discontinued, certainly. In my time, we only ever had the dancing mistress, Peggy Daly, to partner in class or at the periodic dancing exams (held twenty miles away in Weston-super-Mare).

Mark Brown (1961–8)

The stable yard today

De Salis

Like Cedars, this house can claim an early connection with Wells Cathedral School, since it was in an outhouse attached to a building on this site in the early years of the fourteenth century that the school became established. Indeed, it was here that Bishop Bekynton decreed that it should stay in perpetuity – although he seems to have changed his mind very quickly, and constructed a new schoolroom above the cathedral cloisters.

It is known that a house on this site was granted to a succession of vicars from the early fourteenth century on, and was later used by canons, including two chancellors. Parts of the current building certainly date back to the late fifteenth and early sixteenth centuries, and it is one of the most imposing medieval houses in The Liberty. The school took it over in 1956 as a boarding house, and it was then that it acquired its current name, conferred on it by its first housemaster, Jeffrey Bigny, after the Bishop of Taunton who had lived there in the early decades of the twentieth century. As Bigny recalls, 'I started my days in De Salis in the "canonical" part, left free by Canon Jones who had moved to a house on the edge of the garden with the right to walk across it with his wife through a door in the wall for that purpose. Mrs Jones, a French lady, assured me that I would freeze in the house, as there were coal fires only in the hall and the splendidly large room with a bow window. The assistant organist lived in the other part of the house and had a very large Austin called "Duchess". De Salis is today a boarding house for the younger boys.

When I first came to Wells in June 1950, I can testify that it was typical of many boarding schools of the time, which fed their staff well and paid them very little; the staff tended to be single, live in, and be kept very busy. Mrs Ritchie was the pillar of the school. She was magnificent at looking after the domestic side as well as the health and welfare of staff and pupils. After supervising breakfast she would come into the staff dining room and we would all stand up. Sometimes she would appear in the splendid uniform of a commandant of the Red Cross, or she would be completely in black on the mornings when she was sitting as a magistrate (I can still hear a colleague muttering, 'Guilty, so take six months'). The main dining room was the present drawing room with the headmaster's chair immediately in front and at one end of the staff table and Mrs Ritchie at the other end. After lunch, when the boys had left, Ritchie, who liked a cigarette, would throw the packet on the table, inviting anyone to help himself!

The appointment of Frank Commings as headmaster after Ritchie's death encouraged four of the five new young graduates to stay on. Commings deserves enormous credit for the huge amount of work he did in raising academic standards, and in appointing staff who were willing and able to follow his example. He said he would come to Wells for ten years to see if he could sort out and settle down the school. He stayed exactly that period and no one else could have done better the task he set himself. He hardly ever left Wells, devoting himself completely to the school. His attitude was that those willing to help him achieve his aims would contribute all the energy and talent they could muster. This meant that there were no heads of department, and when he persuaded me to take over a house there was no additional financial remuneration. He could be a hard taskmaster, but if he trusted you he let you get on with making your contribution. There was therefore a remarkable feeling of being an essential but greatly appreciated member of a band of enthusiasts on a mission with a clear aim in view. So Wells became a successful school, small but the best of its kind anywhere.

Jeffrey Bigny (staff, 1950–85)

Michael Carter

Mike Carter was one of the new members of staff who came to Wells at the end of Ritchie's tenure as head and the beginning of that of Frank Commings, and who stayed for the rest of their teaching lives. He and the others can rightly be credited, under the influence of the headmaster and the new regime he brought with him, with the transformation of academic standards at Wells. Mike Carter's subject was maths, and it was not long before he transformed that department, achieving excellent exam grades and encouraging more pupils to study it. Even after retirement in 1986, he continued to teach maths in the sixth form. Like all his contemporaries he was active in extra-curricular initiatives too, developing a very successful chess team, coaching middle school cricket, and encouraging his first sporting love, golf; he was also a useful left arm medium fast bowler for the Willows. He was knowledgeable about church architecture, had a great love for Wells Cathedral, and regularly played the organ there.

Geoffrey Williams

Arriving in September 1950 for one term, to stand in for a sick member of staff, Geoffrey Williams stayed for the next thirty-four years, devoting the whole of his professional life to the school. He came to teach history, the subject in which he had graduated, but he was also an outstanding linguist. He taught French, and soon introduced German, a subject that has continued to be taught at Wells ever since. He also mastered Russian and Welsh, and while visiting a local German speaker to keep his conversational skills going in that language, arranged to be taught Spanish; to learn a new language in a language not one's own is a feat indeed! A true scholar, he was also assistant housemaster of De Salis, and is remembered by both colleagues and pupils for his self-effacing devotion to the school and his inspiring teaching. After he retired in 1984 he remained at the school as examination coordinator and to help in the library; when he stopped carrying out those duties he retired to Bridgwater, where he died in the spring of 2008.

Alan and Sheila Quilter greet The Prince of Wales

The Quilter years: challenge and change

Frank Commings' successor as headmaster was Alan Quilter, whose memories of his first visit to Wells Cathedral School were recorded in the 1985 *History*: 'I can well remember the dark November evening when Major Henfrey skilfully conducted my wife and me around The Liberty, showing us the school on the day before my interview for the post of headmaster and carefully choosing to show the finest parts of the school and avoiding the horrors.'

Quilter had a somewhat unorthodox background for a schoolmaster, having left school during the war, without taking A-levels, to join the merchant navy. He came to Wells in September 1964 after gaining his second mate's certificate, reading English at Cambridge, and teaching at Wellington and Uppingham. He inherited a school that had survived and moved on from the uncertainties of ten years before, but was still not

firmly on its feet. There were many issues he had to face up to: living accommodation for both staff and pupils was stark; the buildings needed maintenance – he was bemused by the judicious buckets that had to be placed by the stairs in the Cedars during particularly heavy rainstorms, and the cardboard and drawing pins that kept out the snow from the classrooms by De Salis; and the kitchen arrangements were basic, with two coal-fired ranges as the only cookers and two large discoloured earthenware sinks the sole means of washing up for the whole school.

And then there were the challenges offered by the growing youth culture of the decade. Short hair, conservative tastes in dress, a more deferential age – all were to yield within a mere ten years to the 'swinging sixties' ethos and the cult of the teenager. The school sought to maintain high standards of behaviour among the pupils; but the tenor of the times could not be totally resisted. The old regime whereby the boys were expected to be tough and manly, and to break the rules sometimes and take their punishment – which was still usually a beating – was crumbling. Quilter himself disliked caning the boys; Brian Creese (1963–6) declared himself 'quite privileged, as one of the few to be beaten by the headmaster after being caught smoking at Cheddar Gorge'.

I remember one occasion towards the end of my time at the school when Alan Quilter stood up at assembly and said 'All boys who have stolen from the tuck shop this year are to come to my office after assembly.' The entire school turned up! Not to be defeated, he dished out a punishment anyway: the whole school, day boys included, had to turn out at 8am for a cross-country run on three consecutive Sundays. In similar fashion, his detention was a three-mile run around Cedars at 6am.

Chris Nicholas (1959–68)

I liked Alan Quilter. He gave me the impression that he was a man who was playing at being the stereotypical headmaster – he would peer at you over the top of his spectacles in a very headmasterly way and make headmasterly statements such as 'Andrew, I don't see you as a straight-line career person', which I took as a huge compliment. I thought it meant I was interesting and windswept, creative and different – whereas in truth it probably meant that I lacked focus. There was a rule in those days that no boy's hair should be so long that it strayed over his collar. My hair, left to its own devices, was so naturally curly and gravity-defying that it would never reach my collar no matter how long it was left untrimmed. At one of our regular prefects' meetings with 'Punk' (for this was AKQ's nickname), having gently admonished several of our number for allowing their locks too free a rein, he gave me that over-the-glasses look and with a wry smile said 'Andrew, I don't quite know what to say about your hair except that there's too much of it – get it cut!'

Alan was an eminently sensible man. He decided that, once pupils had passed their eighteenth birthday, they could occasionally, with the permission of their housemaster, go to the pub for a drink. The nearest such venue was the Fountain, which was also the favourite watering hole of a group of the younger members of the teaching staff, including Peter Thomas, Paul Johnson, and others. In my upper sixth year we considered this group to be not just our teachers but our drinking buddies too – so much so that Les the landlord would call 'Time, ladies and gentlemen, please – and that includes Peter and the cathedral school!' I remember having to persuade Charles Sarland, a bearded, Land Rover-driving, somewhat maverick, and, on this occasion, well-oiled member of the teaching staff to react to Les's familiar catchphrase one night. Charles was a housemaster of the Cedars and lived on the premises. In order to walk him home, we had to pass Edwards, which was not only an annexe of the girls' boarding house but also where Alan Quilter lived with his family. As we meandered up The Liberty, Charles staggered ahead and, with mischief aforethought, jumped up onto the wall outside the headmaster's residence, balancing on one leg and giggling uncontrollably. At exactly that moment, the unmistakeable silhouette of Punk appeared at the front door. His right hand rose slowly to his face, and as he lowered his spectacles to the end of his nose, the better to peer over them at us, I feared the worst. We were late. We were drunk. We were done for! 'Ah, Andrew,' said the familiar voice; 'taking Mr Sarland home, I see. Thank you!'

Andy Jones (1962–72)

More fundamental, perhaps, was the fact that boarding itself as an automatic educational choice was becoming less popular, and there was increasingly intense competition for applicants within the independent sector; Quilter recalled interviewing only two prospective sets of parents during the whole of his first Michaelmas term in 1964. And there was still an underlying tension between those running the school on one hand and members of the dean and chapter on the other. This, at least, was a problem quickly solved, with the support of the dean of the time, David Edwards; he was a thoughtful, shrewd man who was easily persuaded that there was an immediate need to appoint lay governors, who could bring to the management team skills and experience beyond those that could be offered by churchmen. The first two lay governors were David Tudway Quilter, a banker who had just inherited the Tudway estate from his uncle, and Lord Waldegrave, an ex-government minister.

All those who remember Quilter's first few years at Wells recall the wackier ideas he came up with, from which on several occasions he had to be gently dissuaded. But he had inherited in his staff a close-knit community who enjoyed a lively camaraderie

I was eight years old when I arrived at Wells, when Claud Holmes was head of the junior school. I enjoyed the school play and started as an extra in Emil and the Detectives, graduating to sharing the lead with Nigel Hyslop as one of the cubs shipwrecked on a desert island in one of Claud Holmes' own creations. I moved on up to the Cedars into the tender care of Alan Tarbat. Looking back, this was the least happy period at Wells for me. Being in the big school was a bit of a shock to the system and it took time to adjust; but eventually I left the Cedars and went into De Salis, sharing a small study dorm and listening to Radio Luxembourg after lights out. I joined the gardening club and spent many happy hours tending the large garden out the back and admiring the wisps of smoke leaking out of the bushes. We diehard footie fans used every spare moment to play in the yard between the cookery department and the sports hall. We were only evicted when the CCF wanted to parade up and down.

Tim King (1965–74)

Above left: A portrait of Alan Quilter

Left: Lord Waldegrave, the second lay governor to be appointed during Alan Quilter's headship

and high morale; and they all also quickly recognised and appreciated his enormous energy and enthusiasm, and most of them were generous enough then and later to acknowledge the huge difference his new ideas and somewhat iconoclastic approach made to the future of the school.

However, it was clear in the mid-1960s that the school was chronically short of money, deficient in many of the facilities that were becoming increasingly essential for an institution that hoped to flourish within the independent sector, and facing an uncertain future within a rapidly changing world. Quilter realised that there had to be fundamental

innovations; and over the first few years of his headship he set about achieving these through three main initiatives: active fundraising; the admission of girls; and tapping into government funds by establishing music as a speciality in the school. The first of these was a strategy increasingly deployed by independent schools in the 1960s, and attracting a new brand of professionals who were able to offer help and advice; and the second was a rapidly growing option for previously all-male boarding schools which needed to fill their dormitories. But it was the third initiative – the development of music at Wells – that was to prove the decisive catalyst for the

The Queen Mother at the opening of the sports hall in July 1969; in the foreground Giles Thorman, who had just delivered the prologue to the Elizabethan play put on in her honour

Alan Quilter was a truly amazing man. He taught me briefly in 1969 and had not set eyes on me for ten years, but when I returned to the school in 1985 for an old boys' weekend, and approached him with Richard Leigh, he immediately said without a second's hesitation, 'Richard, Giles, how nice to see you both again.' I can't imagine how many hundreds of pupils he must have seen during those ten years.

Giles Thorman (1968–75)

An innovation was the arrival of girls in the school. First there were one or two and then there seemed to be floods of them, even earning their own house halfway down The Liberty. I was particularly put out when I failed to become top of the form again because a new girl called Julia usurped my position. She was the one who took to the stage to receive a prize from the good old Queen Mum as I sat sulking in the crowd. O-levels came and went. Britain was in the throes of mighty industrial unrest in the early 1970s and we had to contend with the three-day week. The power would go off with great regularity and I remember sitting on the stairs of De Salis in the glow of candles and gas lamps unable to do any homework and with Mr Bigny fretting over our plight. Eventually I made it into the sixth form and in my last year was promoted to prefect. I was in the cross-country team with future Olympian Danny Nightingale and went to far-flung places such as Milton Abbey to run through the mud. My interest in films had blossomed and, together with George Bushell, I ran both the school and the sixth form film societies. We bought a widescreen lens and constructed a bigger screen so we could enjoy Clint Eastwood westerns in their full glory. And there is still one of many mysteries to solve about my school days – who kept nicking the film posters I put up to advertise film society screenings?

Tim King (1965–74)

school's flourishing development during the last three decades of the twentieth century (for which, see pages 138–59). And it was the forward-thinking nature of this initiative – that the new specialist music scheme at Wells should be established and developed within the environment of a normal school offering all the normal school subjects and facilities – that was to turn Wells into an establishment which is probably unique in the world.

However, Alan Quilter's first, urgent priority was to build the largest covered space that could be afforded. Not only was there no school hall large enough to accommodate everyone who needed to be there on formal occasions such as prizegiving, but there were no facilities for playing indoor sports or for allowing the boys to exercise in bad weather. A sports hall was needed, as well as – if it could be afforded – a swimming pool. It was also clear that Ritchie Hall, which had been carved out of the Bernard Building, could be made more useful if it could be opened out at one end and a permanent stage created.

Raising the money for these initiatives was Quilter's first foray into fundraising. He was greatly helped by the new lay governors, as well as by professionals brought in for the purpose, and the whole enterprise proved both hugely time-consuming and hugely successful. Not only did it raise covenants totalling £50,000, which allowed building work to begin, but it also brought him into contact with all sorts of supportive and useful people from all over the country. The massive amount of extra work necessitated by the project was not helped by the fact that Peter Henfrey had decided to retire in 1965 and the first bursar appointed as his replacement did not last long. Quilter had to endure a difficult six months acting as both headmaster and bursar; he recalled spending part of Boxing Day that year totalling school bills on an antiquated manual adding machine. However, things eased when the new bursar, Jerry Coote, arrived. He proved to be an excellent appointment, and immediately set to work both to reorganise the school's finances into an up-to-date form and to manage the building of the sports hall.

Imagine being a just-orphaned fourteen-year-old, sent off to a boarding school in a strange country, faced for the first time with male classmates, an intensive music programme, and the realisation that she had brains. I arrived at Wells, fresh off the boat from Belfast, the day before my fifteenth birthday in April 1973, and was stunned by the beauty of the place. The reports sent from my Irish school had indicated that I was not very bright and hopeless at maths; accordingly I was placed in the bottom stream of the maths O-level class. When I achieved a final exam score of 97% at the end of that first term, apologies were profuse and I was moved up to Mr Johnson's middle stream class, where I flourished under the best maths teacher the school fielded. My real love, however, was Latin. I devoured every aspect of the classics course taught by Mr Bishop, ending up as the only student taking A-level in my year and taking O-level classical Greek at the same time. This passion for the classics was ironic, as my mother and I, prior to her death, had chosen Wells as the best place for me to pursue my presumed future career as a musician. I did take O-level music, and I started on the A-level course, but I dropped it after a week, realising that four A-levels would seriously cramp my leisure time. However, I remained a consistently 'serious' musician, playing viola in the chamber orchestra and in a very demanding two-viola quintet, as well as singing in the chamber chorus, which was the highest level to which a girl could then aspire in the choral world of the cathedral.

I have many memories: playing for an eighteen-year-old Simon Rattle with some Japanese students at the International Festival of Youth Orchestras in Aberdeen in 1974; climbing Glastonbury Tor on Sunday afternoons; the pouring rain that penetrated the dreadful old Nissen huts that formed most of our classrooms; playing the organ, in a state of almost catatonic terror, for evensong in the cathedral; late night trips in the bus after attending RSC productions at Stratford; playing Albinoni's Adagio for Strings *on Jimmy Saville's TV show in London. I also remember trying to hide how much I was crying on the last prize day when I received the school shield as the first head girl; that shield hangs in my study at St Francis Episcopal Church in Great Falls, Virginia, where I now serve as rector.*

Wells was a remarkably healing place for me. The sheer beauty of the architecture and the rural surroundings were a great contrast to the industrial grit of Belfast, and the encouragement that I received from the staff helped in their different ways to hold me together at a devastating time of my life. The school motto, Esto quod es, *has stayed with me and has played a significant role in my formation as an Anglican priest. I am still in awe that I attended a school that had served boys for over a thousand years (and girls for about four) when I arrived.*

Penny FitzGibbon (1973–6)

Senior school assemblies could now be held in the new sports hall; Ritchie Hall is still used for junior school assemblies

I remember Matron Staniforth singing 'Good strippings (perfect fifth) and curtains for a little air', while striding into each Cedars dorm and opening all the windows, even in the depth of winter. Mr Gillen would immediately close them again to save the heating bill — we had a single-bar electric fire per room. I also remember her wash-check: boys standing in a queue and showing her, in that order, palms, back of hands, left ear, right ear, neck, and teeth. If anyone got things in the order wrong he would be sent to the back of the queue. Then there was Mr Gillen's 'compulsory enjoyment' on rainy Sunday afternoons: eight laps of Cedars field.

Matthew Train (1979–89)

I was looking for something in my loft the other day and came across a number of ancient items from my time at Wells, including a programme from the Wells concert tour of Norway, Sweden, and Finland in 1973. It was from our first concert in the Johanneskirken, Bergen, on Friday August 24. Although I had technically just left the school and was awaiting my A-level results, I was one of several recent leavers who were invited back to swell the numbers. I can remember driving by coach all the way up from Wells to Newcastle Airport, where we caught a flight to Norway.

My claim to fame, if you can call it that, during this trip was to be taken seriously ill during the first part in Norway. We were scheduled to perform in Bergen on August 24 and then go on to Sweden and Finland, returning again to Stockholm to catch the ferry back to England. I can remember feeling unwell on the coach trip from Bergen and then going into hospital at Karlstad in Sweden as an emergency to have my appendix removed. I should have been reading something in Helsinki Cathedral once we got to Finland, and was very disappointed not to make it. I also found two postcards sent to me from Uppsala — a get well card in two parts, addressed to me in Ward 44 of the Centrallasavettet in Karlstad from Mike Stubbings and other members of the tour. I came home with my appendix in a jar, but it's not in my loft with the other items any more!

Richard Lambert (1966–73)

The sports hall, now (in 2008) with a new floor

Prizegiving at the Regal Cinema

Until the building of the new sports hall, the only room in Wells large enough to accommodate the school for the traditional prizegiving ceremony was the Regal Cinema. Alan Quilter recalled its limitations: 'The cinema (a minor gem of an Art Deco building) had been excellently devised as a cinema but not as an auditorium for a live production. The stage was woefully cramped; its edge was fortunately marked by a line of exotic pot plants which were always brought in for the occasion by a local nurseryman, and which at least ensured that an elderly member of the chapter was not suddenly projected into the front stalls. On the other side sat the parents, eager for a proud glimpse of a son or fearful of yet another announcement of a fee increase. What the parents did not see was the sight below the stage that preceded the ceremonies. There, in a dusty, brick-lined cellar, the governors, headmaster, and traditional distinguished guest quite literally crouched and waited for the signal to start. The cellar was about five foot in height; the dean was six foot six! Moreover, the proceedings had to be carefully timed, for the proprietor was often lurking in the wings and could be heard whispering such anxious advice as "Hurry up. *The Guns of Navarone* starts at 4.45 and we've got to get the screen back!"'

The Regal Cinema was also the setting for the final singing, in 1965, of what had become the somewhat outmoded school song:

England, dear motherland,
Queen of the sea,
Chief of a thousand states,
Home of the free!
Sons that are brave and true,
Here and afar,
May they in life's stern fight,
Be what they are.

Boys, sons of Britain, hear!
Know ye your race?
Ye spring from sires that dared
Legions to face;
Naught could their spirit break,
Their honour mar;
Strive to be brave as they,
Be what you are!

Boyhood will grow to youth,
Manhood come soon;
Life's morning mist will melt
Into clear noon:
Evening will cloud the sky,
Shadows fall fast,
Soon the dark night sweep down,
And life be past!

But the whole day be brave,
Heroes in fight,
Girt with the arms of truth,
Stainless and bright;
What though the conflict bring
Many a scar,
Still to yourselves be true,
Be what you are!

Quilter recognised the construction of the hall as a watershed in the development of the school. As he memorably noted, it was one of the largest buildings in terms of floor space to be built in that area of Wells since the cathedral. 'I can remember the sense of anxiety as I saw those bare enormous girders rising above the old Cedars kitchen gardens. It looked so much more imposing than anything that the school had previously possessed…'.

The next challenge was the move towards coeducation. There were several cogent reasons for Alan Quilter to consider at the end of the 1960s that

the admission of girls was the logical next step in both ensuring the school's survival and preparing it for the future. Indeed, such changes were already afoot within the sector, for example at Marlborough which now accepted girls into the sixth form. Moreover, the tenor of the times was a factor: the days were gone when the only officially sanctioned contact between boys and girls of neighbouring schools came about through embarrassingly artificial inter-school dances, with staff patrolling the grounds with torches to keep the sexes apart anywhere other than on the dance floor.

There was a great deal of debate about the issue, among governors, staff, and parents, and the final decision was that it would be best not to limit the admission of girls just to the sixth form, but – in order to allow boys and girls to grow up together through the school and eventually to achieve a mature mixed sixth form – to start coeducation in the junior school. But while it was also felt that the sexes should be mixed for all possible school activities, the housing accommodation had to be rigidly single-sex, so that boys and girls could, when they wished, get away from each other.

The trigger to open the school to girls came when the headmistress of Shepton Mallet Convent School telephoned to say that they had made the decision to close, and to ask whether Quilter would consider taking some of their girls. After further rapid discussions the decision was taken – Wells Cathedral School would go coeducational from September 1969. Twenty-nine girls arrived in the junior school, twelve of whom were boarders who were housed in what had been the organist's house and is now Polydor.

This first intake resulted in a crash course in coeducation undertaken by everyone in the school from the headmaster down. As he later recorded, he came to the rapid conclusion that girls were far less shy than boys and much more inclined to make their feelings known rather than bottle them up or put apparent unfairnesses down to experience. One ferociously bright girl, as he remembered with affection, set him challenges 'not so much by

Matron Staniforth used to help the senior boys with the arrangements for dances in Ritchie Hall. On one occasion, she did her usual stint with the boy who was arranging everything – doing the flowers, helping with the food, seeing that the boys' lavatories were made suitable for girls – when, almost at the last moment, he came dashing up to her wailing 'Matron, matron, we've got everything ready – but I've forgotten to order the girls!'

breaking the rules as by asking very firmly indeed why the rules were there in the first place'.

The curriculum now had to accommodate subjects, like home economics, which formed a traditional part of girls' education; but at the same time it was decided that all subjects should be open to both boys and girls. It did not take long for girl applicants to come forward at all levels of the school, including the sixth form – indeed, by the middle of the 1970s there were girls in every year throughout the school – so the provision of houses for the girls had to expand quickly too. And it was now essential to appoint senior female staff who would not only teach but also act as housemistresses.

Plumptre House

A crucial early appointment was that of Mary Nash (now Mary Williams), who joined in 1972 to teach English and RE and as housemistress of the senior girls' boarding house; in 1975 she also became senior mistress, in overall charge of the girls. Until she arrived, the older girl boarders had lived at the top of number 23 The Liberty (now Edwards), with Sheila Quilter looking after them. But now number 21, Plumptre, was vacated by the boys, who moved into the newly named Shrewsbury House in Vicars' Close, and it became the first complete senior girls' house under Miss Nash. The younger girls, aged eleven to fourteen, lived in Claver Morris, with Elizabeth Green as their housemistress, until she and her husband decided to live outside school and Caroline Gingell was appointed to replace her. Along with Angela Tippett, who arrived soon afterwards to teach science and look after the growing numbers of girl boarders who had by now taken over the whole of Edwards, these housemistresses quickly established the sort of firm but caring regime which was of inestimable value in laying the foundations of successful coeducation at Wells.

While the practicalities caused some upheaval, the culture of the school quickly began to change as the nuances of coeducation asserted themselves. Changing out of uniform into casual clothes after school became the norm. Corporal punishment, now anyway reserved to the headmaster, gradually disappeared. And the 'them and us' approach of traditional boys' schools began to seem inappropriate – an attitude perhaps characterised at the beginning by the dilemma of what to call the girls in class. It didn't seem right to carry on calling boys by their surnames if the same was not true for the girls; but calling girls by their surnames did not come naturally. Mary Nash dealt with the issue by calling all her pupils Mr and Miss.

Dormitories, once firmly out of bounds during the day and reserved strictly for sleeping, now became homes from home, adorned with posters, photographs, and the general clutter of teenage bedrooms; it was increasingly recognised that young people needed spaces like this where they could be

private. Counselling sessions replaced punishment in some instances, or urgings towards the 'stiff upper lip'. Even the question of illicit smoking was addressed, when sixth formers were given a room in which they could, with parental permission, light up – though this concession did not long survive the arrival of the new head in 1986. During his first speech day address John Baxter announced that he would not be continuing the policy and that smoking would now be banned – to a sustained burst of spontaneous applause from the audience. But this was all part of the growing recognition in the 1970s and later that young people approaching adulthood could usually be trusted to behave responsibly. And Wells shared in the experience of other formerly single-sex schools which introduced coeducation in the late 1960s and early 1970s, that going mixed had beneficial social effects as well as providing a wealth of new talent and skill.

With the school firmly established as a coeducational boarding school with a flourishing musical speciality, Alan Quilter spent his final ten years as head building on and strengthening the

It was a somewhat challenging experience being one of the first women on the staff at Wells. The common room was very much a male domain, within which I trod with caution, and – along with all other departments at the school – there were few creature comforts and a great deal of making do. There were no female changing facilities or lavatories in the main buildings – staff and girls had to dash back to the houses – and my own accommodation in Plumptre at first consisted only of two rooms on the ground floor, a shower room on the first floor landing, and a kitchen which I shared with the cleaners. I was the only resident adult in the house, in the evenings, and had just two evenings off duty a week plus two Saturdays or Sundays a term. A fellow staff member, who ran a bit of a sideline in antique furniture, would advise me when he saw a useful item going cheap in a local auction, which I would then sometimes buy to enhance the meagre furnishings of my rooms. It was a relief when the little cottage next to the house was converted for me; it had been the canoe shed, and I still recall with amusement the sight of a canoe being manoeuvred out of the little upstairs window, looking like a giant tongue.

The workload was heavy. In addition to a full teaching timetable and running the house, I was also asked to take on the library, and one year managed the school timetable as well – and of course I then became senior mistress in overall charge of the girls and their welfare. We female staff also had to run the girls' games, and found ourselves refereeing netball and hockey matches without knowing the rules. It was much easier to organise improving walks on the Mendips, with a picnic, for the girls who chose that activity rather than sports.

There were some mutterings when Plumptre was redecorated and refurbished for the girls, but in truth it was hard for them to be the pioneers in this previously masculine environment, with few peers of their own sex and equally few female staff to go to for support. They needed their privacy, and although they did enjoy the boys' company, it was necessary to have strict rules about when they could go into each others' houses and when they could go out into town with each other. But it didn't take long for things to settle down, and it quickly became clear that coeducation was working well, and had been exactly the right move for the school.

Mary Williams (née Nash, staff, 1972–82)

changes he had introduced. More lay governors were appointed, including women; classrooms were built in the junior school and in the stable yard; well equipped science laboratories were constructed; a new library and dining hall were built, and the interior of the Cedars was refurbished; a wider range of subjects was offered, including technological skills and craft and design, and more emphasis was placed on art and drama. And in common with all other schools, Wells had to learn to cope with IT, both as a subject to be taught and as an increasingly vital tool in school management and administration.

The school generally, and the specialist music scheme in particular, benefited from the assisted places scheme, introduced at the end of the 1970s; academic standards continued to rise, and extra-curricular activities expanded; and in 1979 election to the Headmasters' Conference was an apt acknowledgement of Wells Cathedral School's enhanced reputation, along with that of its charismatic head. By the time the *History* was published in 1985, when Alan Quilter was a year away from retirement, the school had transformed itself almost entirely, and his successor, who arrived in September 1986, inherited a flourishing and vigorous institution.

Onward and outward
John Baxter

There are a number of places in the world which, seen for the first time, provide unforgettable memories. Vicars' Close in Wells is one such place, and my first sight was as a candidate for headship being given a tour of the school. Living and working in such a beautiful city for nearly fifteen years was a real privilege.

Inheriting the headship of such a fine school after twenty-two years of Alan Quilter's iconic stewardship was another privilege, and it is impossible to do more than touch upon some of the many glorious recollections that now enrich retirement. The first group I came to know was, of course, the governing body; but I was also honoured to meet, in the first month of my headship, the school's enthusiastic patron, Prince Charles. I was attending the confirmation at Windsor Castle of Lord Nicholas Windsor, a member of my house at Westminster, and the prince is one of his godparents. On hearing of my new post he expressed pleasure that he would see a

familiar face when he came to open the newly restored cathedral west front and, typically, made a point of speaking to me on Cathedral Green. He later made an official visit to the school, musicians performed for him at St James's Palace and at Hatfield House, and he generously hosted a fundraising event at Highgrove in my final term.

The best advertisement for a school is often the pupils. From the moment I met Wells students on my introductory tour of the school to my final days, I could not have wished for a more delightful student body: polite, cheerful, exceptionally friendly, and eminently sensible about their 'work-life balance'. Their relationship with staff was invariably cordial and respectful. My wife visited Bath during our first term and was surprised and delighted to be greeted in the street by a Wells pupil she did not know. Many of those pupils have become friends. Many are now parents themselves, and tragically, a few are no longer with us. The loss of a pupil hits a school hard. The sudden death of Mamokete Mongale on her return home after two years at Wells, where she had been supported by the Bishop Simeon Trust, was particularly painful. To be asked to speak at her funeral in her township was both an honour and extraordinarily emotional.

On arrival at Wells I was acutely conscious of the enormous goodwill and support emanating from the parents. Unusually, there was no parents' association so Philip Peabody and I quickly created one. We persuaded Mike Hay, father of two children in the school, to become the first chair. The association was not formed to raise money, although from time to time it did so with characteristic verve and generosity. It was created to provide a productive partnership between the school and the parents, and a number of important initiatives were generated from that source.

It was music that attracted me to the post of head at Wells, and of course the unique attraction of a school where a specialist music scheme operates within a conventional framework. Among the many delights of working with musicians was to watch 'home-grown' students develop over the years to reach specialist standard, to watch specialists play rugby and netball or, in at least one case, take a leading part in school plays, and to know that musicians would benefit from academic teaching of the highest standard among students whose gifts in mathematics, languages, sciences, or the arts equalled theirs in music. It is also one of the great privileges of the teaching profession to provide opportunities for students with great musical potential but with specific learning or social difficulties. For these Wells was probably the only school capable of providing appropriate help and tuition.

I also quickly realised that Alan Quilter had left a school of potential world-class excellence. He and Frank Commings had established sound foundations for closer relationships beyond Europe. Musicians and choristers had already visited Asia, North America, and New Zealand, and a number of pupils, principally but not exclusively musicians, came from overseas. An unusual and little-known statistic revealed in 1990 that Wells educated more children of service families

John Baxter with The Prince of Wales

than any other independent school, a consequence partly of geography, but mainly of coeducational boarding from the ages of eight to eighteen and Quilter's decision to fix the boarding fee at the level of the services boarding schools' allowance.

At the same time, however, we took a clear policy decision not to follow the increasing number of independent boarding schools who were seeking to boost numbers by aggressive recruitment, especially from Asia. We did not wish to sacrifice quality for quantity, and we were determined to maintain the 'Britishness' of boarding education which all parents sought for their children. We did, however, wish to seek closer relationships with schools of similar distinction throughout the world, a decision which was to provide exciting opportunities for both staff and students.

On a personal level, I just about coped with the role of narrator in *The Snowman* with Penny Stirling's 'Second Orchestra', a wonderful vehicle for the many students for whom special provision for music was made available in the timetable. But Roger Durston's invitation to narrate *Peter and the Wolf* was an altogether more terrifying experience. Three performances were given, two in the Colston Hall in Bristol and one in Wells Cathedral. On each occasion the venues were packed and I learnt something of the pre-performance nervous tension that is an essential part of any significant event. One of the most touching gifts on retirement was a composition by Tim French, entitled 'Fanfarewell', performed at the final concert of the school year in 2000 and constructed using the letters of my name in Morse code as the rhythmic basis of the piece, ending on a B major chord corresponding to the first letter of my surname.

In a city as small as Wells it is inevitable that the cathedral school should have a conspicuous role. It was always pleasing to be told by residents that pupils had been greatly missed during the school holidays. Relations between the city and the school were always constructive and usually warm. The school contributed significantly to the economy of the city, not only through the 200+ employees, but also through the many visits by parents, friends, and audiences. Among the local issues in which the school played a part were the fate of the Cottage Hospital, the long-awaited relief road, and the development of the Mendip Hospital site. Plans to build a new concert hall at the top of Cedars field created more than a slight flutter in the Civic Society, and the provision of new rugby pitches at Tor Furlong angered the Ramblers. The *Wells Journal* always welcomed school material, but strangely never reported sports results.

The inaugural match on the new Cedars cricket square; John Baxter batting for the Willows

It was good to share a warm relationship with successive heads of the Blue School. Annual sports fixtures involving both pupils and staff, the interchange of pupils in a few specific subjects, and a joint initiative to establish a Children's University in Wells were all indications of a wish to support all children irrespective of educational (and social) background. The warmth of local relationships extended to both Mendip District Council and Somerset County Council where the chief executive and chair, respectively, worked in harmony with the school on a number of initiatives. One, in particular, was launched soon after the dreadful accident at Chernobyl. The school quickly became an active part of the Children of Chernobyl initiative, a charity which embraced a wide range of devoted supporters in and around Wells, and helped a large number of children from Belarus, damaged by the effects of radiation.

I was assistant houseparent in Plumptre in the late 1980s, and remember one time when I was woken by a frantic knock on my door one night at about 2am. It was one of the year 9 girls who'd rushed down to find me because there was a man outside their window trying to get in. I quickly roused my dogs who saw him off – and when I went into the dorm to reassure the girls, who were all good hockey players and not at all wimpish, I was amused to see that they had all lifted their sheets and hidden behind them. I phoned the police, of course, only to be told that the only car available was in Taunton! They turned up about an hour later, but the intruder was long gone. I also remember my Romeo and Juliet story, though one with a happier ending – two sixth formers who had been going out together since year 9 and who always had to say goodnight to each other even after a late concert or outing. I once commented jokily that they had better invite me to the wedding – and three years later they did just that!

Susie Jameson (staff, 1985–9 and 1992–present)

The Mamokete Mongale Award

Mamokete Mongale, from South Africa (1992–4), was a very popular student and often in the middle of things during her time at the school. It was a huge shock and sadness to hear that she had died suddenly only a few days after finally leaving Wells and returning to South Africa. Her death deeply affected the school; the headmaster went to her funeral in South Africa, and there was a fantastic memorial service held for her in Wells Cathedral. Moreover, the strong feeling that her coming to the school had enriched everyone there led to the decision in 1995 to set up an award in her memory. The Mamokete Mongale prize is awarded annually to the competition entry which, in the judges' opinion, reflects most sensitively and perceptively any aspect of life relevant to racial harmony, best meets the objectives of raising awareness of cross-cultural issues, and encourages students to explore and respond individually to these issues.

That first year, there were fifty-three entries for the award from the middle and senior schools, and the first prize went to Freya van Hensbergen. The prize has continued ever since, and its 2007 winner was Annabel Jones (2002–present; pictured), who won for her song 'Be what you are', the final verse of which appears below. Her words on winning: 'I was a girl chorister for three years and am now a specialist singer, a member of chapel and chamber choir, and a Big Band vocalist. Songwriting is my passion and music is in my blood (literally: my dad was also a chorister at Wells), so I consider myself privileged to be a member of such a creative and caring environment, where I know Mamokete would also have thrived. When I heard about the competition I knew it was the best opportunity for me to highlight some of the issues that she faced and that still fester in our society today: prejudice, racism, and as a consequence poverty and death. To be yourself is imperative for happiness, and I think that's why our school motto *Esto quod es* is so relevant. I only wish it could be a universal motto, and that there were no forces that said otherwise. Until then, there's my song… and hope…'.

You can't break our spirits,
You can't put us down,
You can throw your sticks and stones,
But how much good will that do now?
'Cos we're all united wishing on the same star,
Looking for peace, looking for freedom,
Looking for love to light up the world;
Esto quod es: be what you are.

Andrew's Tandem Weekends

At the beginning of the 1989 summer holidays, Wells student Andrew Plowman was killed in a tragic accident on a Cornwall beach. Shortly afterwards, his parents set up a trust fund in his memory which would offer disabled children the opportunity to experience the sort of outdoor activities that Andrew had loved. Working closely with John Baxter, they decided to dedicate the fund to what they called 'Andrew's Tandem Weekends', named after an initiative Baxter had launched in New Zealand whereby blind children could enjoy cycle rides by riding tandem with sighted children. Both he and the Plowmans were heavily involved in the weekends, which were an annual event brilliantly run by Dick Crane.

The first was in May 1990, when children with visual handicaps from a school in Worcester arrived to spend a weekend with their Wells hosts at a camp on Crane's own land at Birdwood on the outskirts of Wells. The younger children were supervised by members of staff and sixth form students from both schools, and a variety of activities were on offer, including caving, climbing, and shooting, and culminating in a good old sing-song round the camp fire. As their hosts quickly discovered, the fact that the children were either partially or totally blind made little difference to anything; indeed, the sighted joined in the caving expeditions without lamps so that they all had the same sort of experience.

A couple of years later children with Down's syndrome from Portsmouth demonstrated how adaptable they were despite obvious difficulties. Once again they experienced all sorts of regular outdoor activities, as well as others specially devised to accommodate their disabilities. The visitors had a thoroughly good time, and their hosts too experienced both a tough mental and physical challenge and a great sense of achievement from helping to make the weekend so enjoyable and fruitful. The weekends went on for several years, until Dick Crane left and the increasing pressures of league tables and academic monitoring meant that no other member of staff had the time or the resources to organise and run them.

To live and work in such glorious buildings in the shadow of a magnificent cathedral is, of course, a huge privilege. Pupils might not always have enjoyed the experience of regular attendance at services in the cathedral, but all will look back on their exposure to the stunning architecture with pride and gratitude. For the school, however, the pleasure carried with it heavy responsibility and significant financial burdens. The Liberty Restoration Programme was already in existence before 1986, and the school was committed to regular renovation of the medieval and Georgian houses it occupies. Moreover, such work had to be carried out to high and expensive standards insisted upon by English Heritage. Nevertheless, despite the attentions of august bodies, the school was able to complete additional work in Mitchell's Mews, a new sixth form common room, a new science building, a music technology building and classrooms, a pre-prep building, further classrooms, and the acquisition of properties in New Street.

A school is only as good as the staff it employs. It is no exaggeration to say that it gave me the greatest joy to work with a most devoted, professional, conscientious, and friendly staff for nearly fifteen years, and the premature death of ten of them during my headship was a great sadness. The support staff are sometimes overlooked, but they play a huge part in the larger Wells 'family'. This was a very important aspect in the lives of so many pupils, many of whose parents lived and worked thousands of miles away. The superbly attractive grounds were kept in immaculate condition by dedicated ground staff. The many 'temporary' buildings required constant maintenance, we all needed feeding, the areas in which we lived and worked required cleaning, and the business of the school needed to be efficiently administered. In the sick bay, the library, the book store, the technicians' labs, the matrons' areas, and the clothing shop there was nothing but warm, positive assistance. The secretaries were brilliant, particularly mine, a crucial area as the first point of contact is often an enquiry made to them. The full-time teaching staff were supplemented by part-time staff, notably in the music department. It was a pleasure to get to know distinguished instrumental teachers who regularly travelled every week to Wells, in some cases for over thirty years.

I can identify three features which mark the quality of the professional staff and the pleasure of working with them at Wells. The first is dedication. Nothing was ever too much trouble. Commitment both to work in the classroom and to extra-curricular activities was total. The second is professional excellence. This is partly reflected in the fact that during my headship six members of the senior staff and one of the junior staff became heads of schools elsewhere. Sad as it is to lose good staff, such promotion reflects well on a school. The final feature is the sheer enjoyment, the sense of fun. Playing cricket for the Willows, travelling to the new Millennium Stadium to watch Wales play rugby, winning 'coach of the week' at the morning staff meeting, attending the hugely enjoyable annual Christmas dinners, being invited to tour with the rugby team in Paris and Brussels (and having to control the parents!), and touring with the musicians all provided huge delight. And the one activity that combined these three areas, and unequivocally defined for me the special ambience of my time at Wells, was the Andrew's Tandem adventure weekends (see 74). To have been headmaster of such a splendid school for fifteen years, and to have had the pleasure and privilege of leading it into the new millennium, are honours beyond price.

Left: Sometime tuck shop and bookstore, and now the clothing shop, this building on its staddles is the longest surviving traditional Somerset granary

Below: Alan Hutt, long-serving specialist trombone teacher, gives a lesson as part of the music department's outreach activities

Another new millennium
Elizabeth Cairncross

I came to Wells in 2000 from Christ's Hospital, where I was deputy head. I was aware before I came for interview that this was a very different school from most others, because of its unique offering of both specialist music tuition and a rounded education in an ordinary school environment. I knew too that it achieved this difficult mix at an extraordinarily high level. I recall being both intrigued and fascinated, but also having a few personal qualms as to whether it was the right move for me at that time; Christ's Hospital is a difficult place to leave. It was only when I left after my final session with the governors that it struck me like a blow that I would be deeply disappointed if I were not offered the job. Then I reached home and the phone rang…

The school's retiring head, John Baxter, and his predecessors, Alan Quilter and Frank Commings, had achieved a massive turn-round in its fortunes over a mere fifty years, building on a tradition of real focus on trying to look after people well by the standards of whatever the time was, and always with the golden thread of music – for a long time largely through the choristers – running through the core of the school. The staff I inherited were enormously accomplished and committed. The pupils too were a stimulating mix of talents and backgrounds – whether they were specialist musicians or had other artistic, academic, or sporting aptitudes. Thanks to government assistance, many of them came from families who would not otherwise have been able to send them to an independent school, so there was a good social mix as well as a healthy leavening of different nationalities. The whole placed buzzed with an innovative, 'can do' attitude, which had its roots in the needs of the choristers and the music specialists, with the demands they made for hard work and dedication – as well as flexible and pragmatic timetabling – but had clearly become integral to the whole culture.

There were, however, problems in sight, not least the fact that the government was phasing out the assisted places scheme, which would mean the loss of 100 students with no immediately obvious way of replacing them. Unlike many other independent schools, Wells was not the default option for the children of its alumni, so recruitment was a growing and continuing priority, and efforts put into it had to be ratcheted up very quickly. Moreover, the sorts of fundraising and development initiatives that are so ubiquitous now within the independent sector had never taken real root. There had been campaigns, but their limited ability to deliver against raised expectations had led to scepticism about their purpose and value. Inevitably, the eventual introduction of a proper development office, properly staffed and properly led, with good governor support, was not easy for people at a time when we were having to be very careful indeed financially; as the school has grown again, it continues to be a challenge for people to be financially disciplined to the degree that is necessary if we are to develop into the future and not sink into a Wells sunset. The most important factor in this evolution has been the real love that Wells inspires in its community. The development director and his work are now firmly at the centre of fundraising and recruitment activities, and of the desire and need to get in touch with our alumni and build them into a force for the good of the school.

When we worked with the Peak Performance Organisation to focus our minds on what we really believed about Wells, and included students, alumni, staff present and past, support and teaching, parents present and past, and governors, we found that we agreed that our 'character' as a school was to be 'loving, joyful, including, can do, bold, creating, competitive, and inspiring'. It's a list of which we are proud and to which we aspire every day. It enables us to change as well as to innovate – two things which Wells has always been good at, I think, hence its survival for so long and in so many guises. Change means stopping doing some things as well as doing new things, and that can be hard; focusing on our 'character' helps.

All the positive things in the school were very positive indeed, at all levels and in every discipline. I soon saw that what is so stimulating at Wells is that the ethos gets itself everywhere, and that everyone partakes of the atmosphere it inculcates. Whether in academic subjects, or sport, or drama – and of course in music – there is a willingness to say the unsayable, to say 'yes' not 'no', to make things happen.

There is nothing unusual, for example, about the whole of the junior school suspending its entire timetable so that the children can all participate in some special extra-curricular activity that challenges them in different ways. Equally, we don't mind that we are at the bottom of the national league tables for GCSE maths – quite simply because we get excellent results in the International GCSE which the government statisticians do not recognise but the universities do. Our pupils are not disadvantaged by our decision to go down that route – but it took some guts and some persuasive powers to introduce something which would certainly result in negative publicity but which we felt was for the general good in our particular environment. On one level we offer Mandarin, taught by wonderful teachers who come from Shanghai for a year; and on another, although we don't offer a formal GCSE in the subject of food and nutrition, we insist that everyone learns to cook.

In sport, we have taken advantage of the arrival of a new staff member with a particular expertise to achieve phenomenally high standards in shooting in a very short time. There are scores of other similar examples of this 'can do' culture, both in our day-to-day life at school and within our wider strategy.

As I quickly discovered, Wells Cathedral School is small but infernally complex – or beautifully sophisticated, depending on the nature of the challenge! Above all, I found that the balance between the central position music holds in the school and all the other vital things that go on can be tricky to maintain. We have to work very hard to dispel the impression that 'music gets all the attention', and to ensure that the immense sense of purpose that runs though a large part of the school – through our specialist musicians and our choristers – encompasses everything else we do as well. And we do that crucially by encouraging and focusing on the importance of teamwork, and by using the specific strengths of our musicians to foster similar strengths in all our other talented pupils. Music has a very public presence at the school – we hear it trickling out of our buildings all the time; and we use that ubiquity to bind the school together rather than allowing it to become either divisive or off-putting.

I therefore make no apology for focusing on music at Wells as a metaphor for all that we are achieving here. Music makes demands on its practitioners on all sorts of different levels, starting perhaps with inbuilt ability but swiftly moving on to dedication, commitment, and sheer grinding hard work. It requires individual skill combined with teamwork. In ensemble work it brings together people of different ages, different abilities, different levels of achievement, who are required to work together to a common end. It demands that individual feelings and likes or dislikes are put aside for the greater good of the whole. A solo virtuoso performance is wonderful, and will certainly have needed hours of solitary practice; but equally wonderful – and equally hard to achieve – are the joint individual contributions that make up a soaring

piece of ensemble music. Our musicians have been known to comment that they found chamber music in their adult lives disappointing after their experience at Wells; and this is because they had been well taught here to 'adjust around each other' – a quotation from Peter Maxwell Davies, who uses it to describe groups of musicians genuinely working together rather than merely playing the same piece of music as other virtuosos – groups he actually enjoys conducting rather than those where he feels he's merely keeping them in time.

And music also requires listeners, and interaction with non-performers. It is here, in my view, that the musical metaphor for the school cuts deepest – in the effect it can and does have here on those whose main purpose at school is other than to study and play music. The teamwork point used above for music can apply to every area of school life; but there is more. A small boy who is struck dumb by the sheer musical ability of one of his friends can be led, through his perception of just how good that friend is at what he does, to see that he too has talents which he needs to believe in and work on. And when he sees just how much time and effort go into the endless practice his friend does, and how much blood, sweat, and tears are necessary on top of innate talent for progress to be made, he realises that he too must put in the effort necessary to do well in his chosen area of excellence.

When I first came here I spent a lot of time thinking about what the school is and what we believe in. It quickly became clear, in talking to past and present staff and pupils, that there is – and has been for many years – a vigorous sense of community at Wells, and that this is strengthened by the many different talents and personalities we have here in all parts of the school. Specialist musicians, who may well feel like fish out of water in another environment, quickly recognise that 'there are people like me here'. And they also quickly see that they don't have to explain themselves to their fellow pupils – their friends understand them and enjoy them for both their similarities and their differences. You don't have to be one kind of person

at Wells – and that is why our motto is so completely right!

There has been change over the eight years since I arrived, and there will be more. A school that becomes complacent and stuffy is a school that is moribund. My job is to maintain the balance between the special values we have here and the need to move forward within the particular political and economic climate of the beginning of the twenty-first century. We are fundraising for new buildings and we are open to new ideas in every area of school life. And just as I acknowledge that we at the school now are firmly cut down to size by our 1100 years of history, I also look forward with pride and anticipation, in the knowledge that we are planning for a future that we don't entirely understand. Just as my main focus for pupils is 'what will they be like in ten years' time, after they've left Wells', so my main focus for the school has to be that it can continue to exist, with its own remarkable character, in whatever form is necessary and right for the future.

Head and deputy head: Elizabeth Cairncross and Charles Cain in 2000

THE JUNIOR SCHOOL

WELLS CATHEDRAL JUNIOR SCHOOL started life in 1948, when Prebendary Ritchie decided to set up his own school in a building he bought for the purpose in New Street (now Ritchie House). St Andrew's, as he called it, was quite separate from the cathedral school and outside the jurisdiction of the dean and chapter, and he intended to concentrate on it after retiring as head of the senior school. But he died only a few weeks after announcing his retirement in the spring of 1954, and although his widow continued to run the junior school for a while, she soon offered it to the dean and chapter; in August 1955 it was taken over by the cathedral school, with William Webb-Jones as its first master.

The choristers now joined the junior school, and most of its pupils went on to the senior school in due course. Webb-Jones remained as master until Commings left, when it was among Alan Quilter's

first duties to appoint his successor, Claud Holmes, who arrived with Jane, his wife, in August 1964.

He took on a school of 122 boys, of whom twenty-four were boarders, with his own accommodation in among the boys in Ritchie House. As he recalls, 'We were responsible for cooking and serving meals during term, as well as looking after the choristers during their stay-ons, when the senior boys in the choir would also come down to live with us. My wife was in charge of the domestic side, along with a cook who lived up to her name, Mrs Angel. We suspected that many day boys came in on Saturdays just for her lunch. We had five

I arrived in September 1962 and was shown to my dormitory by Mrs Webb-Jones, the charming, rather 'Queen Motherly' wife of the extremely scary junior school headmaster. I'd won a choral scholarship and sang in the cathedral choir under the guidance of 'Dapper', Denys Pouncey, from 1963 until my voice finally broke in 1968. What with all the other practice we had to put in, being a cathedral chorister added up to a commitment of about twenty hours a week. And then we had all our schoolwork to do on top! My abiding memory of junior school life was being forced to write letters home every week. There was an appointed time for doing this, we were supervised (almost always by Webb-Jones himself), and our efforts had to be inspected and passed fit to send. I remember being sent back to my desk on several occasions to start again because 'there is no such word as "alright"'. I did eventually learn to enquire whether my parents were 'well'. Thanks to the kleptomaniac tendencies of my mother, I have a shoe-box full of those letters crammed with fascinating facts such as 'Next weekend Bates is going on exeat' and 'Last week Lewis got fifty out of fifty in his maths test'. What possible interest this information would have held for my parents I can't imagine, but I guess we had to fill our letters somehow.

Andy Jones (1962–72)

The original junior school building in New Street, now Ritchie House

St Andrew's Lodge, Jocelyn, and Polydor

St Andrew's Lodge is the only building within the cathedral school estate that started life as a school. It was built in 1713 as a charity school for boys, known from the colour of the uniform as the Blue School (girls were also taught, but in separate accommodation). For a short time at the beginning of the nineteenth century the cathedral school and the Blue School joined forces, but this arrangement ceased when the Blue School moved too far away from the cathedral. The building became part of the junior school in the early 1970s and is now the school's medical centre.

The 1970s was also when Polydor became part of the school, taking its name from Polydore Vergil, early sixteenth-century historian and archdeacon of Wells. It was one of several houses on The Liberty which had been canons' dwellings, and was the home until 1970 of Denys Pouncey, the cathedral organist. Although the eye is immediately drawn to the shell hood with cherubs' heads over the front door, which probably dates to the late seventeenth century, the buttresses flanking the door give the game away: this was a medieval canon's house, and its arch-braced roof on corbels confirms that it dates to the fifteenth century. It ceased to be a boarding house in 2005, and is currently used for the concerts department, the department of vocal studies, and music operations.

Jocelyn, another canon's house named for the thirteenth-century bishop who oversaw the rebuilding of Wells Cathedral, became the boarding house for the junior school boys when it was vacated by the cathedral. It now houses classrooms and other facilities for years 5 and 6.

One day my friend Phillip Simpson and I each purchased a quarter of a pound of fudge to fuel our first trip up the cathedral tower. I seem to remember that this was a special privilege for cathedral choristers who were deemed sensible enough to be trusted to climb the tower unescorted. We were given access by Mr Morris, the deputy head verger, and were adjured not to rush and to behave ourselves. How misplaced was his trust in us that day! We raced round and round the seemingly endless spiral staircase to the top, emerging to be greeted by breathtaking views over the Bishop's Palace and out to Dulcote and beyond. But much more interesting to two twelve-year-old boys was the bell of the famous Wells clock that stood behind what looked to be eminently scaleable railings in one corner. This was the bell that, once Jack Blandiver's legs had chimed four 'ding dong' quarters far below, would strike twelve midday soon after we arrived at the summit.

We had been in such a rush to get to the top of the tower that I had not had time to eat any of the fudge that now was calling to me from my blazer pocket. 'Eat me! Eat me!' it said, 'or you could… climb over the railings and put one cube of us just where the hammer will hit the bell and see what happens!' Without further ado I scaled the railings and positioned the condemned confectionery exactly as instructed. I remember thinking that it was a pointless exercise really – at the first stroke the giant hammer would undoubtedly splatter the tiny piece of fudge to the four corners of Wells and the bell would ring out just as it always did. At the appointed time Jack Blandavier ding-donged once – twice – three times – and… at last, the fourth time. As the echoes of his efforts ricocheted into the distance, there was a whirring sound and the giant hammer began to lift very slowly… And then suddenly the hammer fell, slamming down on the wretched kamikaze fudge with a resounding THUD! The bell didn't ring at all – it was like hitting a mattress with a pillow. I couldn't believe it – THUD! – and again – THUD!

Twelve thuds and 386 heart-stopping steps later Phillip and I re-entered the cathedral checking left and right for the enemy. But our luck was out – Mr Morris appeared out of nowhere, grabbed each of us firmly by the ear, and led us painfully to the north door for a severe tongue-lashing, the exact detail of which escapes me. Except that it did, I'm ashamed to say, include reference to another misdemeanour. There were no toilets en route up the tower and the beady-eyed verger was adamant that it wasn't Scotch mist he had seen pouring out of one of the summit gargoyles.

Andy Jones (1962–72)

Far left: Polydor House in the 1960s; left: Jocelyn House; above: St Andrew's Lodge

classrooms, four of which were outside, as were the changing rooms. For art and music we went to the senior school, being seen across the main Bristol Road by a member of staff, and raising our caps when a car stopped for us. One driver was so impressed that he wrote to tell me so.'

He remembered his slightly shocked realisation, when one child arrived from the Far East with his suitcase on the first day of term, that he was totally responsible for him, as well as for several other boarders whose parents were overseas, for the next three months. 'Opposite us was a garage and the proprietor used to take boarders to London Airport at the end of term – he always used to go once around the block and return before actually setting off so that the boys could check that they had everything: several times he had to return to collect forgotten passports.'

Holmes' secretary was also the assistant matron, and there were four members of staff, with Alan Tarbat giving a good deal of his time as well. His

pupils remember in particular the high standard of drama at this time, with many of the plays they performed coming from the headmaster's own pen. Indeed, it was his desire to concentrate more completely on drama that led to his decision to leave the school in 1972.

His final three years at the school coincided with the arrival of the first girls, most of whom started in the junior school. Coincidentally, the cathedral canons were vacating their old houses on The Liberty to move into new accommodation, and so the junior school was able to take over two more houses. The twelve girl boarders were accommodated in what is now Polydor, and the junior school itself moved into St Andrew's Lodge where classrooms were set up, augmented by new prefabricated buildings at the back. This was a considerable improvement on the old cramped facilities at Ritchie House.

When Claud Holmes left, Alan Quilter was worried about finding the right person to succeed

Choristers queue up to kiss Bridget Webb-Jones after singing at her wedding to Peter Lyons in 1957

Daphne Peabody – flowers and parties

As wife of the master of the junior school, and later as houseparent of Haversham, Daphne Peabody was at the centre of school life for the entire twenty-three years that she and her husband spent at Wells. Not only did she memorably tackle the much-needed decoration and rejuvenation of many of the buildings around the school – becoming well known, as her daughter says, for her 'artistic use of colours and textiles' – but she planted flowers everywhere possible, organised parties, and, most importantly, cared both for her charges at the school and for her own family.

When she lost her battle with cancer in the autumn of 2007 her daughter, Jane Graham, who has followed her mother into Haversham House where she is matron, spoke movingly at her funeral in the cathedral: 'Many people feel a huge sense of gratitude to Mum for all that she did, looking after hundreds of pupils who came from all over the world from as young as six to live away from their own families. I remember her getting up at 6am on Christmas Day, year after year, to make eggs and bacon for a dozen young boy choristers who were staying in Jocelyn. One comment from the many letters we have received sums up so many feelings: "her caring, cheerful, and warm personality resulted in her occupying a unique and cherished place in many young lives".

'Many will remember her wonderful parties: events to celebrate weddings, christenings, birthdays, and ends of term; cricket matches and picnics on Cedars field on long August bank holiday weekends; summer balls, barbeques, jubilee celebrations, and even, in the distant past, Mansfield Town football club promotion parties! Our lives with our mother were imbued with unconditional love. She was a magnificent woman.'

him: 'This paragon would have to be master of a coeducational junior school while also acting as housemaster of the boarding house – and looking after choristers for some three additional weeks in the holidays, including the privilege of having sixteen children around you on Christmas Day and Boxing Day.' The best applicant was one Philip Peabody – but his current post was headmaster of the British Embassy school in Jeddah. Quilter wrote offering to pay his expenses from the time he set foot on UK soil, and did not really expect him to turn up. But he was there for interview early, and impressed both on his own account and through the feedback Quilter received on the sterling qualities of his wife, Daphne.

The Peabodys arrived in the autumn of 1972, with Philip intending originally to stay only a few years. But they remained at Wells until he retired in 1995, with Daphne meanwhile taking on the role of first houseparent of Haversham when it became a senior girls' boarding house; this was on top of her hands-on involvement in the junior school and her DIY and gardening activities. Their children were pupils too; Alan Quilter reported that their eldest, Jane, 'kept us all under very strict control when she was head girl, particularly with her strong views on our feeding habits. I have never known a time when I enjoyed brown bread and lettuce so much.'

One of Daphne Peabody's parties: this one in 1995 celebrated the fiftieth anniversary of VE day; she dressed accordingly (below)

Conservation in the junior school

Andrew Parker ran conservation activities in the junior school from the mid-1970s to the mid-1990s. 'They provided an activity for those pupils who did not excel at games, or who were interested in their environment. They were taken in some form of transport to Ebbor Gorge, an area of land managed by the National Trust just above Wookey Hole, where there were always paths needing to be cleared in the autumn, and sometimes new gravel to be placed in the more muddy sections. Work on ponds in a glade was hard but rewarding, and the stream was always in need of attention to ensure that it flowed smoothly. Trees often had to be felled for safety reasons, and there were the annual bracken-bruising sessions when the invasive weed was transmogrified into the shape of any member of staff who had fallen out of favour. There is still evidence of the school's involvement in the form of a log bench and a very good wheelchair-friendly path near the car park.

'There was, however, more to conservation than Ebbor Gorge, and the group spread their wings, or rather their wellington boots, as other local conservation groups, such as the Somerset Trust for Nature Conservation, the Somerset Wildlife Trust, and the estate workers of the Royal Society for the Protection of Birds at the reserve at Ham Wall, near Meare, became interested in the school's involvement and enlisted it on several varied and fascinating projects.

'It was the visit of the late Mr Doug Woods from Cheddar which began a project of national significance which still continues today. He thought that the pupils might be interested in monitoring dormice at a certain site and duly came along to talk to the group. Producing a dormouse in torpor from his pocket was all it took to enthuse the pupils, and shortly after that they spent some time putting up the boxes. This was at a time when interest in these mammals was very high, and because it was known that the pupils were quite relaxed about cameras being present, the group featured on *Blue Peter* and *The Really Wild* Show at the time of 'the great nut hunt'. The project has been running for nearly twenty years and has expanded from the original site, and now students working towards the Duke of Edinburgh awards have taken over the monitoring of the dormouse population.'

Philip Peabody remembers the state of the accommodation when he arrived. Polydor, the girls' boarding house, was almost derelict and Jocelyn – which was where he and his family lived, along with the twenty-eight boy boarders and their matron – had the reputation of being the coldest house in Wells. As with so many other aspects of the school at the time, finances were tight and facilities were very hand to mouth. His wife's decorating skills were very welcome.

An inspection in 1972 was scathing about the teaching facilities, and there was a lingering prejudice that the junior school was still primarily focused on the choristers and therefore on music. The new headmaster – or 'master', as he continued to prefer being called throughout his tenure – therefore set about developing other aspects of school life, including rugby, with teams taking part in junior tournaments all over the Mendips area and, despite his efforts, usually greeted with the cry 'Here come

The Christmas Celebration

Established in the school calendar in December 1970, the Christmas Celebration has been a vital part of the junior school year ever since. It has never been a service, but is what it says it is – a celebration of Christmas through music and readings, given by all the pupils aged seven to eleven; everyone is involved, whether as a speaker, a member of the junior school choir or the cathedral junior choristers, a musical specialist, or part of a group. The event, always in the last week of the Michaelmas term, has expanded from a single performance into two evenings of songs, instrumental music, and readings. In its infancy, the atmospheric setting in the chapter house provided the venue; but the demand for seats necessitated a move into the nave. Many of the songs, including the one entitled 'The Christmas Celebration', were specially written for it by Nigel Hayward. It is moving to recall that it was the final school

event which David Tudway Quilter was able to attend in December 2006, a month before his death at the age of eighty-six. As his wife, Elizabeth, now says, 'He was determined to be there, and it took a lot of effort to help him into the cathedral, but the celebration was its usual brilliant self and we were all so happy that he was able to enjoy it.'

The Christmas Celebration is renowned for its sense of theatre and its aim of leaving people moved by what they have heard and seen, with a fitting balance between religious and secular items. Judith Burns is very clear about how the material is chosen: 'I am adamant that the music, poetry, extracts from plays, or whatever we include are the real thing, never the "junior version". I want to give the children standards that they will understand and appreciate for the rest of their lives.'

the choristers'. He also set out to enhance still further the academic quality of the school and the breadth of its academic range. One of his initiatives was asking the staff to produce termly plans, since there was at that time no set curriculum; but as he recalls with amusement, this did not always produce the desired result: 'Major Carslaw, who taught geography and history to year 6, came up one term with the plan, "We are going to study the universe"; the plan for the next term built on this: "We have studied the universe, which will continue."'

Going coed had a very positive effect on the junior school, which by the late 1970s and into the 1980s was over-subscribed. This was partly because service families could now send both sons and daughters to the same school, and it became a preferred destination for the children of the professional military.

The girls' first houseparent, Mrs Williams, was there for only a year; the new incumbent, who arrived for the start of the Michaelmas term of 1970, was the recently widowed Jane Hewson (later Jane Stockhill), who was apprehensive and gloomy when she arrived with her two sons: 'John, Julian, and I were still in shock after losing my husband and the boys' dear dad to cancer only a few months before. We could not have chosen a nicer, more friendly place to settle, especially within the community of the school. We were greeted by Jane Holmes, who kept an encouraging eye on us for the rest of the first year.'

She found herself in charge of ten little girls aged between six and eleven, and recalled that 'Polydor was a very happy family house and the girls had lots of fun in their free time. I had put together a box of clothes for dressing up and they made up plays and imaginary games. For a few years there was no television in the common room, so when programmes such as *Blue Peter* were scheduled they would crowd into my sitting

The Dean's Lodging,
The Liberty,
Wells.

November 4th, 1973.

Wells 72192.

Dear Miss Jones,
The Dean and Chapter have considered your request to bring a donkey into the Chapter House during the Christmas celebrations of the Junior School.
We are prepared to allow this on condition that:
(1) Entry is from the Vicars' Close by way of the Chain Gate;
(2) The School is responsible for clearing up any mess afterwards, so that the Vergers do not have extra work.
I hope your throat is better.
Yours sincerely, Patrick Mitchell.

Above: The opening of the new pre-prep facility in 1984

room to watch. During a series of power strikes we were often without electricity for up to three hours. The girls came back from prep, got ready for bed by candlelight, and then I would read to them in my room by torchlight while they had their bedtime milky drinks. They all thought this was very cosy as well as exciting.'

Wells Cathedral School's beautiful buildings and grounds, as well as the cathedral itself, encouraged all sorts of activities in the junior school. One of these was 'lawn speaking' which took place under the mulberry trees on Jocelyn lawn and was an open day for parents, when their children could show off to them through speech and drama, and sideshows and stalls would be set up. School sports day was another, including the swimming jamborees; and then there were the Father's Day cricket matches, when the parents would dress up according to whatever theme had been agreed.

An even bigger event was the junior school's Christmas Celebration, an extravaganza of speech and music overseen by luminaries such as Tim Goulter and Judith Jones (now Burns), which became, and remains, the highlight of the end of the Christmas term for the whole school and the parents. The hundreds of people who attend are

treated to a splendid celebration which has reached ever greater heights – even, one year, featuring a live donkey, permission for which was granted by the dean and chapter 'on condition that the school is responsible for cleaning up any mess afterwards so that the vergers do not have extra work'.

Looking after the choristers was always a special role for the junior school head, and Philip Peabody made it an aim to integrate them as fully as possible into the general life of the school despite the restrictions imposed by their cathedral duties. He recalls that their so-called privileged position was not always to their advantage; they could be pitied rather than envied because of the extra work they had to put in and because they had to stay on after the end of term; and they could also be treated as scapegoats if timetabling difficulties caused problems for their fellows. He was fortunate in the organist during his time, however: unlike some other holders of his office, Tony Crossland was happy to recognise that the choir had a school life too. Many was the time when the cherubic choristers would be wearing muddy rugby kit under their cassocks, or would be allowed to open the batting so that they could get back to school in time for evensong. For their master, having them there with

Extracts from the *Yellow Pages*

September 26 1986 One of the boarders feels that the Yellow Pages deprive him of the opportunity of writing the full and informative letters he would like to write home. My apologies therefore to Major and Mrs Philpott in particular, and boarding parents in general, for depriving them of the literary masterpieces which they might expect from their offspring. Might I suggest that long, interesting letters be written to grandparents who, not receiving the dull, factual notes of the *Yellow Pages*, might be overjoyed to receive a missive from Jocelyn or Polydor.

January 16 1987, when the temperature was -14°C

Everyone woke to the first snow of winter on Wednesday morning. Despite the snow continuing all day the great majority of the school came in, though we finished early. Not so many people made it on Thursday.

Casualties: Mrs Tucker's car was abandoned in the Ritchie Hall car park, Mrs Burns couldn't get her car out, Mr Stokes had to stay overnight in sick bay (he recommends boarders' breakfasts), Mr Thompson couldn't have a bath, a pipe burst in St Andrew's Lodge bringing down part of a ceiling, ruining a carpet, and spoiling a collection of the world's most boring books. No assemblies. No games.

Benefits: Boys were able to wear their tracksuit bottoms and boarders wore their bobble hats, a snowman appeared outside Polydor complete with shower hat, Hugo's toboggan, snowball fights, icicles outside the pre-prep, lovely patterns on the roofs, footmarks in the snow, being inside and warm.

This letter, dated September 16 1986, purported to come from one Mrs B Reynolds, but was actually a spoof from Richard Booth:

Dear Mr Peabody, I have a concern about the over-emphasis on rugby in the school. I would much prefer to see my boys being offered alternative opportunities on activities afternoons such as Morris dancing and perhaps crocheting. This would appear to be well in keeping for young boys attending an established independent school in the south of England. I would agree that the boys themselves may change their minds in the senior school, particularly if they wish to take up a career in the police force. I look forward to raising this matter with you at the next parents' evening, as I am sure other parents share my views.

Picking teams

When we pick teams in the playground,
Whatever the game might be,
There's always somebody left till last
And usually it's me.

I stand there looking hopeful
And tapping myself on the chest,
But the captains pick the others first,
Starting, of course, with the best.

Maybe if teams were sometimes picked
Starting with the worst,
Once in his life a boy like me
Could end up being first!

When asked, as I often am, to provide information about Mansfield Town, a quick glance through the official year books or the marvellous *Mansfield Town, the complete record 1910 to 1990* by the wonderful Stan Searle fills in any gaps in my encyclopaedic knowledge of the great Stags. A reference to my almost complete collection of home and away programmes from 1947 to the current season would also be able to determine such esoteric matters as climatic conditions, sponsors, and which linesman carried the yellow flag in the Mansfield Town v Accrington Stanley game of 1953. However, I have no such records in my possession of Wells junior school soccer teams – no Wellensians, no team photographs… so does that make me into a total anorak or a failed social historian? Probably both! So I apologise in advance for inaccuracies or omissions, and for the opinions, which are mine alone.

When I joined the school in 1972 soccer was the main boys' game, but within a year, for various reasons, it changed to rugby. We did, however, carry on playing soccer, and I seem to remember that our first match was against Hazlegrove; our feelings after a heavy defeat (I seem to remember 7–0) were that we could only get better! Our fixture list seemed to be against prep schools, but we did join the local leagues and our first breakthrough in recognition was when Giles Bailey and Stephen Bethel were chosen to represent Mendip Schools. The A and B teams played in Divisions 1 and 2 of the local Schools League. Once our A team finished bottom, but our B team were champions of Division 2. We never won the league (though we were runners-up in 1977), but won the cup twice.

Our goalkeepers always had a great deal of practice and every opportunity to show off their skills. In defence, we had some cultured full backs, along with several exponents of the 'if in doubt kick it out' style of no-messing-about football often seen in the Third Division North teams! Of midfield dynamos, ie those who ran around a great deal, we always had an abundant supply; true wingers are hard to find, though some showed flair. Those who could perhaps solve England's problems with a natural left foot were few and far between – and so to strikers, often isolated figures who laboured manfully and with some success. We had a few, and there were some magic moments.

Philip Peabody (master of the junior school, 1972–95)

his family for Christmas dinner was a pleasure, and he much enjoyed singing 'Good King Wenceslas' with the youngest chorister, who would take the page's part. And an added bonus, as the Wells Cathedral choir became more famous, was the travelling that he could enjoy in their company.

In 1983, a pre-prep department was founded, in the charge of Kathleen Thomas (now Davidson), who was to remain its head until her retirement in 2004. It started with one small class in a room at the side of Ritchie Hall, but already by the end of the first year numbers had expanded into two classes, and it was not long before more space was required. The demolition of a stable building provided both the site and the materials for the new pre-prep facility, which was put up by the school ground staff and was ready in 1984; soon afterwards the Queen Mother came to visit, and planted a tree on the lawn. After a move to New Street, the department eventually came to rest in Mitchell's Mews, named for the dean of the time, where the children could enjoy light, airy classrooms and both a playground

Philip Peabody and the Handsome Men's Club

Andrew Parker writes: 'The outings that we undertook in the junior school remain etched on our collective memories. To pursue studies outside the classroom was actively encouraged, and patterns soon emerged. The annual outing by members of the Young Ornithologists' Club to the Wildfowl and Wetlands reserve at Slimbridge just before Christmas became very much a fixture (left); these were long, cold days, but always successful, and there was always something to talk about on the way back to Wells: the unpleasant odour of the flamingo compound, close encounters with feeding geese and swans, and the floodlit feeding. The group travelled far afield; there were the bitterly cold avocet cruises on the Exe estuary, and visits to the Forest of Dean, the bird of prey centre at Newent in Gloucestershire, the peregrine falcon breeding crag at Symonds Yat, Kenfig Pool near Bridgend – quite a trek, that one – as well as regular local outings to the Dorset coast, the reservoirs, and the Levels.

and access to Polydor's lawn. The pre-prep benefits from the input of specialist Wells teachers who make time to introduce the four-to-seven-year-olds to sport, music, and drama on top of the normal curriculum; and the staff always ensure that there is daily interaction between themselves and parents, so that any worries or problems are dealt with immediately and parents feel confident that their children are receiving the best of care.

Amid all the focus on academic standards and sporting achievements, the overall sense of fun has always persisted in the junior school; one of Philip Peabody's initiatives was the foundation of the Handsome Men's Club, membership of which was restricted to boys who wore glasses. Another new development of the 1980s was the junior school newsletter, known as the *Yellow Pages*, which began publication in September 1985. Along with the usual day-to-day material, the newsletter was enlivened by quirkier pieces, such as the relieved announcement that 'Michael Wilson, who swallowed a 20p piece on Thursday night, stopped being a human money box the following Wednesday morning'. It has become more factual over the years, but remains in

'We sometimes incorporated a viewing of the Severn bore at Stonebench, just outside Gloucester, with a visit to the National Waterways Museum at Gloucester Docks. The highest tides and therefore the best prospect of a good bore, coupled to a civilised time of viewing, usually occurred in February; and on one occasion our bank-side viewing was dramatic, after substantial rainfall made it obvious that the river was rising rapidly and that the road would soon be impassable, and we were marooned in the safety of a farmer's yard for a couple of hours. There were also other places to visit in connection with canal topics, like the Kennet and Avon Canal, Caen Hill Lock "staircase", and the museum at Devizes.

'Watchet Harbour, Westonbirt Arboretum, Saunton Sands, and Dartington Glass at Great Torrington were all long days out in connection with studies, and always furnished material for the end of year open day displays. The basket works at North Curry was a favoured location, as well as the peat works on the Levels and on one occasion Sheppeys Cider Mill at Taunton, where sampling the brew proved popular. Then there were Cleeve Abbey, the wonderful rock formations at Kilve, or the nuclear power station at Hinckley Point. There were always the Quantocks to provide the venue for "playtime", and the Sedgemoor battle ground, with the church, at Westonzoyland fitted in brilliantly with the curriculum. Some of these occasions were really happy events; the children were a delight to take anywhere and always showed their appreciation in a most spontaneous manner.'

production to this day, still printed on yellow paper – though a collectors' edition appeared on March 16 2001 when the school had run out of yellow paper and the newsletter, for once in its life, became the 'Red Pages'.

In 1995 Philip and Daphne Peabody retired after a hugely successful and productive twenty-three years at the school. The new head was Nick Wilson who, when he arrived with his wife, Jane, and their children was, in his own words, 'struck by the atmosphere which was friendly, extremely supportive, and displayed a charm which was simply magical'. The family moved into a newly acquired property in New Street, and immediately stilled any worries that they would find the Peabodys a hard act to follow. Jane Wilson is a phenomenon; in the words of school governor Helen Ball, 'She is worth three, four, five times her weight in gold. She makes all the costumes for the school plays – and they are splendid; she organises all the trips and social events; she takes on any extra duties that need doing; and she is there as a wonderfully comforting presence for anyone – child, parent, teacher – who needs her.' She now also has a formal role in providing pastoral care for the choristers.

Jane Wilson fits one of her costumes

I have known you, Mr Peabody, for so long that it seems you have been present all my life (which is almost the case). You have been a significant influence on my total outlook on life and the way I conduct myself. I remember arriving at Jocelyn to a hearty welcome, and at assembly the next day you were there with all the staff on the stage, but not at all as intimidating as my fears had told me. My teacher that year was Mrs Thomas, whom I will always think of as a secondary mother. A memorable occasion was singing on the stage with you in front of the whole school. I must remind you that you went wrong, and we stopped and I corrected you before we carried on. I apologise belatedly for being so up front!

For some reason I was very homesick during my second year, but with help from the class and my friends I was kept busy and well looked after. But in my third year, sadly, racism started to cause me problems, although it was overcome with strong support from you. A year later I remember vividly, and with profound gratitude, the assembly when the whole junior school was taught about racism and the need to treat everyone with respect. Esto quod es.

A great memory is of being selected to sing along with the senior choirs and three soloists in the moving and beautiful Haydn's Creation. We sang the whole way through the concert, even though we had been told earlier that it would be difficult for us to sing some of the passages – it was satisfying to surprise the senior choirs with our ability. At around the same time, by contrast, a few of us were caught returning from the girls' house, Polydor, during the night (I wasn't actually caught, but had the honour of being sneaked on!). My parents laughed and said it served me right for breaking the rules and that I had to suffer the consequences.

Of course the longest-living thing that came from the junior school, and I hope will last throughout my life, has got to be my nickname, Chokky, which was given to me in my first year by Evan and Noel. It was used through my school life by other pupils (some of whom did not know my real name), teachers, and parents. Some of those who heard it for the first time were a bit shocked, but I was never offended by the name and still use it today. And to this day, whenever I see you, Mr Peabody, I check that my tie is straight, my socks are pulled up, and my shoes will pass muster.

Phillip-Luke Simmons-Hedges, 'Chokky' (1980–91)

*Nick and Jane Wilson with pupils
and guinea pigs*

That the school continues to flourish is clear; Helen Ball again: 'I will never forget the first Christmas Celebration I saw after becoming a governor. As a primary school head myself, I know full well that school productions can be a bit hit and miss; but this was professional beyond belief, and so enjoyable. There is no doubting the poise and the confidence that you can see in the junior school children; and as their confidence grows, you can see them beginning to fly.'

The new head was clear that, while accepting and absorbing national changes in the curriculum and the closer monitoring of academic performance, he was not prepared to compromise the distinctive creative curriculum which is such a huge benefit to junior school pupils. But there would inevitably be

changes, and new initiatives. One major development was the new nursery department, which opened its doors to its first twelve children in September 1996. But it was also clear, by 2005, that junior boarding was declining, so in that year Polydor, which for some years had housed both boy and girl junior boarders, closed and became part of the music department; the remaining boarders joined the lower school houses of Claver Morris and De Salis. And in September 2007, in a move that horrified traditionalists, the junior school uniform changed – most significantly with the disappearance of the school cap. The new uniform came as a relief to the staff who would no longer have to take to task boys who had employed their caps as frizbees and lost them in the trees; and the long trousers now worn in winter also relieved them of the constant need to tell boys to pull their socks up.

In 1998 the junior school celebrated its fiftieth anniversary, with a tea party, a dinner dance, the creation of a huge wall mosaic, and the burying of a time capsule in the garden of 8 New Street. The work on the mosaic, masterminded by Jane Tucker, enabled all pupils to contribute by sketching ideas, sticking broken tiles to the patterns, and buying special tiles for the surround, engraved with their names. The previous two junior school masters, Claud Holmes and Philip Peabody, were both present at the unveiling.

The particular creative vitality of the junior school has gone from strength to strength. One of

The fiftieth-anniversary mosaic

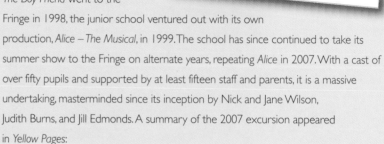

Based on the adventures of Alice in Wonderland, this riot of colour, music and effervescent fun will delight children of all ages.

August 15th, 16th & 17th 12.30pm at Augustine's(152) Tel: 08452 26 27 21

Nick Wilson's early initiatives was the introduction, in September 1996, of a pre-prep violin scheme for pupils in years 1 and 2, with all of them having their own violins for the year, taking part in group lessons, and playing in two concerts. Drama flourishes too throughout the school: the nursery and pre-prep children have one speech lesson and one music and drama lesson a week, and put on two productions a year; and the older children have two or three weekly lessons and are all involved in the summer production of a play with music which they take to the Edinburgh Fringe every other year. In May 1999 a drama exchange began with a school in the Czech Republic, and has since transferred to a similar school in Germany; and in May 2004 the first Arts Week took place, with all pupils from nursery to year 6 involved in workshops, collaborative art, dance, and music on an annual theme. All these initiatives were crowned in November 2006 when the junior school was awarded Arts Mark Gold by the Arts Council, in recognition of the amount of arts work in the curriculum across the whole school. In making the award, the Arts Council took into account the opportunities for performance both locally and nationally, the work that outside practitioners do with the school, and the chances pupils have to visit theatres and galleries.

The Edinburgh Fringe

After the whole school musical *The Boy Friend* went to the Fringe in 1998, the junior school ventured out with its own production, *Alice – The Musical*, in 1999. The school has since continued to take its summer show to the Fringe on alternate years, repeating *Alice* in 2007. With a cast of over fifty pupils and supported by at least fifteen staff and parents, it is a massive undertaking, masterminded since its inception by Nick and Jane Wilson, Judith Burns, and Jill Edmonds. A summary of the 2007 excursion appeared in *Yellow Pages*:

'This year's colour was a vibrant, sunshine yellow. At 6pm on August 13, those yellow sweatshirts, wrapped around the excited cast of *Alice – The Musical*, hit Edinburgh. Seemingly not tired by the nine-hour journey from Somerset and the intervening tour of service stations, the 2007 visit to the Fringe was underway in earnest and with gusto. The routine was quickly established: morning rehearsals, costumes and make-up, performance at Augustine's, singing and dancing in costume along the Royal Mile, back to the boarding house to change, out to a show, hot chocolate, lights out – followed by another equally demanding day of the same! Those yellow sweatshirts certainly did the trick – the sun shone for the cast in Edinburgh after a damp summer. It was quite an experience – in the shadow of Edinburgh Castle, the Royal Mile was a marketplace of performance talent, colour, and music. It was alive with excitement, and the cast of *Alice* – the youngest cast at the Fringe – impressed the throng with their dramatic and musical prowess. It is to their credit that they filled the auditorium at Augustine's with three sell-out shows. As seasoned performers, the cast made audience participation an art form at the shows they visited each evening, with the children thrilling to a dazzling display of break dancing, giggling through an evening of stand-up comedy for young people, inspiring an entire audience to join a conga at a display of oriental drumming, and gasping at the daring of the Cirque Surreal. But there was still energy enough to put on an evening talent contest!

In September 1999 one of our parents, who had been involved with the Edinburgh show, was trying to get away from school by travelling to Brazil, of all places. She thought she was dreaming when she heard the strains of 'We're all Mad as Hatters' in her ears. Opening her eyes she was amazed to see on the in-flight screen fifty junior school pupils and staff singing and dancing in the Royal Mile, Edinburgh. CNN were featuring the school's production of Alice *as part of an item about the Fringe!*

Drama exchanges to the Czech Republic and Germany

The first link with a school abroad was in 1999, when a relationship was forged with a school in Brno in the Czech Republic. The schools visited each other on alternate years between 1999 and 2002, and gained much experience from working together on drama projects and living within another culture. Because of issues at the school in Brno, this link ceased in 2002, but since then a new relationship has started with a school in Prum, Germany, and the numbers of pupils involved have increased from sixteen to thirty-six.

The first visit to Brno, in May 2000, was described by Alice Bruegger, Charlotte Gillard, and Ben Kolb:

'We spent our first evening and day in Prague shopping and sightseeing. We then drove to Brno in horribly hot conditions, and were met by our host families (most people live in flats). On Monday we went to the school for the first time, and were greeted in the traditional way with bread and salt. We then had a drama workshop with the Czech children; it was all about emotion. They also did a performance of *Little Red Riding Hood* in English for us. On Tuesday, we went with some children from the school to the famous caves nearby. Then on Wednesday we had a music workshop where most of us had to make a musical bird story just from the sound of paper and voices, while the others made paper birds, and we then mixed it all together to make a sort of play. Then we went to a tower in Brno, and the following day to Lednice to a stately mansion there. Friday was the day when we were going to perform our show, so we rehearsed and then did the show. Afterwards we were given presents which the children had made. Then on Saturday it was back to Prague to catch our plane home.'

Classic FM Christmas concerts in Liverpool Anglican Cathedral

For four years from 1999 to 2002, Classic FM held a charity concert in Liverpool at which the junior school choir of forty-five pupils was invited to sing as one of only six choirs and the only one made up of children. The cathedral, had over 2000 people in the audience. On the second occasion, we managed to persuade the organisers that it would be a good idea to have one or two readings among our choir items, and also insisted on a piano rather than full organ. When we got there, we made a further suggestion – that it would be splendid to have a group of children processing up the nave with candles. Liverpool was treated to a mini-version of the junior school Christmas Celebration, and they loved it. Some very tired pupils and staff arrived back in Wells at 2.30am on the last day of term.

Junior school choir, May 2008

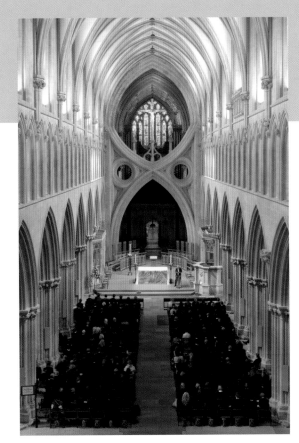

WELLS CATHEDRAL – or more properly the Cathedral Church of St Andrew at Wells – dominates its small city. But it also lies at the heart of the cathedral school, just as beguilingly today as it has over the last 1100 years of its history.

The first church on the site was built at the beginning of the eighth century by King Ine of Wessex; a baptismal font is one of the few relics of that early foundation that can be seen in the cathedral today. Two hundred years later, in AD 909, the church at Wells became the centre of the diocese and was made a cathedral. But it did not remain so: the first Norman bishop, John of Tours, moved his seat from Wells to Bath, effectively demoting the Wells church. But the canons of Wells were having none of this demotion, and fought over the next two centuries to regain their cathedral status. Those two hundred years are a story of shifting power politics as Wells, Glastonbury, and Bath vied for ecclesiastical supremacy in Somerset. And, to quote Jon Cannon (in *Cathedral. The great English cathedrals and the world that made them*), 'It is the church itself that forms the most determined statement of their claims. The canons' knowledge of their own history was reflected in every aspect of it; the result is a kind of manifesto in stone for cathedral status.'

They eventually won. In 1220 the pope allowed the bishop to style himself Bishop of Bath and Wells, the title still in use today; and meanwhile, huge effort and resources continued to be put into creating a building that would definitively see off the rivals at Bath and Glastonbury. Bishop Jocelyn oversaw the steady rise of those masterpieces of the Early English style, the nave and transepts, along with the chapter house and, most of all, the magnificent west front – one of the greatest of all works of Gothic art. Jocelyn lived to see the

dedication of his marvellous new church in 1239, and it was his death in 1242 which precipitated the final struggle with Bath, when they elected his successor without recourse to the chapter at Wells. The dispute went before the pope who finally, in 1245, came down on the side of Wells and accorded it full cathedral status again. The magnificence of the building had triumphed.

It was not long before extensions and enlargements were deemed necessary, and subsequent bishops oversaw the heightening of the crossing tower and the building of the dramatic stretched octagon lady chapel at the east end, where much original glass survives. But further additions to the tower at the beginning of the fourteenth century began to put pressure on the central piers of the crossing, which started to sink; the solution, devised by the cathedral mason, William Joy, in 1338, resulted in the feature unique to Wells among English cathedrals: the double-pointed inverted arches where the nave meets the transepts, known both as scissor arches and, more technically, as owl-eyed strainer arches.

The cathedral was finished by the end of the fifteenth century, and a hundred years later a new charter granted by Queen Elizabeth I created a governing body consisting of the dean and eight residentiary canons. Wells had always been a secular rather than a monastic foundation, in the charge of five key dignitaries, the *quinque personae*, who ran the place. These were the dean, *primus inter pares*; the precentor, in charge of music and the liturgy; the chancellor, responsible for education and general administration; the treasurer, in charge of the finances; and the archdeacon, who had no specific duties within the cathedral but oversaw the running of the parishes. The bishop, whose seat was in the cathedral, had no formal status there but was in overall charge of the diocese. And the canons worked both within the cathedral and elsewhere, either running parishes or further afield as diplomats, teachers, or lawyers.

Wells Cathedral suffered damage from local fighting during the Civil War, and fell into disrepair under the Commonwealth. Monmouth's soldiers did further harm during the rebellion of 1685, tearing lead from the roof to make bullets, smashing windows, organ, and furnishings, and stabling their horses in the nave. Restoration had to start again. But the cathedral today still contains many early features and many marvels: the staircase that rises up to the chapter house which bears eloquent witness to the many feet that have trodden it over the centuries, its worn steps undulating like rolling waves; and the clock, depicting the universe with the world at its centre on its original medieval face, with its knights jousting as the bell strikes each quarter.

And then there is the magnificent west front, with its amazing collection of medieval statuary set into over 300 individual niches: of the original 176 figures, 149 survive, and all of them would have been painted in rich colours. The west front played a very public role in the life of the community, overlooking as it did the lay cemetery in the green in front of it, and acting as the splendid backdrop to ceremonies and rituals. One of the greatest and most important of these was the re-enactment on Palm Sunday of

'Roman' trumpets, borrowed from the Globe Theatre for 2008's Brass Prom

Christ's entry into Jerusalem, when the façade did duty as the gates of Zion themselves and the statues appeared to burst into song when choristers secreted in openings in the thickness of the wall, behind the painted stone angels, lifted up their voices in response to the singing of those processing below. Trumpeters too would add their fanfares; the holes behind which they stood can still be seen high up on the façade, there to allow them to sound the last trump for the dead in the cemetery.

Today's choristers follow in the footsteps of their predecessors who played such an important role in the cathedral rituals; and Wells Cathedral School as a whole also finds its spiritual home in the cathedral, with important parts of the school year celebrated in services there.

Musicians on Wells Cathedral's undulating chapter house steps

I suspect some pupils only came to appreciate the beauty of the cathedral as former pupils, but there can be no doubt that regular exposure to one of the most awe-inspiring buildings in the world is a privilege open to a fortunate minority. Heads of independent schools are invariably expected to preach. I had not done so before Wells and came to enjoy the experience. I was flattered to be asked by the canon-in-residence to preach in the cathedral on one Mothering Sunday. Three days before the service, a gunman ran amok in a school in Dunblane and the sermon I had carefully prepared had to be adapted. It was daunting to be faced in the pulpit by twenty-two candles and to be speaking to a packed nave. To be present in such a strong spiritual atmosphere in that beautiful building was a huge comfort to me and others in the congregation.

John Baxter (headmaster, 1986–2000)

Any memory of Wells for me is dominated by the cathedral in whose shadow we all lived: the sound of the matins bell accompanying me up The Liberty to breakfast; the clock chiming the quarters all through the night when I couldn't sleep – and coming in at inappropriate moments during a concert in the music school. Even auditions weekend often coincided with an attempt at a full peal.

During my years as tutor to the girl choristers I loved the quiet emptiness of a Tuesday evensong in February, when few visitors were in the stalls, it was dark outside, and the girls sang their hearts out to the glory of God. No adult can ever equal the beauty that is in young voices and our choristers, boys and girls, belong to one of the finest cathedral choirs in Britain today. I shall never forget Edmund Comer (known to some as a teacher of English and drama, but previously a head chorister and actor manqué), whose singing of the top part of Allegri's Miserere on Ash Wednesday was spine-tingling, nor Julian Wilkins' breathtaking introduction to an Advent carol service as he processed down the darkened nave singing the first verse of 'Once in Royal David's City'.

The end of year service was always a glorious occasion and in my later years the houses took to wearing flowers. I always found the reading out of the names profoundly moving and never managed to get through all the verses of 'God be with you till we meet again'. One year the hymn was not included and the service felt flat and incomplete.

But the one occasion I recall more than any other was the beginning of term service in January 1999. The school stood round in the nave, empty of chairs as is the custom at that time of year. John Baxter was preaching and with his usual eloquence he spoke of the sudden and far too early death of Chris Taylor, a well loved teacher, on Boxing Day. At the end of the service the organist struck up the 'Voluntary', a sign for the school to leave. Not a soul moved; we stood frozen in time, unwilling to go even when the organ finished playing.

Chris was one of the middle school tutors. I had asked him the previous summer if he would like to continue tutoring in the middle school or have a rest, ie take a smaller senior school tutor group. Would he, I enquired tentatively, be prepared to take on a new year 7 group again? 'Just you try and stop me,' he threatened. Now I had taken over the group, and as I looked at all the sad little faces in front of me I decided to ask them to write down their memories of Chris. Even though he had been with them for only one term, the words poured out. My eyes filled as I read them afterwards. How they missed him already: how much they knew he really cared about each and every one of them.

Diana Davies (staff, 1987–2003; now school archivist)

The school chaplain now is Juliette Hulme, who arrived in 2006 as the first woman to hold the position. 'I remember being captivated on the day of my interview by the uplifting voices of the school chapel choir who were singing evensong in the cathedral on that May evening. That experience, and the presence of the large ginger cathedral cat throughout the service, convinced me that I wanted to come and work here.' Her role involves some religious studies teaching – which is compulsory for everyone up to GCSE – as well as organising and conducting services and events in both the cathedral and the Vicars' Close chapel. The school is, as it always has been, a Christian foundation, but also today plays host to students of other faiths.

The cathedral plays a regular role in school worship; the whole senior school attends a weekly Monday morning service in the cathedral at the start of the school day, when the chaplain or another member of staff leads the service, sometimes with live music provided by the school musicians. There are also cathedral services at the beginning and end of each term, when the chapel choir sings and members of the chapter might speak, and services too for St Andrew's Day, Ash Wednesday, and Ascension Day. The most moving service of all is the Advent carol service, which begins with a candlelit procession and has beautiful singing from the junior and senior choirs; the cathedral is always packed. The boarders go to Eucharists at the cathedral three times a year, and also attend an evening service of a Compline/Iona style in the cathedral every Sunday, after which some of them are invited in groups to 18 Vicars' Close, where the chaplain lives, for drinks, nibbles, and chat. There are also Sunday evening services once a term for the junior school; Juliette Hulme is their chaplain too, and takes a weekly religious assembly for them in Ritchie Hall.

Juliette Hulme in the Vicars' Close chapel

The tiny chapel at the top of Vicars' Close plays a leading part in the spiritual life of the boarders, who go there for house chapels on weekday evenings between supper and prep. These are informal affairs with a varying format, and are there to support the pupils in their spiritual lives, to ask and answer questions, and to allow discussion and interactive worship. General pastoral care, 'overseeing the spiritual life of the school', is of course fundamental to the chaplain's work, relating to both staff and pupils, and she sees her role as both proactive and reactive – responding to individual needs while also seeking to stimulate the spiritual search and connecting the Christian faith with the busyness and secularity of life today, both at school and at home. There are several Christian groups in the school

which provide opportunities for study, questioning, and discussion, and the chaplain also prepares pupils for confirmation each year and leads them in a retreat at nearby Abbey House, Glastonbury, or the Bishop's Palace, Wells.

Charity work is a fundamental part of the life of the school and the school chaplain. There is a charity committee which decides which charities are to be the focus of fundraising and participation each year – Amnesty International and the Rowan Tree Trust, supporting orphanages in Romania, are those for 2008 – and there are also individual initiatives arising from particular issues. As Juliette Hulme says, 'The students here are well aware of their privileged position, living and receiving a fine education in such a splendid place, and are usually eager to organise

Matthew Owens, master of the choristers, with the choir in the cathedral

Right: A house chapel in the Vicars' Close chapel

Below: Jane Peabody's wedding to Mark Graham in the Vicars' Close chapel with the Reverend Peter Hogg officiating

and take part in charitable events.' Even for those whose religious faith is insecure, such activities, bolstered by the ambience of Christian – and other – faith that surrounds them every day, provide a sure foundation for a spiritual dimension to life now and later. And, for the chaplain, it is a privilege and a challenge to have the chance to sow the seeds of faith in these young people – the very age group who are so often absent from our churches.

Every single day at Wells was packed full with so much variation. After a heart-warming breakfast (how I loved those warm croissants) prepared by Molly and the other kitchen staff, with their soft, lyrical Somerset accents, a typical Wednesday morning would begin with a short service in one of the most glorious cathedrals in all of Christendom. As at the Sunday evening services, one of the organ scholars and the chapel choir would serenade us with a reverential piece of sacred music. Then we would be presented with one of Rev Hogg's two preferred sermons: 'Don't take the Bible literally' or 'Be what you are'. But his favourite and most enchanting story, which made his face glow with delight, was this (and for those who never had the honour of knowing the late Reverend Hogg, imagine it delivered in a broad Yorkshire accent): 'One day, while I was at Cambridge, I was going about my day and I happened upon the most fabulous pair of legs, and I said to myself, "Hoggie, follow those legs." And I did. And now she's me wife. And she makes the most fantastic sandwich.'

Even though I never developed much of a spiritual life at Wells, I cannot deny that the short services and a good old sing left me feeling both energised and at peace. And I have no doubt that, although my faith did not flower until my mid-twenties, the seeds began germinating in that beautiful and awesome church and in the intimacy of the Vicars' Close chapel.

Caroline Hamilton (née Cowan, 1993–8)

SCHOOL AS FAMILY

MEMORIES OF LIFE at Wells fifty or sixty years ago echo what was the norm for the time in most boarding establishments: charmless dormitories used for sleeping only and out of bounds during the day; draughty lavatories and washrooms; little privacy and certainly none of the comforts of home – and, as ever, there are mixed memories of the food. Teachers could be formidable, punishment was often a beating, and the matrons could be strict. Yet the overall memory is of a happy place. Living conditions in the school in the middle of the twentieth century may have been stark, but Wells pupils were on the whole content there; and as time went on – particularly when girls arrived – life at school relaxed and formalities dissolved.

In the junior house the washing facilities, on the second floor, consisted of two benches running down either side of the room with a basin at the far end. In order to wash you had to get an enamel basin, fill it up, and carry it to a free space on one of the benches. There were two or three baths in rooms leading off the main washing area as well. The dormitories varied in size, but had around ten beds in each – simple iron bedsteads with a chair at the side to put clothes on. The middle house had no electricity when I was there, and was lit by gas. There was a bit of extra freedom when you got to this house, in that on Sunday afternoons we could go out unsupervised – in fact, most of us had bicycles. In the senior house there were rooms in the basement where we could practise our hobbies – mine was building amplifiers. We used to light and look after the fires, which were fuelled with wood or peat. The hour between midday and 1pm on Saturday was the only time we were allowed into the town – although Woolworths was always strictly out of bounds (I never found out why). If you were punished with a detention, this was the time you had to stay in, so sometimes you couldn't get to the shops for two weeks.

Anthony W (Tony) Smith (1943–9)

The hobbies rooms

These rooms, in the Cedars basement, housed multifarious activities including stamp and coin collecting and swapping, and the making of wool rugs, lampshades, plaster models, and ship and plane models. Some of the boys did painting by numbers, one boy is remembered as trying dress designing, and some of the boys would learn carpentry, pottery, or photography. There was an annual competition which was judged by a wool shop owner and his wife.

Varying views on the food

During her husband's tenure as headmaster, the food at the school was overseen by Mrs Ritchie, and was often maligned (where is it not?). But she went to immense trouble to provide nutritious food at every meal for growing boys and hard-working masters. Cream and milk were supplied daily, and the school even bought its own 'nominal' cow at the farm to ensure a regular supply of clean, fresh milk. As Bill Whittle remembers, 'Her presence in the dining room was formidable; she could silence the whole company by taking a deep breath. But she had considerable culinary skills and could produce some exotic dishes. Who can forget those delicious bowls of cream, the jam sandwiches fried in batter, and the tasty fish spread? We never went hungry; and there was always a supply of bread and dripping available at the hatch after second prep.' John Barrett (1935–44) remembers her as someone who was 'respected and feared, if not much liked, but she did feed us well – though I remember one time early in the war when we must have been the recipient of a consignment of apricots from the Americans, and they featured at every meal for weeks. I have never been able to eat one since.'

There was a ritual about dinner (as it was called) at 1pm. The meal was served by pupils who took it in turn, and there had to be complete silence until everyone was served – Mrs Ritchie was on hand to ensure that this rule was complied with. Then you could talk, but you had to have cleared your plate before 'packing-up plates' time, when complete silence ensued again. Then dessert was served.

Anthony W (Tony) Smith (1943–9)

Ann Ritchie (now Brierley) with Millie and Terry the dog

Patricia Staniforth recalls the 'crispy crusts spread with scrumptious dripping' too. 'The dripping came from the joints of meat that Millie and Peter, the school cooks, roasted. Peter was a big, tall, strong chap, and Millie was tiny. She had to stand on a box to reach and stir the porridge with a large wooden paddle. Every Sunday evening, Mrs Ritchie would sit at the kitchen table spreading slices of toast as we matrons made them in a wire cage on the stove. We also served soup from a huge pan, and washed up the teaching staff's dishes as they brought them down from their dining room. Sometimes they would help us and chat. But Mrs Ritchie didn't really approve of fraternisation.'

The headmaster's wife was well known for her resourcefulness. One winter when burst pipes meant that there was no water on tap, she had the matrons filling buckets with snow from the Cedars lawn which she then boiled up and used to make a delicious steamed lemon pudding. Ann Brierley, the Ritchies' youngest daughter, was living at home at that time: 'My mother was helped on the food front by Millie – a diminutive figure who had come to Wells with my parents from Liverpool in 1924 as their cook. Millie, though tiny, was immensely strong, lifting large, cast-iron Aga pots with ease. When the war and rationing came, and numbers rose, feeding everyone became much more of a challenge. The three large walled gardens went into full production, the top of Cedars field was ploughed up for potatoes, and hens were kept up there. Most of the school's fruit and vegetables came from our own resources. We kept geese in the mower shed, and two pigs, Nausea and Nostalgia, in the old stables by the museum garden. All were intended for the pot but we

Food rationing began early in the war, but this didn't really make much difference as generally the food had always been very healthy but fairly simple. For example at breakfast we had porridge from a large black pot and then bread with either butter or marmalade but certainly not both. At one time there were rather a lot of small black objects in the porridge, which were widely thought to be mouse droppings, but were probably dried husks. There was also quite a lot of rabbit. One day I got just the head on my plate and I haven't really liked either porridge or rabbit since.

Michael James (1934–42)

When I started at Wells food was rationed, and one of my memories of Wells is constant hunger. We used to sneak pieces of bread and margarine out of the dining room (forbidden, of course) and toast them on the boiler in the senior house – rather gritty, I recall, but tasting wonderful to our youthful palates. Another forbidden act was to sneak out to Thomas Street to buy a lardy cake which would be brought back and devoured with relish in the basement wash rooms. Thomas Street was strictly out of bounds as loose ladies were reputed to live there – though I never knew what a loose lady was!

David M Parnell (1941–5)

grew too fond of the geese, which would come flying round to the Cedars steps when we called. Others did, however, eventually eat them. All this food production was in the charge of Stanley Weeks, the head gardener and groundsman, with whom my mother could become quite cross when a crop in the school gardens was poor but prolific in his.'

One of Alan Quilter's priorities in the mid-1960s was to improve the food, and he therefore engaged a catering company to take over the kitchens. Along with the company came Bill Tamblyn, who had served twenty-two years as an army caterer and was well used to feeding hundreds of hungry mouths. It was not long before Tamblyn pointed out to the headmaster that money could be saved if he was allowed a free hand as catering manager, and so he took over and immediately introduced new, professional ideas into the catering operation. Like everyone else during those straitened years he had to struggle to obtain finance for new equipment, but it was acquired bit by bit, and the improvements in the kitchen facilities quickly led to improvements in the food on offer.

One of his popular innovations was a choice of menus, particularly at lunch, the main meal of the day, when the menu would consist of some sort of stew, probably a

Our breakfast bacon was cooked in mutton fat and was disgusting, but we were supposed to eat up everything on our plates – so we would lift the grates at the side of the floor and drop the bacon down them. Or sometimes we would put the bacon into envelopes in our pockets and chuck them over the wall into the Bishop's Palace. Cheese too offered us an alternative entertainment on Sundays; if you chewed the cheese for long enough it reached a consistency ideal for throwing at the ceiling where it would stick. At the end of each Sunday cheese and fruit meal the ceiling was covered with little clods of cheese.

Brian Creese (1963–6)

Bill Tamblyn

Peter Hillard, the school cook, with Mrs Brown (second right) and Mrs Emery (right), 1955

I can happily and incontrovertibly state that the favourite lunchtime menu with the boarders in those early-to-mid 1960s was most definitely 'mock duck' (over-baked sausage meat) with peas and gravy, with rice pudding topped with a dollop of shaving cream and a slip of demerara sugar to follow for pudding. And it was always on a Tuesday, at about three- or four-weekly intervals. Contrast this with the Absolutely Worst meal of the whole school year: graveyard stew (actually a thin gruel-like substance made from neck of mutton, served up complete with bones, and barley beans). Nightmare food. In the Cedars years, it struck fear and trembling into our hearts as we trooped into the dining room to realise that, once again, we were trapped! If the introduction of outside catering around 1966 achieved nothing else, it will be forever blessed for putting an end as much to the fear as to the actual horror of such a culinary travesty.

And who remembers the horse-trading at supper on the first evening of every term, when deals were done and clandestine agreements reached between consenting table-mates over who would agree to eat your detested food in return for surrendering something popular in payment? But don't let Matron Staniforth hear what you're doing. I could command more scrambled eggs and peas from certain friends because I would (willingly) accept their lumpy porridge or roast parsnips. But me, I loathed and detested kippers (every fourth Sunday, for breakfast) which nobody else on my table ever wanted. So I had to smuggle my kipper out of the dining room wrapped in the envelope from my father's latest letter-from-home. His envelopes were always best-quality bond – nice and thick, unlike my mother's envelopes which would fall apart in your pocket if you put any food in them which wasn't totally dry and odourless (no plastic bags in those days). And of course how do you smuggle food out of the dining room without getting caught by matron and told to Turn Out Your Pockets, and without sweating with nerves and looking shifty? A practised art, I can tell you: always use the jacket pocket on the blind side of where she's standing; and always let your arm hang loosely down by your side so it covers said pocket. Look straight ahead, and never ever take a sideways glance at matron as you walk past. If it smells, you've had it! Use two, no three envelopes if you have to. And, no, I never got caught in all those years in the Cedars.

Mark Brown (1961–8)

Angie Brock

piece of grilled meat or fish, several vegetables, and something cold, as well as a choice of puddings. The coming of girls brought a surge of interest in salads, and there was always fruit on offer, usually in the evenings when there was a smaller choice at the supper table. His wife, Vera, hardly saw him during term, because he would be at the school all day every day, catering at weekends for visiting teams as well as the boarders, and running a kitchen which by the time he retired in 1991 consisted of over twenty staff, most of them part-timers working shifts. Even in the holidays he would be summoned in to deal with visitors; and as he now says, 'If you had a good idea, you could be sure that you would be listened to, and if it was possible, the idea would be taken up.' As Alan Quilter said in the *History*, generations of staff and pupils had every reason to be grateful to Bill Tamblyn for the high standards he consistently achieved.

One of the chefs who joined the kitchen staff under Tamblyn was Ray Jones, who arrived in 1984 and is still there today. 'I never intended to stay so long,' he now says, 'but the friendly atmosphere and the family feel to the school have kept me here.' He has seen constant improvements to the food on offer, with increasing choice and lots of healthy options, including the well-stocked salad bar. 'We don't have any particular specialities in the kitchen, but all turn our hands to anything that's required. And we are all aware of the needs of the children, and tend to keep an eye out for any potential problems. It's often their attitude to food that is the first symptom of a worry.' Molly Joy has been here even longer, arriving in 1982 to work in the kitchens and now, in 2008, about to retire. She will miss the children, she says – 'seeing how they grow and change, even though some of them have been known to ambush me and lock me in the Cedars cloakroom as a joke; I still get Christmas cards, and there's more than one mother who's said to me that her son knows me better than he does her, since he spends so much time here as a boarder.'

The menus are prepared by the head chef, but in close consultation with the food committee which has representatives on it from teaching, house, and kitchen staff, and pupils. The assistant catering manager today is Angela Churches, another long-serving member of staff who has worked her way up since 1989 when she joined as a kitchen assistant. She recalls that the food when she first arrived was wholesome and tasty, but there was limited variety: 'Bill Tamblyn had a very small catering budget and we had to do the best we could. We still don't have a great deal to play with, but the catering company, Sodexo, can offer economies of scale and therefore more choice. I think the food is good value for money and is well presented – and we have a very good team here who work well together.' The kitchens are open and functioning whenever there are choristers to be fed, when there are special events to be catered for, and also during the three weeks in the summer holidays when the choristers are away and the houses are let to visiting choirs. As Ray Jones says, 'The quality of what we provide for visitors is often remarked on; they are not used to such varied and tasty food at a school.'

Geoff Shean (left) and Mark Biddiscombe

School matrons in 1955, left to right: Edith Heywood (who was also the housekeeper), Patricia Staniforth, Mrs Bennett, Mrs Ford, Pauline Wormald

I wonder who hid a well-thumbed copy of Lady Chatterley's Lover *under the dorm floorboards. And of course no Cedars boy would have dreamed of getting onto the roof to peep through the skylight into the surgery which just happened to double as matron's bathroom… or would he? And who was it who played 'woo-woos' on the Cathedral Green at dead of night, wrapped in a white sheet? I don't recall how many ex-Cedars boys I caught smoking at the top of De Salis garden… and believe it or not, I didn't tell. I wonder who left his burning cigarette on a piano in the new music block? It was all so very exciting, with three fire engines. I often wonder why the police thought it must be Cedars boys scampering along The Liberty at dead of night in their pyjamas. Strange to say girls also wear pyjamas and also took part in dares, just as girls have been known to take a peek at 'doubtful' literature. But it was a boy who one night painted the four stone storks that stood around the pond on Cedars lawn – and it was the night before sports day too, when Captain Tudway was presenting the prizes. Strangely enough, the miscreant owned up – and spent the morning scrubbing the storks clean.*

Patricia Staniforth (staff, 1953–83)

Opposite: Edwards House

Matron at the Cedars for thirty years from 1953 until she retired in 1983, Patricia Staniforth is remembered with affection – despite her strictness: 'I know I was called names like Hag, Nag, or Bag; but strangely enough, whenever there was a disaster, the cry would go up, "Matron, come quickly." It might be a lad with dysentery who had broken his potty – "and I had just used it, matron"; or there was the time when Bruce Parry (now of the television programme *Tribe*) fell over the Cedars banisters and landed on the tiled floor. I don't know who was greener, him or me.'

When not dealing with disasters or looking after the sick, her days were filled with 'sewing on name tapes, washing socks, mending socks, in fact mending all the clothes – shirts, pyjamas, underclothes, turning up, turning down, taking in trouser legs (flares were not allowed!)'. When she had a bit of time available, she delighted in doing flower arrangements and always tried to have a vase of flowers on every table in the dining room. But despite permission for this having been granted by Mrs Ritchie, picking the school flowers involved running the gauntlet of Stan Weeks, head groundsman and gardener. Many was the time when – to the delight of the boys – she was charged by Mr Weeks on his tractor shouting 'It's those bloody matrons again!'

Her love of fresh air was legendary – and remains the same in her retirement; when the editors of this book told a current, long-serving member of staff that they were going to visit Miss Staniforth in Ilminster in the depths of February, they were advised to wrap up warm.

The teachers did little better than the boys when it came to home comforts. Peter Bishop (1965–2003) recalls the first words he heard from Major Henfrey, then on the point of retiring as bursar, when he arrived to join the staff in 1965: 'Tell him to bring his own electricity then!' This was in response to the suggestion that if he wanted such a thing as an electric blanket, he would have to bring his own. 'Henfrey's successor was describing the furnishings of the attic room in number 4 (now Claver Morris) which I was to occupy as assistant housemaster. I would be given a bed, a table and chair, a (so-called) easy chair, and a one-bar electric fire. "Anything else you want," said Squadron Leader Ashton, "you'll have to bring with you." That casual remark elicited the comment above; obviously Henfrey was alarmed at the profligacy of the new regime. I had never used an electric blanket and did not intend to start then, but I did wonder whether it might have been a wise investment during the months that followed. My room was at the top of the house facing north and east, and the ice used to form overnight on the inside of the windows as well as the outside. I shared a bathroom with the housemaster, Stuart Burt, and the senior boys; but I did at least have my one-bar electric fire; the only heating for the boys was provided by two night storage heaters in the common room (elderly armchairs and TV) and games room (table skittles). Alan Quilter used to say that he thought it was good for boys to be a bit hungry, cold, and uncomfortable. Well, number 4 was a tough house and I think our boys took some sort of perverse pride in their Spartan conditions. But it was the advent of the first girls in 1969 that really began to make a difference. Girls were provided with carpets and heating: so much for sexual equality! In 1970 Dean Edwards vacated number 3 and I was transferred there to help Alan Quilter run the new house, where we had central heating and I had my very own bathroom.'

I used to be involved with my local village pantomime to which some of the school pupils would come. One year I was playing Simple Simon in Dick Whittington, and part of my role was to steal some money and plant it on Dick, who would then be falsely accused and be driven out of the village. I was up on stage about to do my thieving when a little voice piped up from the back of the hall: 'Don't do it, Ray.' It was one of the Wells boys, who obviously didn't like to see me branded as a wrongdoer!

Ray Jones (staff, 1984–present)

Caroline Gingell recalls that, although comfort and homeliness did begin to creep in in the early 1970s as more girl boarders came, it was often achieved in the teeth of the ever-persistent shortage of money. She arrived in 1972 as houseparent of Claver Morris, where she looked after almost forty middle school girls until she retired in 1985, and was shocked to find that 'When I first arrived there was nowhere for them to put their clothes, which often ended up under their beds from where the cleaners had to fish them out so that they could polish the (really old and beautiful) wooden floors. We eventually managed to get hold of some small chests of drawers, and some rugs to make the rooms a bit more comfortable. We would go to a remnant shop near Bristol to buy cheap materials for curtains, and make them up ourselves. If we needed medical supplies, we would just heave a sigh and buy them with our own money – the tiny amount we were given for such things each term was soon spent.'

Claver Morris was soon crammed with boarders; Miss Gingell recalls fighting to retain a small room as a sick bay, and giving up one of her own two rooms so that she and the matron, who came in four mornings a week, had somewhere to work. As the school grew, more buildings had to be taken on as residential accommodation. A building on New Street was purchased as a senior girls' boarding house, Haversham, with Daphne Peabody as houseparent. Being a DIY fanatic, she immediately set to on decoration – the phrase 'Daphne's flowers' could be applied both to her ubiquitous flower plantings in the gardens and to her choice of wallpapers. At Haversham she chose light blue, pink, and yellow as the colours of the paint and was one day greeted by the builders with the comment that they felt that they ought to be wearing sunglasses. Being houseparent suited Daphne Peabody, particularly since she now had a position in the school in her own right and was no longer, in her own words, 'standing in my husband's shadow'. He, on the other hand, was sometimes heard to remark that he felt he was 'doing a Denis' (Thatcher).

The need to create a structured and caring environment for the boarders became more central as time went on. Caroline Gingell again: 'The girls and boys who had grown up in the school together from the junior school were easier to deal with; they were used to each other as friends and fellow pupils, and treated the coeducational life as normal. It was

girls who came into the school later, often from a single sex environment, who would react to suddenly finding themselves with BOYS! They would either start to act a bit madly, or retreat into themselves. The boys were the same, of course, and I sometimes had to deal with inappropriate behaviour, such as when a couple of boys took it upon themselves to climb the fire escape at the back of Claver Morris and knock on the windows of the dorm at the top. One of the girls came to tell me about this, and I went out into the back garden and gave the boys a dreadful shock when they came down the fire escape and found me standing there waiting for them.'

She says she was certainly regarded as an 'old dragon – but I hope as a caring old dragon'. She was strict, but it was for the good not just of the individual girls but of them all together, living cheek by jowl. 'I saw more of the naughtier ones, and had to make sure that the quieter ones did not feel excluded. My door was open day and night – it had to be – and I felt that I was there as a parent substitute, however distant and firm I was, and however strictly I had to impose the rules. Some of them, particularly perhaps the specialist musicians,

Edwards House

In the break between classes, we would all head back to house. On the walk back to Haversham, one could either stroll along The Liberty and cut up the side of Ritchie Hall, or cut through the junior school playground, where you would undoubtedly be mauled by some of the littlies, past the science department, and then sneak through the back door. All of the three senior girls' boarding houses had a different feel. Haversham certainly did not have the splendour of Edwards and Plumptre; from the front aspect on New Street it was little more than a terraced house, but once inside, as well as being like the Tardis with one corridor leading up and over into another, it had the most homely feel. When Shirley Smith took over as houseparent, the house was extended further and in all my time there it was always at full occupancy. So there was a real energy to the place akin, I imagine, to the stately homes of old, which were only ever really alive when they were brimming with people.

Madame Meare was one of the teaching staff who did an evening duty at Haversham – yet another wonderful teacher who graced our school, and one of the most glamorous with her chic French fashions and flowing skirts. One evening when she was on duty, myself and dorm-mate Alix were celebrating the end of GCSEs. With music blaring, we decided to get all our notes from the last two years and shred them right there in the room. The pile was already a foot deep and had begun spilling out into the corridor and down the stairs when Madame Meare popped her head round the door to explore the source of the mess and the terrible racket. Rather than being cross, she delighted in the idea and joined us in what she called a 'paper dance'.

There was always fun to be had. We had some wonderful parties, sometimes jointly with Ritchie House, and there were the sixth form balls and Christmas parties. But just as special were the Saturday evenings in Hollies Cottage, once we had returned from the Crown or the Star, spent watching The Ugly Bug Ball *or* Great Expectations *– what larks, eh, Pip!*

Caroline Hamilton (née Cowan, 1993–8)

worked so hard that they needed to be told that they had to go to sleep, that they couldn't stay up late and chat.'

Charles Cain, now deputy head, arrived in 1986 as head of history and was also houseparent of Shrewsbury until 2000 when he took on his current responsibilities. He remembers how he felt about the school when he arrived: 'It was quaint – there were these grand domestic houses where staff and boarders lived, but they were furnished in a homely sort of way – quite makeshift, even shabby! Alan Quilter had had to make the school pay by packing them in – there were over twice as many boys in Cedars then than there are now. But I was also immediately struck by how friendly the school was, and the strong sense of family. There was no age hierarchy, the approach to coeducation had been

On February 5 1992 Edward Nowell (right) and Andi Kinnersley (left) went to the Queen Elizabeth II Conference Centre in London, for the presentation to Edward of his Child of Achievement award. He was one of 180 children to receive the award, in the presence of the special guest, John Major, the prime minister, along with many personalities from children's television. Edward was presented with his award by Anna Ford, the newsreader, and he was also given the autographs of all the famous people present, including John Major's.

Edward suffered from Hunter syndrome, an incurable genetic condition; but despite his illness, he was a happy, popular boy with many friends at Wells. He was at the school most of his life, and died shortly after leaving. John Baxter, whose wife taught Edward for three years while his schoolfellows were playing sports, spoke at his memorial service in the cathedral, and recalls the very moving ceremony later when a bench, donated by his family in his memory, was placed at the spot outside the dining room where he used to hold court before lunch in his motorised wheelchair, surrounded by friends.

very enlightened, and there were – and still are – no "gods". You might be a prefect, or a member of the first rugby XV, or a high-level specialist musician – but you were and are treated just like any other person, and respected both for yourself and for your talents, whatever they might be. The ethos here is to treat people like adults and to trust them. We tend to need disciplinary action not when someone has done something wrong but when he or she has not done something they promised, and were trusted, to do.'

When John Baxter arrived, he immediately saw that the physical quality of the boarding accommodation had to be improved at the expense of numbers, and set about doing just that. Boarding was anyway starting to decline; many of the choristers were now local day boys, and the balance between boarders and day pupils varied at the different levels of the school, with fewer boarding in the junior years and many more towards the top of the school and the sixth form. Nowadays over half the boarders are sixth formers, some of whom arrive at the school at that level. Charles Cain again: 'One of the attractive qualities of the school is its constantly changing population. From nursery, through pre-prep and the junior school, and then into the senior school, we get people arriving and others leaving. There will be an intake in year 7, and then another in year 9 when pupils come from their prep schools; and then new faces again in the lower sixth. It is also a feature of Wells, which is unlike many other independent schools, that the children of many staff members come here – and it's not the

The exchange with Preston Manor

In the spring of 2006 Wells Cathedral School participated in an exchange with Preston Manor school in north London, which involved three London students spending a fortnight in Wells, partnered by three Wells students, who then returned to London with them and spent a fortnight at their school. The six pupils – all in year 10 – were Libby Orrett from Wells partnered with Michelle Yembra, Tom Lloyd Jones with Moeed Majeed, and Jeremy (Jez) Lloyd with Mustafa Saai. The exchange was televised, and was later shown in three hour-long episodes on Channel 5, so the six young people not only had to be prepared to cross into other cultures on all sorts of levels, but also had to learn how to do so with cameras constantly following them.

The initiative was very successful, particularly in the fact that it has established ongoing ties between the two schools. On a personal level it was also a fascinating experience for all those involved, and not just in absorbing new cultures, a different school environment, a different pace of life in two cities of vastly differing sizes. They also made real friends, with their partners and with other students, and they are confident that these friendships will last – though for now they are all so busy with their A-level work that they have little time for regular contact.

What comes across both from the programmes and from talking to the Wells students now is that it was important for them to recognise and accept the similarities and the differences in environment and experience. They all remember being shy and overwhelmed at first, and making a complete hash of their first lessons; but they also quickly realised that – although Preston Manor class sizes were bigger – pupils at both schools were learning the same subjects at the same levels. Jez: 'We might be paying to come here to Wells, but we're not paying for lessons to be harder.' The exchange needed to ensure that their studies were not interrupted; Preston Manor provided Tom with an Italian teacher, for example. And they all had to get used to the bustle and sheer size of a large urban school, after their much more sheltered lives at Wells; Libby remembers often getting lost and rushing late into lessons, fully expecting to receive the standard detention, 'though they were nice, and didn't punish me'. And, as they pointed out, over 230 hours of filming had to be boiled down to three one-hour programmes, so there were focuses and biases which did not always reflect the day-to-day actuality of the experience. 'It was not exactly life-changing,' they now say, 'but it was a marvellous initiative in which to be involved, and none of us would have missed it for anything.'

sort of problem that it can be elsewhere. I remember when I had my daughter Naomi in my class, and she called me "Mr Cain" in a lesson; all the others rounded on her and said "Come on, Naomi – he's your dad, for goodness' sake."'

There was no such thing as a school sanatorium until 1980, when Vivienne Leigh, a qualified nurse whose son had been a chorister in the 1960s, became the first resident 'sister of the sick bay'. Previously, sick pupils had been looked after in their houses by the matrons, who usually had a room they could use for the purpose; though at times when epidemics like measles hit the school, whole dormitories would be put aside to accommodate the sufferers in isolation.

Patricia Staniforth recalls being told soon after she arrived by Mrs Ritchie that she had a 'bleeder' among her boys. 'I was shocked, and decided that I would never mention to the parents that the headmaster's wife used such language. How innocent I was! I soon learned what was meant by a "bleeder" when the poor boy in question had a tooth extracted. And did he bleed! The school doctor and dentist attended to him in his dormitory until the flow stopped.'

The school doctors all came from the same Wells practice, then and now. In the 1950s the doctor was George Mullins, who had been a ship's surgeon and has given his name to the house where he lived and which is now part of the music department. The matrons would weigh and measure all the boys at the beginning and end of each term, and would deal with a whole catalogue of minor medical tasks: taking temperatures; poulticing boils; dealing with chapping behind knees; combing for nits – and of course getting up in the night if any of them were poorly.

The first dedicated 'san' was set up in 1980 in a house in New Street newly acquired by the school (called Haversham, and later part of the larger girls' boarding house of the same name). As Vivienne Leigh recalls, 'It was nowhere near ready when I arrived: the floorboards were up, there was little furniture, and the whole building had to be decorated. I had to settle into temporary

accommodation elsewhere before setting to, with two helpers, to decorate, make curtains, and install furniture. There was little spare money, so we made do. I remember being given a few plastic boxes as vomit containers, and I ended up using my own money to buy a fridge so that we could store medical supplies and food. I had a basic kitchen in which I could cook breakfast, bake cakes, and heat soup for supper, but I mostly had to run up to the main dining room and bring back food for my patients when I had any. We did have some outbreaks of illness, but sometimes my charges were simply children who needed a bit of a break from school or some general tlc. Alan Quilter had a habit of scooping up kids who seemed a bit "droopy" and consigning them to my care for a while.'

Medical care is much more sophisticated today. The well equipped sanatorium occupies the whole of St Andrew's Lodge, and for many years there have been two fully trained nurses on the staff, currently Louise Wiscombe and Kate Saunders. The school doctors hold a surgery there every day, and a recent addition to the medical strength has been Deirdre Sisson, a professional counsellor. The school staff, particularly the matrons, have always kept their eyes open for troubled pupils, but in recent years the issue has been approached in a much more forward-thinking manner, and there has been increased concern to ensure that problems are confronted and dealt with.

Behind the scenes – the support staff

In 1996 Nicholas Le Breuilly wrote an article in *The Wellensian* about 'the many people who do vital work for the school, some of whom you might never have heard of.... Whether we personally know them or not, as pupils we owe them a huge debt of thanks for all the marvellous work they do for our sake. So maybe next time you get up for a day at school, spare a thought for all the people who make the school what it is.'

The same of course is true more than ten years later – and the long service at the school of so many of the support staff bears eloquent witness to the loyalty they feel and how much they enjoy the friendly and supportive atmosphere. Menna Searle, the bursar's secretary, came to the school in 1992 and is still doing the same job today – though, as she says, 'My busiest time is actually out of school term time, when I organise the summer lettings of the school houses to visiting choirs.' Jill Walsh has been here almost as long, joining in 1995 as secretary to the deputy head. As she says, 'No day is the same – things are always happening, in and out of term. I'm often the first point of contact when a pastoral or disciplinary issue comes up, and I try to deal with any problems immediately so that they don't fester. All the office staff get on together really well, socially and as working colleagues, and we also get to know the pupils.' Like Mrs Searle, she loves watching them growing up from little tots to strapping sixth formers.

When she retired in 2005, Barbara Smith had worked for two bursars and three heads, and had also been the registrar, dealing with admissions. She arrived in 1977 to work for Jerry Coote and then his successor, before being poached from the bursary as Alan Quilter's secretary. After running the next two heads' offices, she became full-time registrar in 2003, taking over from Peter Bishop who had in his turn taken the job over from her in 1997 when he retired as a teacher; she had previously combined it with her secretarial work. She remembers the change in atmosphere among the staff that John Baxter encouraged – the greater rapport and camaraderie which then became the norm throughout the school. For the first time non-teaching staff were included in staff meetings to discuss policy at the start of the school year, and the head would make a point of eating in the dining hall, surrounded by children so that he got to know them better. Mrs Smith has just returned from a trip to the Antipodes, the money for which was her farewell present from the school when she retired; and while there she met up with ex-pupils and gap students, staying with the musical Tan family in Malaysia and with other Wellensians in New Zealand and Australia.

Buildings and maintenance work is the province of Pete Penfold, facilities manager since 1998. As he puts it, 'I look after just about everything that doesn't move of its own accord: buildings, grounds, vehicles, equipment...'. He is responsible for managing the processes of rebuilding and refurbishment, with all the complications that an estate of so many listed historic buildings entails. John King heads the small team of staff who look after the day-to-day maintenance of the whole site; their skills and expertise are constantly in demand. Meanwhile, heading the grounds staff are Craig Keast, who manages the sports facilities, and Paul Barnett for the gardeners: the fifty-plus acres of the estate that they all look after, including the outlying sports fields and the gardens, form a well loved and splendid adjunct to the beauty of the school's environment.

Sally Greenhalgh, houseparent of Plumptre, has followed her mother, Shirley Smith, as both domestic services manager and houseparent. She oversees thirty-two cleaners who are assigned to the different houses, and not only keep them clean but also keep an eye on the pupils. Some of them have been at the school for decades: Josie Melmoth, who works in De Salis, is the longest serving cleaner, having joined the school in 1973; then there are May Madden and Jenny Mitchell, who arrived in 1979 and 1984, plus others new and older. Plumptre itself is home to thirty-five senior girl boarders, plus thirty day girls who use it as a base, and Mrs Greenhalgh lives among it all, with girls living and sleeping above and around her. It's a full-time job.

John Dennis, who attended the school from 1935 until 1944, sums up his educational experience as a chorister at Wells: 'By any standards the pattern of education for choristers was limited, constrained as it was by the requirements of attendance at services and practices at the cathedral. This is shown by the subjects I took in public examinations: history, religious knowledge, French, mathematics, English language, English literature. I failed Latin, and had to retake it at a later date in order to qualify for entry to Bristol. In many respects this was an education that severely limited one's choice of career. No maths after the age of sixteen, no Latin until older than sixteen, no physics, no biology, no chemistry, and no geography. The reasons are understandable. In addition to the restrictions on time available for lessons, the very limited number of students in the fifth and sixth forms would have made it impossible to plan for a broader range of topics in the senior years. Several choristers took advantage of their training to make music their careers.'

During the first half of the twentieth century this range of subjects was broadly what was on offer at Wells. The school's basic raison d'être was to provide an environment in which the choristers could be educated; but it could not survive on choristers alone – places had to be available to other pupils if the school was to be financially viable. There were undoubtedly many bright boys who flourished at Wells – and much of the teaching was exemplary, as old pupils recall with gratitude. But Prebendary Ritchie did not primarily aim at high academic achievement. He regarded the school as there to provide a basic education for choristers and the sons of local farmers and tradesmen, regardless of their intellectual abilities. The Ministry of Education inspection of 1951 saw this clearly: 'There is a considerable tendency to leave without completing

the normal course of a grammar school. Only eight boys are in the sixth form. Of the sixty-five boys who in the last three years finished their school life here, no fewer than twenty-nine took up farming, in most cases on their fathers' farms.'

The report went on to comment on the somewhat confused organisation of the school, 'which no doubt arises from the mixed intellectual calibre of the boys'. But this was in accordance with Ritchie's educational philosophy; his ideal teacher was William Carl, who had been at the school when he began his headship and stayed until his sudden death in 1941, and who 'could teach anything to anybody. He had no educational ideals; he merely "got boys through". On the other hand, his bête noire was Dr Lowndes, the science teacher on whom praise had been lavished by the inspectors and whom Ritchie's daughter, Ann Brierley, remembers 'walking down The Liberty to the Bernard building resplendent in his red doctor's gown (DSc not PhD, he insisted)'. But Ritchie disliked his all-embracing focus on science alone: 'Dr Lowndes has resigned his post and will leave at the end of the current term. All that I wish to record is that the school will be much happier without him, and that it need not lose in efficiency…'.

There were some remarkable teachers on the staff, long remembered by their pupils as having been a strong early influence on their lives. But the norm was for young staff to stay for only a year or so before moving on to schools which would offer a greater challenge. This changed when Frank Commings became headmaster in 1954. Not only did he immediately start to pay the teachers properly and give them greater responsibility, but he put a great deal of effort into raising academic standards. His challenge was a formidable one: he not only had to develop the curriculum so that it offered a much broader range of academic subjects, but also to

I came to be at school at Wells because my schoolteacher mother's school had been evacuated to Wells from London. My first year there was not very happy because I was put in a form a year ahead of my age. But the following year everything changed: I was with my own age group, I made friends, and I thoroughly enjoyed the course work leading to the school certificate. My contentedness was to a large extent due to two outstanding masters: Alan Tarbat for English and Mr Walker for French and, in my case, German.

Mr Walker – I don't think I ever knew his first name – came to Wells in 1941. He had retired from teaching modern languages at King's School, Rochester, and was trilingual. I got to know him so well because I had studied German at my London school and, even though Wells did not teach German, Mr Ritchie thought I should take it as one of my subjects for school certificate. Our lessons were very informal, sitting in armchairs in the staff sitting room. Most of the time our conversation was in German, and we used as our main source Die Zeitung, *a paper produced in London by Jewish refugees from Nazism. I eventually got a credit in my exam. Mr Walker was a cultured, lovable old man, who discreetly showed me the wealth of German culture, so alien from the monstrosities of the Nazi regime.*

The legendary Alan Tarbat was a gifted teacher, who widened our appreciation of English literature and indeed our skills in writing our beautiful language. One particular joy I remember was when he used to read aloud to us on Saturday mornings, from writers like Mrs Gaskell, Jane Austen, and J B Priestley. Occasionally too he would read us poetry, which he held dear. He was an exacting critic of our written work, and would set us essays to write in the school holidays. Two of the titles have haunted me all my life: 'Sunt lacrimae rerum' and 'Qui s'excuse, s'accuse'. We kept in touch for many years after I left school, and I remember both these men with affection and a profound appreciation of their friendship and wisdom.

John Burbridge (1940–5)

appoint talented new staff and provide them with the facilities which they needed to teach their subjects effectively.

By the end of his ten-year tenure, the academic standing of the school was very different. The expansion of science and other subjects had been greatly facilitated by new classrooms and laboratories – albeit often constructed out of temporary materials which it later fell to Alan Quilter to replace with more permanent structures; and there were some fifty boys in the sixth form, most of whom were intended for university or other forms of further education.

The teaching of science is perhaps most illustrative of the change and development in the academic approach that took place during both Frank Commings' decade as head and Alan Quilter's early years. Science above all needs a well-equipped teaching environment, and as John Hard's memories of arriving in 1973 indicate, some of this was in place but much of it was still rather makeshift. Colin North had been the first head of science – and specifically of biology – and Hard was being interviewed to replace him as head of biology:

'My interview with Alan Quilter was pleasant, though I was a bit taken aback when he asked to be excused and climbed out of the window. It turned out he wanted to give a message to his wife who was in the garden – and I was then told that Mrs Quilter would take me to the science department to meet

We boys were cheerfully unaware of the tremendous pressures on the school's managers and only dimly of the inevitable restrictions they brought – there was, for example, no gymnasium, science laboratory, art or music room. Books and basic equipment, the sort of things now taken for granted, were in short supply. It was only when I became a teacher, and in due course a headmaster, that I came to wonder how on earth the school had kept going at all. Three teachers in particular exerted life-shaping influences on me and, I am sure, on many of my fellow pupils. Though strikingly different, they shared (but certainly never planned or, probably, even discussed) intense concern for our well-being and personal development, and took practical steps to bring it about, to a degree perhaps more common then than now. Alan Tarbat taught English by the effective but now unfashionable means of simply presenting us with works of literature and allowing our own judgments to form without imposing his own views (though Tennyson could make his eyes go misty), together with rigorous insistence on correctness in our own writing. Studying English at university provided no more than a top-up to his teaching. Linzee Colchester (irreverently called 'Horse') was essentially just such another. He ran the senior house humanely, capably taught Latin and French, and, through his energetic management of what was laughingly called the scout troop, instilled in us a delight in the outdoor life. Once towards the end of my time, when I was in a singularly stroppy mood, he gave me a tent, half a crown, and the weekend off with the instruction to get up onto the Mendips and come back 'when I could behave'. He took a group of us cycle-camping in Belgium at his own expense. At night in his room, as prefects, we drank his appalling coffee, listened to scratchy Bach, and read books on stained glass.

Michael Peterson, then cathedral sub-organist, was not on the regular staff but lived close to the school. I went to him, first for piano and then for general music lessons, his only pupil. His house was a haven; I spent much time there, playing and listening to music, and on Sunday evenings half a dozen of us sang madrigals and motets round his table. Later on, he pushed me into trying for Oxford, and everything that's good about my life, including my long marriage, has flowed from that. Michael was a man of simple, unthinking goodness, but it was only after his recent death that I found out how much good he had done to so many people, and always by stealth.

Bryan Bass (1946–52)

the current head of science and his successor. Mrs Quilter and I got lost on the way – as she explained, she did not often visit the scientists, usually described by her husband as "that mafia at the other end of the place". My meeting in the science department was informality itself. I was asked to help unload a minibus after a biology field trip, and then we drifted down to Sadler Street to a café to drink coffee and chat about cars, football, and the price of wine. I got the job!

'Early in my first year I discovered that the sinks in the old biology lab (long gone now) were not connected to the drainage system. This accounted for the peculiar miasma on some Monday mornings after a warm weekend, and also for the fact that any mouse, gerbil, or hamster escaping from its cage and seeking refuge under the floorboards usually drowned. The department gradually expanded and I found myself teaching botany and zoology alongside biology. One particularly good year produced ten medical students, two vets, two nurses, and a clutch

of biologists. Teaching botany was always enjoyable as the characters wishing to study such a subject tended to be a little out of the ordinary – not to say quirky. In the case of two such students I cannot remember ever having formal lessons as I think we spent all the time arguing. I must have enjoyed my time at Wells, as I stayed until 2006.'

Nigel Walkey, who came to the school as head of maths in 1983, is now deputy head with specific responsibility for the curriculum, and is a national key figure in curriculum development. When he arrived he was shocked at the small numbers then doing A-level maths; but his enthusiasm and teaching skills quickly ensured that numbers increased, and within only three years one of his pupils, James (Jock) Angus, became for two years

Martin Ashton and his pupils in an English lesson

Paul Johnson

For thirty-two years after his arrival in Wells in 1967 to teach maths, until his death in 1999, Paul Johnson was a loyal and dedicated member of the school staff. He was well known for his individual approach to teaching his subject, and to the care and attention he lavished on less able mathematicians. And then in mid-career, he was faced with the daunting task of embracing the new discipline of information technology, which he taught himself and then imparted to his pupils. It is to him that the school owes the initial setting up and development of this vital subject; it is amazing now to remember the days before IT, and both the excitement and the challenge offered by an academic subject and a technology that blossomed alarmingly quickly.

PJ also loved sport of all kinds, and sportsmanship; he was an outdoors man who tended his garden and went fishing. Although without a military background, he revelled in his work with the CCF, particularly in being able to share with his students his love of the Lakeland fells where he organised many sessions of adventurous training.

Paul Johnson

one of the six members of the British team at the maths Olympics. Today there are well over 100 pupils doing the subject in both years of the sixth form. Maths, indeed, is diagnostic at Wells of the school's enlightened and confident approach to the academic curriculum and academic change, and of the huge improvement in attainment that the last two decades have seen. Under John Baxter and then Elizabeth Cairncross, there has been considerably greater focus on the sixth form, A-level entrants have grown steadily in numbers, and results at both GCSE and A-level have rapidly got better.

Wells is unusual for an independent school in its progressive take on academic matters. Not only are all year 7 students exposed to Mandarin, studying it as a modern language along with either French or German, but all students in years 7 to 9 have dance

Maths at Wells

The consistently high numbers now choosing maths as an A-level option are a tribute both to the teaching team and to the encouragement the students receive to approach maths, not as a subject that is too difficult for any but the brightest, but as something that anyone can tackle – and enjoy. As the charismatic head of maths, Susie Jameson, says, 'Before Nigel Walkey came it was only for the clever; he widened it out to the clever and the interested; I want it to be for both of those and also for those who are prepared to have a go.' Ms Jameson has had two stints at Wells: the first from 1984 to 1989, and the second when she was tempted back in 1992 to become head of the department. Her enthusiasm for the school and the subject is infectious: 'We are a very friendly team, very approachable; no one's a dragon, so the pupils don't become scared of the subject or convinced that they can't do it. My philosophy is always to encourage them to believe in their ability to tackle complexities by saying yes not no, by offering them an escape route with honour, by telling them that it's ok to make a mistake, that mistakes are good things – there to be learned from. They may be ignorant, but that's not the same as unintelligent.'

She regards A-level maths as a positive, functional subject, a useful option for university entry; further maths is more challenging, more philosophical, 'maths for maths' sake'. It is telling that over a third of the 2007/8 lower sixth are doing further maths. Similarly, the decision to take the IGCSE maths course – despite its non-recognition in government statistics – has proved highly beneficial: it is, says Ms Jameson, a more rigorous course, a better feed into A-level, and offers a clearer approach for students at all levels – challenging for the brightest while also less confusing for weaker candidates. The success of this policy is amply demonstrated by the results in March 2008, when twenty-three out of the twenty-five who took the IGCSE six months early achieved either an A* or an A. In September 2008 70% of the lower sixth form will be studying maths and 30% will be studying further maths; this runs counter to national trends.

The maths department will benefit in autumn 2009 from a new maths block; the old one has already gone, and is much missed. It was familiar to non-mathematicians also, because it contained the lockers used by members of the lower school, who would slide down the metal railings on the steps outside and creep into their lockers to hide and talk to each other. Ms Jameson recalls the badger which used to live under the building and was christened Bernoulli after the talented European mathematical family; it would sometimes appear during the day and disrupt lessons by running along outside. She also remembers the mural based on Escher's 'Metamorphosis' that gradually came to adorn the blocked-up windows of the building before it was demolished. The mural has been stored, and the school looks forward to seeing its reinstallation in the new classroom building.

Nigel Walkey (left) with Andrew Thompson (right) and a pupil whom he is sponsoring

lessons as a matter of course. Latin continues to flourish, and – again unusually for an independent school – key stage 3 assessments are made so that pupils can see where they fit on a national scale, and subjects like Italian are made available for those who want to study them.

Above all, there is flexibility – an approach that is perhaps easier at Wells than at other schools because the timetable anyway has to be able to accommodate the particular needs of specialist musicians. The sciences are studied separately, which not only

I used to bring in my bearded collies, first Harry and then Bramble, to lessons when I wanted to demonstrate dentition. Dogs were ideal to show how teeth worked, because I could offer them a hard biscuit and it was clear to all how they could grab on to it and worry it. They were also useful if I wanted to deliver a light-hearted rebuke to a cheeky pupil: all I had to do was position the dog with its back to the child and tell it what a good dog it was. The result was a vigorously wagging tail which would often catch the cheeky one unawares. And when not being part of the lesson, the dogs would happily fall asleep under the lab benches and be no trouble at all.

John Hard (staff 1973–2006)

Ray Robbetts had set up an experiment to examine bacterial decay in milk, which involved a row of bottles with varying amounts of milk allowed to go off for varying periods of time standing in a row in the open air at the back of the biology labs. The bottles had been in place for a good part of the half term over which the experiment was being conducted, when the headmaster, John Baxter, happened to spot them one day while walking past the labs. In disgust, he emptied them all down the drain – half a term's work wasted!

Another experiment which went wrong was with a stillborn baby llama, which I had begged from a farmer near Wedmore. I kept it in a tank of formaldehyde for several years, and it served me well as a demonstration of differential bone structure – its legs were extremely long in relation to its tiny body. I then decided to remove it from its tank and allow it to decay so that I could salvage its skeleton, and to that end I buried it at the back of the biology lab near where I knew there were several ants' nests on whose occupants I could rely to help with its disintegration. After a suitable length of time had elapsed I went to dig it up, but had trouble remembering exactly where I had put it. Several holes later, I found it – but there was nothing left apart from a bit of its hair: the ants had devoured it in its entirety, skeleton and all. It had been too young for its cartilaginous bones to ossify so they had been able to eat them too. Then to add to my disappointment, I had to endure a telling-off from the head who had fallen into one of my holes!

John Hard (staff, 1973–2006)

provides students with a more demanding curriculum than the integrated approach but also offers a stronger opportunity for in-depth immersion in the individual subjects. Students who are ready can take GCSEs early, and can also study their AS subjects over two years if they wish. And there is flexibility in the courses offered: the IGCSE in maths, elements of the International Baccalaureate, such as critical thinking, available alongside traditional AS and A2, a course in law studied via video conferencing, and the International Computer Driving Licence. As Nigel Walkey says, 'We want to offer flexibility in opportunities for learning in order to balance high musical achievement with high academic achievement.' It is fair to say that Wells Cathedral School is unique in Britain – and more than likely in the world – in this combination; and all within a normal school.

Peter Thomas

Arriving to teach physics in 1970, Peter Thomas later became head of science and was indefatigable in developing and lobbying for his department, and in introducing imaginative innovations to the science curriculum. An outstanding teacher, he inspired many of his pupils to go on to distinguished academic and professional careers in science and engineering, and his early death in 1991 was greatly mourned at the school. One sixth former simply summed up the feelings of everyone: 'He was a great bloke.'

A passionate lover of classical music, he was also devoted to sport, particularly cricket and rugby, and regularly turned out for the Willows. At his memorial service, John Baxter drew comparisons with Albert Schweitzer for his love of science, and Neville Cardus and John Arlott for his love of music, sport, and wine. As he went on to say, 'We are all diminished by his loss; but we are also exalted by the privilege of having known and worked with him.'

'The Electronic Freshman' (with apologies to W S Gilbert)

Richard Lambert (1966–73) remembers this being written collectively and dedicated to Peter Thomas, the recently arrived head of physics; it was performed at an end of term concert in Ritchie Hall. He particularly remembers the 'English public school choral tradition' pronunciation of 'information' and 'hesitation'.

I am the very model of a modern electronical
I know it all, though not as yet with thoroughness Teutonical
Its underlying mysteries which puzzle some, don't puzzle me
And diffidence I don't possess and so it doesn't muzzle me.
And thus I go about the place and air my views ad nauseam
And people view me doubtfully and ask me on what course I am
And though I can elucidate with devastating clarity
I find it doesn't help me to develop popularity.

If you can pose a problem in a circuit that's transistorised
Which I can't solve in half a mo then I'd be quite a bit surprised
I can as quickly recognise a crystal of Germanium
As any horticulturalist can pick out a geranium.
The laws of electronics seem as clear to me as light of day
I sometimes read a textbook just to pass the time of night away
With solid states and microwaves I've learned familiarity
Twixt me and my professor I can see no great disparity.

The workings of computers whether digital or analogue
I understand as easily as falling backwards off a log
I undertake to clarify and answer curiosity
With confidence which some would say was next door to precocity.
The striving and retrieval of all programmed information
I can explain in full without the slightest hesitation
Whilst programming and punching tape are matters of simplicity
Which I perform at any time with satisfied felicity.

Although I've only started yet and only have a smattering
This will not of necessity inhibit me from chattering.
In short, you'll see quite clearly if you've really read this chronicle
I am the very model of a modern electronical!

Slavery then and now – extracts from a poem by year 9 history student, Hannah Wood

They came on horse and yelling loud,
Cracking whips above the crowd,
Some tried to run from this fierce horde,
But were soon cut down by flailing sword.

Roped in lines with children wailing,
Off to the coast they'd soon be sailing,
'Keep your silence', these evil knaves,
To the coast they went to be shipped as slaves.
…
Slavery then was an awful trade,
Worked to death and never paid,

We all must take a share of blame,
The thought of their plight puts us to shame.

Slavery we think is a thing of the past,
But no, it's back and the shadow cast,
Even now in these modern times,
Evil people commit evil crimes.
…
We all of us must be prepared
To help and show that some do care.
Stand up and fight these evil men.
Think back to the old slaves, 'Never again'.

The art room and A-level art

Art

Art at Wells has produced some distinguished artists, notably Justin Mortimer who studied the subject in the 1970s under the then head of art, Sue McDougall, and has gone on to forge a high-flying career. It is a popular subject at both GCSE and A-level, with the work exhibited both in the art department and, for AS and A2, in Wells Museum. As the current head of art, Jan Tapner, says, 'The department focuses on fine art, mainly drawing and painting with sometimes a sculpture workshop. I try as far as possible to teach one to one, to focus on the individual so that I can help to bring out individual talents and skills.' The work is on show round the school too, so that the achievements of artists at all levels are on public display.

Right: Justin Mortimer

Drama

School drama productions during the first half of the last century, despite being somewhat hampered by lack of resources for costumes and sets and, of course, by the need to persuade boys to take on the female parts, were encouraged by the staff. Linzee Colchester is remembered for his energy and resourcefulness in set building and production, and the junior school under Claud Holmes benefited enormously from his deep interest in drama and his playwriting abilities. When Paul McDermott arrived to teach English in the mid-1980s he reinvigorated drama at the school, and several of his pupils have gone on to become successful actors. When he left, he was replaced by Mike Theodorou as the first full-time drama teacher, and he was in turn succeeded by Edmund Comer; under them both drama, particularly musicals, continued to flourish.

Jeffrey Bigny had done a great deal to foster both school and house drama by presenting trophies known as the Tarbat Shield and the Bigny Cup, the former for the lower school and the latter a house competition for the upper school. Both have recently flowered into different formats. The Tarbat Shield is now the week-long Tarbat Festival in early June each year for everyone in the lower school. Each year group has its own day in De Salis garden, taking part in workshops on poetry or dramatic themes, with a competitive element self-judged by the participants. In 2007 it was enlivened by a resident poet, Marcus Moore, who performed 'poetry slamming' and encouraged the pupils to have a go too. The Bigny Cup is now an autumn house competition for the upper school, when girls' and boys' houses are paired off and they write and act out performances on a given theme, with only a week allowed for preparation. Points are awarded for originality and acting skills, and also for good planning and organisation. Carolyn Meade, head of drama, is adamant that drama is a discipline that takes time and dedication as well as skill if it is to be a success: 'The best performance doesn't necessarily win if their organisation was bad and they just blagged it.'

Mrs Meade and her predecessors in recent years (as well as Judith Burns and others in the junior school) have overseen a huge increase in dramatic activities throughout the school. Everyone in years 7 to 9 does dance and drama, and the choristers too are now taught to step and clap while singing so that they too benefit from dance and movement. There are theatre visits with the English department, drama clubs are growing up, and student groups are encouraged to put on their own productions: a year 11 and 12 English group recently staged *The Importance of Being Earnest* after studying the play; the drama department's only contribution was to hire the lighting for the performance in Ritchie Hall.

Student productions happen throughout the year, starting in the autumn and going on to a major performance by the upper school in January – in 2008 it was *Anything Goes* – and a lower school play or musical in March. In October 2008 year 11 students are going to New York for a theatrically themed visit, when they will go to plays and on backstage tours and visit the School of Performing Arts. And in recent years there have been productions of Shakespeare in De Salis garden after

the exams in summer, when a local director has come with a professional team for two weeks to rehearse and perform with the students.

Meanwhile, theatre studies is available at GCSE and A-level, readers at cathedral events are coached, every year group has at least one theatre visit (exam students have more), and pupils are encouraged to go for auditions at national youth theatres. And although specialist musicians rarely have enough time to become deeply involved in productions, they are encouraged where possible to take part.

Despite the relatively limited resources of Ritchie Hall, the annual school drama show run by Judy Burns was always a resounding success. We did Guys and Dolls, Cabaret, and the poignant O What a Lovely War! There were some really talented singers and actors, but Caromay, a volunteer mum, had quite a challenge getting some of us to dance. What immense fun, though – and after all those months of rehearsals, the production week was over all too soon. Those were some of the times that really tried but ultimately strengthened our friendships. One particularly memorable production was Love you to Death, a Denegri extravaganza. What a fantastic show: young and vibrant with brilliant tunes. It saw two productions during my time, one of which involved a tour to Jersey. About thirty kids and staff landed in Jersey with instruments and equipment, all of whom ended up staying with my family for ten days. Everyone mucked in: friends brought around huge one-pot meals and the garage became our dining room. It was such an adventure and, with TV and radio coverage, a huge success.

Caroline Hamilton
(née Cowan, 1993–8)

I was recently asked by Mike Stirling (a 1968 leaver, like me) whether I remembered being a pirate, as he was, in the 1965 school production of The Pirates of Penzance. A pirate? Me? Hmph! The chance to be even vaguely macho would have been a fine thing!

I was Second Chorus Girl along with Nick Ralph (First Chorus Girl) because we were by then singing alto in the school choir and so ranked senior to all the trebles from the choir who were the rest of the 'female' chorus. What's more, I remember us both arriving at the costume-fitting session after everyone else because it was a Wednesday and so we couldn't get down to the Bernard Building until after scouts. My dress was a bit on the small side, and particularly tight across the chest. I must have been the flattest-chested chorus girl in the production because there wasn't even room to ram a couple of pairs of rolled-up socks down for a makeshift bosom.

Worse still for me was that we had a hockey house match on the Monday before the production. I was in goal and, in one particular goalmouth scrimmage, I was down at ground level trying to save the ball when I got the club-end of a hockey stick in my face, right above my right eye. By the time of the dress rehearsal (and first performance to the junior school as guinea pigs), my eyelid was deep purple, and then turned purple-black the next day for the first of the three proper performances. It's a wonder I was able to keep my eye open at all with all the white muck they plastered all over it each night. I remember that we 'ladies' had to wear gym shoes for 'lightness of step', but I still managed to trip over the 'rocky' staging coming out from the bottom of the wings every time we danced round in a circle on that small stage.

My 'pirate pairing' was with Andrew Williams, Middleton was Ruth, Durston was Frederick (and couldn't pronounce his Rs properly), and our classmate, David Lewis, got the role of the comedic policeman who arrived on stage down the middle of the hall from the main door at the back, and made a lot of 'business' over booking the dean for a parking offence. Other memories are hazy.

Matron Wormald was coopted to sing one of the lesser soprano leads and could hardly sing a note. I think, shortly after that, romance started to blossom between her and Goop (Geoffrey Shaw) who, I fancy, was the artistic director while Bill Whittle was of course the musical director. It was, after all, 1965!

Mark Brown (1961–8)

Opposite: The Importance of Being Earnest

MUSIC

ANY ACCOUNT OF MUSIC AT WELLS has to start with the choristers. It was for them that the school was originally set up 1100 years ago, and it was the need to house and educate them that kept it going during several dark periods over the intervening centuries when it might otherwise have closed. Aelfric's *Colloquy* gives an insight into their daily routine around the turn of the last millennium; and it is fair to say that choristers then might well recognise and feel a kinship with the lives of choristers now.

John Barrett, who was a chorister and a pupil at the school from 1935 until 1944, remembers that in the 1930s probationer choristers would have some theory pumped into them by the deputy organist, but most of their musical education was acquired through imitation of the experienced singers beside them. Academic work was less important; after matins every day at 10am they returned to school in time for morning break,

and naturally missed lessons. Some subjects were sacrificed; as he now says, 'Any science or geography I know was self-taught.'

They didn't at all mind staying on after the rest of the school had gone home for Christmas: 'We got two Christmas dinners out of it after all, one with the Ritchies and another once we returned to our families. Our house then was the building now called Edwards, and I was dared one year on Christmas morning to use the rope fire escape outside our window to descend to the ground. All would have been well, but as I was passing the window of our housemaster's room I somehow managed to put my foot through the glass. Mr Forman was not pleased.' The Christmas 'stay-on', as these times were known, was also a lucrative time for the choristers: after breakfast on Christmas Day they would go to the palace to sing carols to the bishop, for which he gave each of them a newly minted

There was one very special day which changed my life for ever. This was the day when, in the middle of the morning, a priest came into our classroom at my primary school, and invited anyone who liked singing to sing a hymn while he accompanied on the piano. This was the Rev Bawtree-Williams, who was acting organist and master of choristers at Wells Cathedral while Denys Pouncey was away in the RAF, and the hymn singing was in fact an audition to become a cathedral chorister. I was then given a letter for my mother, which explained that in return for becoming a chorister I would also be able to attend Wells Cathedral School – a brilliant gift for me as well as for other local day boys, many of whom, like me, came from families who would not have been able to send their children to public school; and we got a first-class musical experience as well.

Sunday was the day of the week when, dressed in all our formal finery, we had to run the gauntlet of what seemed like hundreds of evacuees. I

have forgotten how many times my mother had to sew the tassel back onto my mortar board. As an eight-year-old I used to have to open the large doors to the practice room above the cloisters using huge keys which I carried in my pockets, and which regularly wore holes in the linings. But these memories pale into insignificance beside the wonderful musical experiences I shared with my chorister friends. By the age of nine I and others could read, sing, and (some of us) play music almost faultlessly at first sight. And the choir was self-managing, relying on a code of discipline taught very early in our careers, which provided great opportunities for team-building and leadership, as well as confidence. I recall shaking with fright at my first solo, but these feelings did not last long and I fully enjoyed singing Mendelssohn's 'Hear My Prayer' ('O, for the wings of a dove') to a packed cathedral at the beginning of my last year as a chorister. I no longer play brass, but I often still 'give forth', especially in tiled rooms containing a bath!

Peter Wade (1944–9)

shilling coin; and then they would go on to the Deanery to sing to the dean and his family, and were given five shillings to be shared among them – sixpence each for the seniors and threepence for the juniors. They also shared out the collection at the Boxing Day carol service – and as they were responsible for taking the collection plates around, they made sure to scour every corner of the cathedral to seek out every last member of the congregation.

James Kench (1978–89) had mixed feelings about 'stay-ons': 'The words of the hymn "God be with you till we meet again", so joyfully proclaimed by most of the pupils at the junior school Michaelmas end of term assembly, inspired a different joy and excitement in my mind. Waving goodbye to my fellow pupils (including my little brother and sister), who were casting aside their cares and heading off to a nice long Christmas break in the comfort of their homes, represented the beginning of a different and often quite gruelling period of the year for me. We would watch the last stragglers leave before heading off to evensong in the cathedral – but even though we were not heading home, there was always a palpable excitement on that last evensong of the term. It represented a change in the daily routine which was exciting to a bouncing, energetic bunch of young lads. The march down The Liberty to the cathedral in a crocodile was usually a particularly unruly one, with the head chorister doing his best to maintain order. But once we entered the cathedral the noise level always dropped. There is a level of respect bestowed upon all who enter that magnificent building, and we were no different.'

As a chorister I attended two Three Cathedral Choir concerts in Sherborne Abbey in 1938 and 1939, and as an honorary vicar choral sang in three post-war concerts in Wells, Bristol, and Bath. I was asked to sing in Edinburgh's Episcopal cathedral while in the navy in 1944, and also sang in the choir under six diocesan bishops. I recently sang at a rehearsal for Truro Cathedral Diocesan Choral Festival, at which one anthem was Haydn's 'The heavens are telling', which took me back seventy years to the time when I had sung the part of Gabriel. At the last Wells choristers' reunion I was the oldest chorister present, at the age of eighty-two.

Derek Goldie (1934–43)

I joined Wells Cathedral School in the summer term of 1935 and left at the end of the summer term of 1944. In May 1935 the school numbered 105 or so boys, and its composition was considerably different from what it is today: boys only, and of these at least twenty per cent were choristers or ex-choristers. The link between cathedral and school was pervasive. Being a chorister set one apart from non-choristers. Naturally we shared meals and (as boarders) lived in the same dormitories, went to the same classes, and played soccer, rugby, and cricket. But life was different in certain crucial respects: the cathedral, holidays, and the pattern of our education.

It is difficult now to envisage the obligations placed upon a member of the cathedral choir sixty years ago. At that time Wells Cathedral maintained the full sequence of choral matins and evensong throughout the week, plus Holy Communion on Sundays. There was some respite: Monday morning and Wednesday afternoon services were men only and, reciprocally, Tuesday matins and evensong were boys' voices only. Thus the duties involved thirteen services per week, which were supported by daily practices – Monday to Friday 8.30 to 9.50, a principal rehearsal after matins on Saturday, and a further rehearsal on Sunday mornings. As a consequence, formal education did not begin until 11am, except on Mondays.

Public attendance at matins and evensong during weekdays was very limited, and frequently at evensong consisted of a single individual – said to be the city librarian. There were other rewards; very occasionally in the dim, gas-lit cathedral a greater horseshoe bat might be seen. Choral activities were not entirely confined to the cathedral. In the late 1930s there was a major concert in Sherborne Abbey with the Boyd Neel ensemble and the choirs of Exeter, Salisbury, and Wells.

Holidays were much truncated by staying on for cathedral duties. In effect, Christmas and Easter holidays were frequently less than three weeks in duration and sometimes only a fortnight. Due to the nature of the cathedral services and practices, the time passed quickly, and, in the case of Christmas, profitably. I remember little of those times except running over the bridge into the Bishop's Palace on a cold and icy Christmas morning, and at some time or other trying to play ice hockey on a frozen pond up the Old Bristol Road with a bar of soap as a puck.

John P Dennis (1935–44)

'And are you the little cherubs who are going to sing to us?' The voice came from a tall, well-dressed lady whom we almost knocked over as we hurtled round the south-west tower of Wells Cathedral. I quickly looked behind me to see whom it was she was talking to and realised that she was referring to us. A cherub indeed! I was at least twelve years old – almost grown up.

My two friends and I were dressed in our Sunday uniform. This consisted of an Eton suit – long pin-striped trousers and a stiff collar which overlapped the jacket collar and, incidentally, roughened up your neck – crowned by a college cap or a mortar board with a neat black tassel. Some three years before, in 1942, I had won a choral scholarship to the cathedral choir. At first I was a probationer, but I soon became part of the daily routine, which went on week in, week out. The great ecclesiastical events still loom in my memory, particularly the Boxing Day carol service when the cathedral was completely packed out. I also remember the enthronement of Dr Wand as Bishop of Bath and Wells. The service was filmed, and a great fuss was made of the ceremony

which came towards the end of the war when people were longing for the relief of some pomp and glitter. We were later taken to the cinema to see ourselves singing. And we had another cinema trip when Dr Wand, who was a kindly person, came unannounced into our vestry one evening a few weeks after his enthronement and asked, 'Now then, who is coming to the flicks with me?' No one said no.

The demands of cathedral life left us little free time. But paradoxically, I remember the freedom we managed to have at the weekends after Sunday evensong, and the glorious times spent exploring the Mendips when we had to stay behind during school holidays to sing the services. We cycled to Cheddar and Shepton Mallet, Dulcote and Glastonbury. We walked to Arthur's Point or wandered out to Wookey Hole. I had become interested in bird watching, and I saw my first raven at Ebbor Gorge. But then eventually my voice broke and I had to return reluctantly to a normal life – a cherub no longer!

John Simms (1942–6)

John Baxter was headmaster when the decision was taken to admit girls to the cathedral choir. 'As a former chorister in an all male choir I observed the boys with particular interest; as the head of a long-established coeducational school I was increasingly aware of the wish of some girls to sing in the cathedral choir. Angus Watson, then director of music, and I pressed the chapter to consider opening the choir to girls. Salisbury was already taking positive steps. One day the full story of the eventual Wells decision will be told. Two important contributors to the debate were "last ditch conservatives", and the words "over my dead body" featured. But the radicals prevailed and two new choral sounds emerged, when the girls sang alone and on the few occasions when boys and girls sang together. A generous grant from the Music and Ballet Scheme helped provide some funding towards the education of the girl choristers at the school, and the story has been a happy one ever since.'

He recalls an amusing postscript to the decision to accept girl choristers a few years later. 'Cathedral

These extracts from the 'matters discussed at a meeting between Anthony Crossland, cathedral organist and master of the choristers, and senior choristers on October 1 1983' have been provided by Matthew Train, who was at the school from 1979 to 1989 and head chorister from 1983 to 1986. Discipline among the choristers was clearly an important issue. In addition to rules about merit and demerit points, procedures before and after services were laid down: once they were robed, and had checked that hair was tidy and shoes clean, conversation was to be kept quiet and to a minimum, and was forbidden altogether once they had moved from the sacristy into the cathedral. Anyone without a mortar board on Sunday mornings would receive a warning, topped up by a demerit point if he was still without it in the afternoon. And they had to keep strictly in their ranks on their way back to school 'until the whole crocodile has come to a stop in the passageway at the side of Cedars and the head chorister, or chorister in charge, has called "Dismiss"'.

The procedures were there to maintain the dignity and gravitas of the offices that this young group of boys was charged with. The document ends, 'It is recognised by all senior choristers that the positions which they hold, together with the duties and powers which they carry, place a special responsibility on them, in effort and behaviour, to maintain proper standards for the whole chorister team.'

Drawings by Rose Fay

My very first service as a chorister was the Saturday evensong after the death of Diana, Princess of Wales. We arrived at the school on the Thursday afternoon and performed Fauré's Requiem to a packed cathedral on the Saturday afternoon, having learned it – as well as the Mozart settings for the two Sunday services – in just those two and a half days.

As a probationer chorister, I was privileged to stand next to head chorister Roger Drabble for my first Advent carol service. We were standing on the flagstones in the quire with the cathedral in darkness apart from our candles. As we started to sing, Roger couldn't see his part very well so he moved his copy over my candle, which promptly set fire to it. The two of us proceeded to do a little dance to put the flames out with our feet, much to Malcolm Archer's angst. Thank goodness we weren't in the wooden choir stalls.

I also remember the midnight mass at Christmas in 2002 when my voice 'went south' after the live broadcast when I was talking to Malcolm. He suggested that my brother Ben might as well inherit my deputy head chorister medal, so I handed it over to him under the Christmas tree in the crossing.

Jonathan Jones (1997–2003)

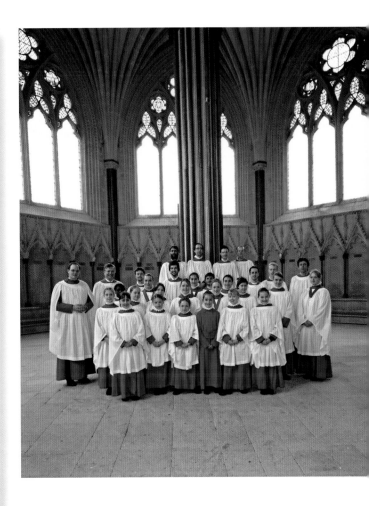

organists and choirmasters were invited to the annual meeting of the Choir Schools' Association at York. At one point the head of York Minster choir and I erected a screen and invited the organists and choirmasters to identify the gender of the voices singing behind it. We provided solo boy, solo girl, groups of boys and girls, groups of boys, groups of girls, and so on. Not one of the organists was able correctly to identify the gender of the singers.'

The girl choristers' choir was formed in 1994, a year after Salisbury Cathedral had taken the plunge. Rose Fay (1994–9), one of the first girl choristers at Wells, remembers a wonderful

evensong which the two new choirs from Salisbury and Wells sang together in May 1995. As she wrote in *The Wellensian*, at the end of their first year, 'All the adults involved seem to think we have improved loads this year; but all the choristers still think we've got a long way to go until we're as good as the boys.' The new choir settled in very quickly: 'At the beginning of the year we were thrown in at the deep end, having to do evensongs without the support of the vicars choral, but we managed and even enjoyed it once we got over our nerves. After a while we gained confidence and the number of services we sang built up as our repertoire grew. We all feel much more sure of ourselves when singing with the boys, partly because of all their experience but also because together we can produce a much greater volume. In September all the adults were convinced that there would be lots of jealousy and rude comments from the boys, but we soon became good friends.'

I am so proud to be able to say I was one of the first girl choristers in Wells Cathedral. Those first years were a truly memorable time, attended by much excitement and anticipation from both the girls and all those involved with us. From the beginning we had amazing support from Tony Crossland, who believed in us so much even when others didn't, and we were very soon preparing for our first evensong, just over a month after we started – and it was particularly exciting because it meant that we were being properly confirmed as choristers of the cathedral by the bishop.

Processing into the quire was a daunting experience, but we felt that we had so much support from so many people – though there were regulars at evensong who didn't come that day as they still hadn't come to terms with girls in the cathedral choir. Soon we were singing regularly, and it was wonderful to be involved in the Christmas services during our second year, and also to be part of the process of choosing a new organist, sad though we were to see Tony Crossland go. We did our first recording soon after Malcolm Archer arrived; we sang with the boy choristers and men, with a mixture of the girl and boy choristers singing individually and together, which became known as the 'great choir'. At the end of our first year with Malcolm, we were off on our first tour to East Anglia. In our third year we finally got our own medals to signify head and deputy head choristers and corner girls, and in the November of our fourth year we recorded our first CD without the boy choristers. Then we began practising for our first overseas tour to America; it was particularly fascinating to sing with the girl choristers in the new cathedral in Washington DC – such a stark contrast to Wells!

It was wonderful to see people's opinions change towards the girl choristers over time, with far fewer people viewing us as pariahs. Being a girl chorister teaches you so much, and not just musically; it has given many girls so many opportunities, and has led to lifelong friendships. I am so grateful that Wells Cathedral took the brave decision to create the girl choristers. I still think of myself as a girl chorister of Wells Cathedral and feel a sense of camaraderie with the present girls.

Naomi Cain (1989–2002)

Naomi Cain and Roger Drabble, head choristers 1997–8

Jazz at Wells

Our jazz band was formed in 1958, and was quite an achievement, considering that only one of us was a trained musician. The rest of us were self-taught and started off in our free time around the piano in Ritchie Hall, listening to jazz records and gradually assembling a few tunes. 'Alcoholic Blues' was one of our first, and 'St Louis Blues', before we progressed to the more challenging 'Muskrat Ramble', 'Tiger Rag', and so forth. The first band consisted of David Hopper on trumpet, Peter Baines (ex-head chorister) on clarinet, Peter Gregson on trombone, Brian Ellery on banjo, and Fred Galvagne on drums. From the start we called ourselves 'The East Liberty Stompers', and our wild antics soon became legendary in Wells. We held the stage at the St Cuthbert's Day fair, and we also held a jazz dance at the school, when girls were 'imported' from Sidcot School and the 'joint was jumpin'!'

On our own initiative we arranged to have a record made at Ray's recording studio in Bristol. We caught the bus from Wells, persuading the conductor not to charge extra for our instruments, and arrived at the studio. We had to play all the tunes on each side of the record with no more than a few seconds break between each one because it was a waxed record — and we were all very nervous. In due course about sixty copies of the record arrived and were sold out on the first day. At least three of us still have copies today, and for most of us that band at Wells was our only musical endeavour.

David Hopper (1950–61)

The 1932 jazz band

The Wellensian for the summer term of 1959 dignified the East Liberty Stompers with their own section under the heading 'Jazz notes': 'Several senior boys, interested in traditional jazz, grouped themselves together and performed an entertaining act in the last Christmas concert. At that time perfection was in the distance, yet they showed great promise. Many Sunday evenings were spent in hard but enjoyable practice. One night, for example, they carried their instruments up to Cedars field for a "session". Unfortunately, complaints were made by quiet-minded neighbours and from then onwards the Bernard Building was their home. During the last two weeks of term they gave two public performances. The first was at St Thomas's church "Evening Revels" where an enthusiastic audience heard them. Gaily lit by coloured lights on the vicarage lawn, they made a fascinating picture both in vision and sound. The other performance was, perhaps, only semi-public, for it was confined to the school. Many went to the assembly hall expecting to be driven out after a short time, among them the head and Mr Tarbat. But they both admitted afterwards that they had thoroughly enjoyed the show. The boys showed their enthusiasm with many rounds of cheers and applause. It was a grand climax to a successful year.'

Yfrah Neaman and Yehudi Menuhin with the school orchestra in Wells Cathedral

Although the choristers and their music took centre stage at the school, there was some musical teaching for other pupils – though for many years the only 'music room' was a small room off Ritchie Hall – and pupils also made their own music. There was certainly a jazz band in 1932, and again in the late 1950s, and Frank Commings encouraged music; in his last year as head he appointed old boy and ex-chorister William Whittle as director of music. But it was when Alan Quilter started the specialist music scheme that it became a central force in the school.

As he later recalled, among the first questions posed by Lord Waldegrave soon after he had become a lay governor was 'For what is this school particularly renowned?' The only answer the head could come up with immediately was its tradition of choral music, and even that had in the past been limited to the choristers themselves. However, a seed was sown.

Among the government's educational innovations in the 1960s was the encouragement of schools specialising in forms of the arts; and in parallel, local authorities seeking to fund boarding places in independent schools for talented children used a musical speciality as one of their criteria. There was also a growing recognition that school-age academies devoted to the teaching of music were lacking. The time seemed right to drive Wells Cathedral School down a new path which would involve specialist teaching of instrumental skills.

The music school

This stunning building (opposite) faces the north door of the cathedral and, like many of the other grand houses on the north side of Cathedral Green, was the home of one of the cathedral dignitaries, in this case the archdeacon. Although much of the interior retains its fifteenth-century fabric, the façade is largely late nineteenth century. But with its great oriel window and the housing for the circular stair, it presents a suitably medieval appearance, enhanced now by the splendid music often to be heard as one passes.

The archdeaconry of Wells was the largest in the country, responsible (before 1974, when it was reorganised) for over half the parishes in the diocese. The last archdeacon actually to use this building as his dwelling was Polydore Vergil, appointed to that office in 1508, though he was also at the same time acting as proxy for the Italian Cardinal Hadrian de Castello who was the appointed bishop.

The building was part of the premises of the Wells Theological College from 1890 until 1971, when it moved to Salisbury. It was fortunate for the newly enhanced musical department at the school that it then became available as the new music school. A grant from the Calouste Gulbenkian Foundation allowed the school to purchase and refurbish the building, and support from other charitable trusts made it possible to buy instruments and other equipment. The music school was opened in 1974 by Lord Goodman, chairman of the Arts Council, and today it houses the wind, brass, and percussion departments and a fine recital hall.

Bill Whittle was an immediate ally; and there was a stroke of serendipitous good luck when Wells Theological College vacated its library opposite the cathedral, and the school was able to take it over as the music school. From the outset Alan Quilter was

I was a sixth former at Wells when girls had not long been accepted and only string players were considered for the music scheme. But when Liz Shenton and I arrived, Bill Whittle saw his chance to put on his beloved Dido and Aeneas (above) – for here were his Dido and Belinda. The fact that neither of us had had a singing lesson in our lives did not deter him, and along with Simon Butteriss as Aeneas and a good chorus we started rehearsals. As Dido I flatly refused to stab myself, but agreed to poison myself instead with a phial of Ribena. One evening, I forgot to bring the phial on stage with me, and had to ask a member of the chorus to go backstage to fetch it, which he did with much bowing to hide the handover. But he had not had time to dilute it, so my brilliant act of dying was almost too true to life when I swigged the neat liquid only to nearly choke for real. Meanwhile Liz had wanted to shed real tears at my untimely death, so had hidden a raw onion in her pocket. But despite her attempts to sniff at the onion to induce tears, it was my close proximity to it that had the desired effect – so it was the corpse who was weeping, not her lady in waiting.

Iona Zuiderwijk
(née Sherwood-Jones, 1972–4)

The start of the specialist music scheme coincided with my becoming a sixth former. As an ex-head chorister, member of the school choir, grade six pianist, school orchestra viola player, and sometime Elton John wannabe I had been at the centre of all things musical at Wells, so I was interested in (and not a little concerned about) the difference the specialist scheme would make to our lives. James Shenton, the first member of the scheme and a shy, quietly spoken lad from Leicestershire, didn't look or act 'special' at all. But with a violin tucked under his chin, the difference was very obvious; the guy was in a league of his own.

Girls were a relatively new phenomenon at the school at this time too, and those of us with any musical talent at all quickly realised that this could be our 'in' with the fair sex! James very quickly attracted the attention of the only girl in the sixth form at that stage, who seemed determined to throw herself at him. One evening while he was watching TV in the girls' common room in Plumptre, his admirer blatantly decided to get changed in front of him. Dressed only in her underwear, she was amazed to be pushed to one side by the maestro and told 'Bugger off, woman – I'm trying to watch the football!'

When Bill Whittle decided to start a Saturday morning music club, with the idea that his A-level music pupils would gather in the music room in Ritchie Hall, listen to records, and (presumably) discuss what we had heard, Shenton wanted to know what kind of music we would be listening to. 'Oh, classical music,' replied Bill, 'you know, Bach, Beethoven, Handel…'. 'But not Mozart,' James interjected. 'Mozart's crap!' This forceful opinion, and especially the language with which it was communicated, made James Shenton something of an instant folk hero. But I have no recollection of the club ever getting off the ground.

Andy Jones (1962–72)

helped in his new initiative by contacts at the music colleges who provided specialist teachers, often part-timers who travelled down from London once or twice a week. The school also benefited from the advice of such highly qualified musicians as the violinist Yfrah Neaman, and quickly began to acquire a reputation for the excellence of its musical teaching and performing. Neaman was to remain a consultant to the music scheme for over thirty years, and was not only a very hands-on teacher, determined to first encourage and then maintain the high standards he demanded from his pupils, but was also a strong supporter of music at Wells for the rest of his life.

William Whittle remembers those early years: 'Alan Quilter's decision to secure the future of the school through a specialist music scheme was boosted by the closure of a local girls' school, in that we had already accepted that the admission of girls to the school was essential to the scheme. As the school would have to finance the initial stages of the new venture, it quickly became obvious that we would have to confine our efforts to one instrument. The violin was the clear choice, and Yfrah Neaman an obvious preference as the eminent musician we needed to advise us. He embraced the idea with great enthusiasm. And then in September 1970 I was able to appoint Timothy Goulter as my first assistant. A

fine young musician with a wide range of talents, he also possessed tremendous enthusiasm and energy. These were exciting times and we worked twelve-hour days as we undertook all the class teaching in addition to the A-level and O-level work. The evenings were filled with orchestral and chamber music rehearsals and we both taught fifteen individual pupils a week.

'It is impossible to mention and give credit to all of the many musicians who visited twice a week to teach and to give a sound start to the scheme in its early years. For the first three years the eight specialist violinists were taught by David Nalden before he returned to New Zealand, when he was succeeded by James Coles and Mark Knight. We were also soon able to extend the scheme to other stringed instruments; Amaryllis Fleming became our cello consultant, and recommended Rafael Wallfisch as our first specialist cello teacher. For some time too we had been able to produce a succession of good double bass players from our organists and those who proved a little too physical with the cello. With a complete string orchestra, formed in the main from specialist musicians, we were able to perform in various venues at home and abroad. And with Tim Goulter there to teach piano, our specialist music provision could extend beyond strings.

Mark Knight, head of strings in the 1970s, and the chamber orchestra in the cathedral

'Special highlights were performances at the
Aberdeen Festival of Youth Orchestras, and the three
trips to Scandinavia with the choir and orchestra in
the 1970s; on one such trip a party of eighty-five
musicians visited Norway, Sweden, and Finland.
Holland and Belgium were the venue in 1980,
culminating in a performance at the renowned
Walloon Festival. A particularly memorable occasion
was the joint concert in 1978 in Wells Cathedral with
Chetham's School – now also developing as a
specialist in music – where Yfrah Neaman and
Yehudi Menuhin were the two soloists in the Bach
Double Violin Concerto. There were many exciting
achievements in those early years, with the musical
reputation of the school boosted by the successes of
the pupils, who came from all over Great Britain as
well as Europe and the USA. It was not long before
we could celebrate over twenty organ and choral
scholarships won at Oxbridge – an impressive
achievement and an exciting start for a scheme then
in its infancy.'

*Opposite: John Byrne, head of
keyboard, with a pupil*

A knock-on effect for the whole school was that
applications started to come in from families who
wanted a school which offered a stimulating musical
environment for their children, even when they had
no particular individual musical ambition or talent;
and there was from the early days a strong
conviction that musically gifted children would
benefit from a broader-based educational ambience,
sharing their school days with fellow pupils who did
not share their speciality. The school was beginning
to develop a specific locus within the independent
sector. Eventually too, it was able to secure
government funding for grant aid to children from
less affluent backgrounds who could demonstrate
and be chosen for their musical talent.

By the early 1980s the music scheme had become
consolidated and properly structured. After William
Whittle's departure to New Zealand, the new
director of music, Richard Hickman, established
four departments: academic and choral, brass,
keyboard, and string and woodwind, each with its
own administrative head and dedicated teachers.

Ensemble work grew, as did lively orchestras and concert bands. Informal concerts, which had begun in the early 1970s in the headmaster's drawing room, moved to the hall of the music school where they attracted – and continue to attract – a devoted following. And as the scheme developed, it became clear that early worries about undue specialisation at too young an age were unfounded. Its intention had always been to nurture the talents of musicians who would have been frustrated without that opportunity, and many of those who benefited went on to study and work in music in their later lives; but in addition, the decision to combine specialist music teaching with an ordinary school life had been triumphantly vindicated, and it was increasingly clear that this was the unique strength that Wells offered.

When John Baxter arrived as head, fifty students were supported by the Music and Ballet Scheme, which had been set up in 1970 to help gifted instrumentalists and ballet dancers and was the bedrock on which the specialist music programme at Wells was based. By 1996 the number had increased to seventy, and as the scheme grew the heads of the four specialist music schools in England held regular

Kevin Murphy, back row right, head of woodwind, with pupils

meetings with the heads of the conservatoires. As Baxter recalls, 'Sir David Lumsden, principal of the Royal Academy of Music, joined the governing body and many distinguished professors at the conservatoires gave workshops and lessons and helped with the audition process. On the retirement of Sir David, Janet (later Dame Janet) Ritterman, principal of the Royal College of Music, joined the board. Specialist musicians are often also blessed with academic gifts, and decisions frequently had to be made between a performing course at a conservatoire or an academic course (not necessarily music) at a university. It was consequently important to create good relations with directors of music and admissions tutors at universities and colleges. It has been interesting to watch the development of Wells musicians after the tertiary stage of their education. Many, of course, are performing and/or teaching. A few are close to the top of their profession and their names can be seen from time to time in major London programmes. And many Wellensians have found their niche within the music industry in sound production and recording.'

Musicians of great international distinction were welcomed at the school: 'Before coming to Wells I would never have expected that Evelyn Barbirolli, Yehudi Menuhin, Boris Beresovsky, Evelyn Glennie, Peter Donohoe, Zvi Zeitlin, Tasmin Little, and a very young Vanessa-Mae would be among our guests – as well, of course, as Yfrah Neaman, consultant to the

> *It was a lecturer at Bristol University who first suggested the idea of 'Friends of Music'. I had been asked to run a workshop for potential teachers at the Education Department and my contact had attended a lunchtime concert in the music school. The director of music and the governors were keen and an energetic committee was formed. The Friends have grown considerably since those early days when membership was drawn largely from regulars at lunchtime concerts. Among them were Mr and Mrs Komolibus, a courteous, music-loving Polish gentleman and his charming wife. They epitomised the deep affection held by members of the public for music at the school and they often travelled to concerts far afield, such was their devotion to music-making by the pupils.*
>
> **John Baxter** (headmaster, 1986–2000)

I attended Wells Cathedral School, along with my brothers Kenneth and Gordon, in the late 1920s. All three of us joined the armed forces during the war, and sadly Ken became a prisoner of war of the Japanese, and suffered terrible mental and physical hardships, which left him with periods of deep depression. About fifty years after the end of the war, Ken rang me with the story of a melody that he had developed in his mind during his imprisonment, which he had imagined as an accompaniment to the John Masefield poem 'The West Wind'. He had learnt the poem by heart while in the camps, as an attempt to maintain a degree of sanity, and had found himself singing it to a melody which gradually became complete.

Ken had no musical knowledge to speak of, but he did have a good ear, and as I was musically trained I set it down on paper as Ken hummed it; the melody was still clear in his mind, even after fifty years. I then contacted the Old Wellensians and asked if it might be possible for the school's music department to arrange it and perform it. This was done as part of a singers' concert, and the hauntingly beautiful melody was sung by Maiko Suzuki accompanied by Lucia Leung. I was there with my wife, but sadly Ken was too ill to attend; he died in 2004.

Donald Baggs (left in 1931)

The chamber choir rehearsing

The average day was inevitably interspersed with trips to the music school for a flute lesson here or a singing masterclass there, or maybe a spontaneous jam session that would manifest itself out of someone tinkling on the piano in the concert hall while waiting for a rehearsal with Paul Denegri, head of brass. He was never seen without his leather jacket, and his long blond hair and vivacious conducting style made him look like Rowlf, the pianist from The Muppet Show. His CD collection was made up almost entirely of Tchaikovsky and Bon Jovi.

The composers' concerts were a highlight in the concert calendar, from the avant-garde style of Kieron Galliard's Concerto for Two Pianos to the lyrical live improvisations of Mei Yi Foo and the epic production of Dylan Thomas's Under Milk Wood. We would spend many an un-timetabled evening singing and playing the ballads of Rogers and Hart or dancing the Charleston. Jazz took off and everyone wanted to be involved. But the most wonderful musical moments had to be on those balmy evenings at the informal jazz BBQs on Cedars lawn.

Caroline Hamilton (née Cowan, 1993–8)

starring Christopher Lee and James Fox. Its success led us to our second project, The Little Vampire, for which we found ourselves writing, producing, and recording eighty-three minutes of music in a mere seven weeks. Wells had taught me how to work hard, and it never came in more useful than then. Nigel and I have since worked on films that stretch from animation to serious documentary.

In 2002 I was invited to become composition fellow at the London College of Music and Media where I completed a two-year MA degree in composition with composer Martin Ellerby. While there, I wrote more concert pieces, and began to develop relationships with chamber ensembles. Again, the early composition lessons that I had with Don Hart at Wells gave me the foundation I needed to pursue concert music. Over the last few

I spent most of my time at Wells practising the piano, with the occasional interruption from an academic lesson to which I now wish I'd listened! I remember clocking up eleven hours in one day; I worked so hard because of the environment and because of my piano teacher, Hilary Coates. The performance opportunities were fantastic. I played concerts both at the school and in the neighbouring counties – an incredible foundation for any aspiring musician wanting a career in performance. My development as a pianist and musician over five years at Wells earned me a place at the Royal Academy of Music to study piano; but I soon found that it was music technology and composition that fascinated me more than anything else. I had experimented with the technology available at Wells, where I had taught myself how to programme music on a computer. At the academy I would very often use one of the computers to write on, and I started to take a composition class with composer Nigel Clarke, which I enjoyed so much that I began to neglect my piano practice. Composition had taken me over, but my request to change course was refused so I persevered with my degree while writing in my spare time.

By the time I graduated as a pianist, I was already collaborating with my mentor, Nigel Clarke, and we had secured our first feature film, Jinnah,

years, due partly to my experience in the world of film soundtracks, I have begun to develop interests in recording, programming, and film editing. Nigel and I formed a company in 2005 called Moviefonics, which acts as an umbrella for a wide variety of musical activities, including film scoring, film editing, recording, programming, session playing, concert music, and classical concert promotion. Since leaving the academy, I have returned to the piano and have played a variety of concerts, both solo and chamber music, as well as arranging and playing with an indie/alternative singer songwriter (something I never expected to be doing). The music industry is going through major change: to be a musician today and pay the rent, one has to be a 'musician for all seasons', and be able to work in any genre or ensemble. For me, it has been about creating a portfolio of work; as a pianist, composer, and programmer, I do a variety of different things in music of all types, and it was Wells that gave me the ability to adapt to anything that was thrown my way. It has sustained me in a career that I love, and provided me with the musical foundation I needed, for which I am truly grateful.

Michael Csanyi-Wills (1989–94)

I'd just like to thank you for my schooling, for the inspiration to be a musician, and the feeling that I could indeed Esto quod es. I have very fond memories of so many tutors, past and present. Since leaving the school, I have meandered down the paths of life: made some mistakes, came to some dead ends, and found my way back to music. It's lovely to hear the music in the listening room section of the web site; to see how the school's teaching of music has changed over time. I am now writing music for small theatrical productions, I've worked as a vocal coach and acting tutor for the New York Film Academy international summer school, and will shortly be performing as Benny with the international tribute act, Abba Forever. I've even found the time to bring my trombone out of retirement, though I'm sure Alan Hutt will read with a wry grin that I'm only playing jazz and blues on it these days. The foundation of piano that I was given by both John Byrne and Hilary Coates, together with composition tuition from Jeff Sharkey and Simon Dearsley, have given me the ability to compose, work in a session studio, and play live as a jazz and blues musician, working with some people who otherwise would only have featured in my wildest dreams. More than that, through the teaching at Wells I have learned how to appreciate music as an art form and that brings me more joy than anything else. So, thank you all for the pleasure you have given me. I hope that for the rest of my life I never have to leave this world, and will continue to follow my path as a composer, musician, and singer. I have to be honest: at Wells I was probably one of the worst singers ever to pass through the doors of the cathedral, but owing to a lot of effort from people like Nigel Perrin and other tutors, I am now at least passable, well, for blues and rock. I hope you continue making other people's dreams a reality.

Charlie Wall (1991–8)

Paul Denegri, head of brass and commercial music (right), with a pupil

school and contemporary of Menuhin, with whom he performed Bach's *Concerto for Two Violins* with the school orchestra at the end of my first term.'

In 1990 Angus Watson arrived as director of music from the Hong Kong Academy for Performing Arts. The school had been without a director of music for a year and, as the new director says, 'Perhaps because of this, there seemed to be some uncertainty among members of the common room as to the role of specialist music in their midst, uncertainty exemplified by a request at one of my early senior management meetings that we should reduce the number of lunch-time concerts. I replied that, on the contrary, we planned to double the number so that every specialist and special provision student could perform publicly two or three times a year. There was a certain unease even among the music staff too, although the level of teaching in some areas was truly inspiring. Michael Young, the funniest colleague I have ever had the good fortune to work with, led a dedicated team of teachers in the keyboard department, including his brilliant successor today, John Byrne, and the invaluable and sensitive accompanist, Barbara Murray; Catherine Lord, a fine violinist who had studied with Galamian in New York, had arrived as head of strings the term before I did and was already setting the exacting standards she still maintains; and the charismatic Paul Denegri was starting to build the outstanding brass department we all know and celebrate today.'

Angus Watson introduced a management structure which involved increasing the number of semi-autonomous departments and giving each its own head, whose responsibilities included appointing new specialist teachers, arranging lessons for both specialist and general musicians, and inviting distinguished consultants, such as Chris Elton, David Strange, and Evelyn Barbirolli, to visit the school to give masterclasses. 'The proposed arrangements were strongly supported by the headmaster and the governors' music sub-committee; and almost miraculously, the right people with the right personalities and qualifications arrived to fill the additional head of department posts. Some have left the school by now: Jeff Sharkey, head of composition, became director of music at the Purcell School soon after I retired, and has now returned to his native America to become director of the prestigious Cleveland Institute; Ioan Davies, the brilliant cellist in the Fitzwilliam Quartet, head of chamber music and later head of strings at Wells, is now director of Pro Corda; and Michael Young is a professor at the Royal College of Music and the Royal Welsh College. Others who joined the staff in 1990 or soon afterwards have remained. Jeff's fellow American, Kevin Murphy, husband of Hilary Wynne Murphy, the excellent head of lower school music, became the new head of woodwind, Alison Armstrong has proved to be the ideal head of senior music at Wells, and Karen Trego, responsible in my time for practice supervision, is now the highly efficient head of musical operations. And of course every music school needs a Jean Windridge as a calming administrative presence

Wells is effectively my spiritual home. How couldn't it be? I had eight wonderful years as a student there and returned as head of strings to 'give something back' to an institution that had given me so much; wherever I go in the world part of me is forever 'Wells'. What were the highlights? Playing to HM Queen Elizabeth the Queen Mother in 1985, the world tour in 1986, performing Sinfonia Concertante with Tasmin Little and the SCO, and conducting Fauré's Requiem in 2006 come to mind pretty quickly. Inspirational people I revere and whose impact shaped my life are or were in abundance at Wells: Alan Quilter, Yfrah Neaman, Mark Knight, Tricia Noall were all colossal personalities who were the pillars of my education. A day seldom goes by without one or all of them offering a word of advice in the corridors of the mind. Wells produces a particular type of student: from a musical perspective they can be immensely talented and a real prospect; but more than that, they are instantly recognisable by their human capacity, communicative sparkle, sense of humour – all sponsored by the Wells formula which makes them particularly attractive when in search of a career in the years ahead.

Philip Dukes (1978 – 85; staff 2001–7)

A bassoon masterclass with David Hubbard

Oh yes, I had a great time as a student at Wells!
Mullins used to be lived in then by the head of
academic music, a very sleepy fellow called Alan Bluff.
When he overslept, we had to break in in the mornings
to practise early. After about age thirteen I tended to be
the tallest of the freezing mob in the car park, so I was
hoisted onto the wall and in through the window of
room 6. Not sure what health and safety would make
of that sort of thing these days! Combination locks are
definitely a step in the right direction. Anyway, you can
put my name to any number of hyperboles about the
school. It was a really wonderful start in life and I'm
very pleased to be back again now.

Richard Ormrod (1985–92; staff 2008–)

when we musicians start getting temperamental.
Eighteen years on, she is still at her post, as wise and
calm as ever.'

Angus Watson retired in 1994, and was
succeeded by Roger Durston, who had been a
chorister, head chorister, double bassist, and pupil at
the school in the 1950s and 1960s, and was one of
those among Bill Whittle's and Tony Crossland's
students who won a choral scholarship to King's
College, Cambridge. He was responsible, with John
Baxter, for exerting relentless pressure on the
funding bodies to increase the specialist places
available, which rose during his time to seventy
government-funded places along with around 150
special provision places; and his tenure as director of
music was marked by his determination to ensure
that pupils leaving Wells became employable in a
fast-changing world. With the head's wholehearted
support, therefore, the students began to give
children's concerts in the Colston Hall and Wells
Cathedral, use period instruments, engage in
community workshops, work in partnership with
primary and secondary state schools, and further
develop work in world, folk, rock, jazz,
contemporary, fusion, music theatre, and crossover
forms of music. New music provision included a

music technology centre with two new classrooms,
more practice rooms, a recording studio, and a green
room. In the recognition that Wells would have to
develop its own young violinists, a violin scheme for
all the pre-prep children was set up with Susan
Thompson, and Alexander technique lessons were
introduced for all students, in part to counter the
danger of repetitive strain injury. More practice
supervisors and a technology technician joined the

Our son, Ross, was at Wells from 1996 to 2000 as a trumpet specialist, having gained a
scholarship with encouragement and practical advice from the head of brass, Paul
Denegri. Those formative years and pastoral care gave us as parents a pride in the
school that has never left us. 'All work and no play' was and is certainly not in evidence at
Wells – we particularly remember a merciless rag concert to the outgoing head of music,
Roger Durston, all in great fun and in good faith! We think the only disappointment Ross
and his friend Nathan Hewitt expressed was that their final concert in the cathedral
(Sheherezade) ended pianissimo, and not with the earth-shattering finale hoped for by
young trumpet players. And now Ross has returned to the brass department at Wells as a
part-time tutor, a post where he can share with other professionals, and pass on, the
enthusiasm, skills, and encouragement he benefited from throughout his time at Wells
and the Royal Academy, and now as a successful freelance player.

Chris and Sue Brown

school, and Wells Music College was launched to offer specialist instrumental lessons to non-Wells students from across the West Country. Durston's successor as director of music in 1999 was – and still is – Dorothy Nancekievill, under whose leadership the department has gone from strength to strength, developing and nurturing all levels of music in the school, and increasingly spreading its wings into all sorts of outreach, at home and abroad.

That the learning, teaching, and performance of music at Wells are special goes without saying. Numbers help to give an idea of what is achieved here: there are approximately 1600 timetabled music lessons a week; about 150 concerts are given each year throughout the school; out of around 700 pupils in the school, 450 or so have one-to-one music lessons, of whom 200 have music as their main focus; of those 200, forty are choristers and the remaining 160 are on some sort of specialist music course, whether on a 'set menu' as specialists or as pupils with special provisions who may be on the same level as the others or aspiring to get there; there are seventy government-funded places available for talented young musicians, on a means-tested basis; there are fifty ensemble performances each week; and almost ninety people are involved in the delivery of music, whether as instrumental, academic, or singing teachers – many of them visiting from elsewhere or assistants supervising practice – and support staff in the various departments.

Wells is unique in other ways too. Jayne Obradovic, for example, is the only dedicated head of percussion in a music school in the country. And of course the specialists are part of a normal school and take part in normal school activities, like sport and drama. This is in contrast to other specialist music schools, some of which, for example, have little or no sports provision. And as with other departments in the school, the philosophy is to emphasise that those lucky enough to study here are privileged, and need to give something back.

Hence perhaps the huge amount of outreach initiatives that the music department fosters. Musicals have been written and performed with the

Bristol City Academy and Somervale School; there are collaborations with the South West Music School, the Bournemouth Symphony Orchestra, Dartington Plus, and the Wiltshire Music Centre; there are singing classes for primary schools and free orchestral concerts for around 5000 children in Bristol's Colston Hall; non-Wells pupils are invited to masterclasses; there are online resources, such as a virtual lesson in playing the Javanese gamelan. The expertise and talent at Wells, in short, is made available beyond the school, whether in helping to encourage music in primary schools or inviting local people, often in their retirement, to attend the piano club at the school. The aim is to enable listening, which will lead on to doing.

And of course the musicians themselves take their music outside Wells, whether it is the Big Band performing in Scotland, the string chamber orchestra going to Shanghai, the chamber choir playing in Beijing, or the brass and percussion players forging a link with Stanford University in the USA. In April 2009, the symphony orchestra will be going to Hong Kong; and there is an ongoing partnership with the Zinghai Conservatory in Guangzhou, China, which five Wells pupils visited in April 2008, funded by the British Council.

Perhaps a fitting footnote to the story of music at Wells is the attitude towards it of the rest of the school, as characterised by teachers who encourage specialist musicians to flower in other subjects despite the pressures on them to give so much time to learning, practising, and performing their music; and by the musicians' non-specialist fellow pupils, who both accept them for their similarities and their differences, and are in their turn encouraged to develop and work hard at their own special aptitudes.

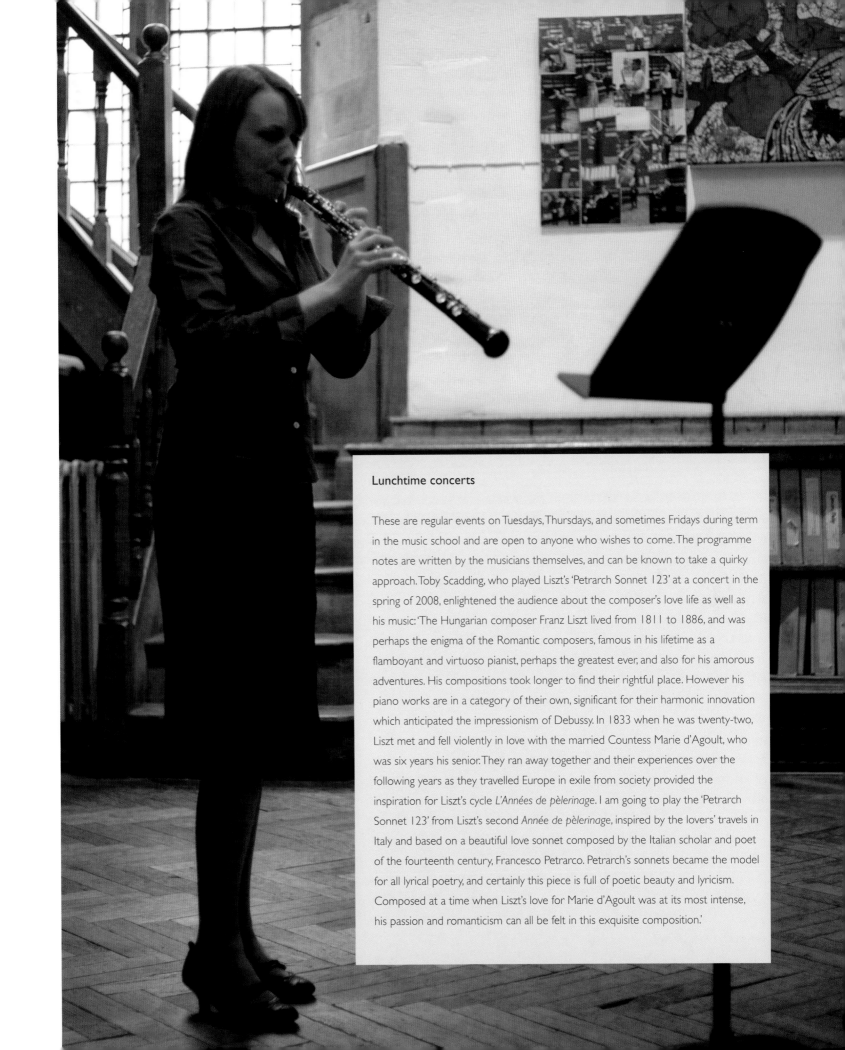

Lunchtime concerts

These are regular events on Tuesdays, Thursdays, and sometimes Fridays during term in the music school and are open to anyone who wishes to come. The programme notes are written by the musicians themselves, and can be known to take a quirky approach. Toby Scadding, who played Liszt's 'Petrarch Sonnet 123' at a concert in the spring of 2008, enlightened the audience about the composer's love life as well as his music: 'The Hungarian composer Franz Liszt lived from 1811 to 1886, and was perhaps the enigma of the Romantic composers, famous in his lifetime as a flamboyant and virtuoso pianist, perhaps the greatest ever, and also for his amorous adventures. His compositions took longer to find their rightful place. However his piano works are in a category of their own, significant for their harmonic innovation which anticipated the impressionism of Debussy. In 1833 when he was twenty-two, Liszt met and fell violently in love with the married Countess Marie d'Agoult, who was six years his senior. They ran away together and their experiences over the following years as they travelled Europe in exile from society provided the inspiration for Liszt's cycle *L'Années de pèlerinage*. I am going to play the 'Petrarch Sonnet 123' from Liszt's second *Année de pèlerinage*, inspired by the lovers' travels in Italy and based on a beautiful love sonnet composed by the Italian scholar and poet of the fourteenth century, Francesco Petrarco. Petrarch's sonnets became the model for all lyrical poetry, and certainly this piece is full of poetic beauty and lyricism. Composed at a time when Liszt's love for Marie d'Agoult was at its most intense, his passion and romanticism can all be felt in this exquisite composition.'

Sport

Craig Keast, who came to the school in 1988 as a groundsman and gardener and has been head groundsman for the last fifteen years, sometimes stands at the top of Cedars field and marvels to himself, 'They actually pay me to work here!'

Cedars field, with its splendid trees and views down to the school buildings with Wells Cathedral towering over them and the Somerset countryside beyond, must be one of the most beautiful school sports fields in the country. And through Keast's devoted attention to the cricket square on which the school's first XI play, it is also one of the best. Laid in 1995 with Ongar loam on a hardcore base, its quality is such that for many years now junior county games have been played here, and its reputation will improve when, as is hoped, funds become available for a pavilion.

Sport has for many years enjoyed a high profile at Wells. Fifty years ago the boys played rugby, hockey, and cricket, and were often very successful in inter-school matches and tournaments. When girls arrived, the range of sports on offer widened to encompass their needs, with netball and tennis becoming available. Now the boys play rugby, hockey, and cricket, the girls hockey, rounders, and netball, and tennis and athletics are open to everyone. Cross-country running is also an option, as is croquet on Cedars lawn in summer.

The school's move to the Cedars in the 1920s made the splendid grounds available for sporting activities – old photographs show boys being put through their paces over vaulting horses under the shadow of the large cedar – but the slope of the ground meant that most of the major sports were played on Mundy's Meadow, behind the school. Tor Furlong was purchased in the 1950s to provide

further facilities, but it was the coming of the new relief road in 1995 that provoked the need to make new arrangements for sport. This road cut across the middle of Mundy's Meadow and halved the space available there. So what was left was turned into a car park and an Astroturf pitch, which is used today for hockey in winter and tennis in summer, and more land was bought next to Tor Furlong in Bekynton. This now houses rugby, hockey, and cricket pitches and facilities for track and field athletics, and is also the base for cross-country running. At the same time, Cedars field was levelled and the precious Ongar loam was imported to form today's splendid cricket pitches.

Head of sport today is Martin Swarfield, who manages a team of three full-time staff, one of whom is head of girls' sport, plus a sports technician. He also has the help of gap year students, and many of the staff who teach other subjects are also involved in coaching various sports. He oversees two distinct areas of sporting activities: the games programme, whereby every pupil is involved in at least two games lessons a week plus after-school practice; and the physical

> In the late 1930s when I was at the school there was no gym or swimming pool – our swimming was done at the Wells City baths. We played rugby, hockey, and cricket and did a considerable amount of cross-country running – in all weathers, even deepest winter. Our route was usually through Milton Lodge grounds and along the Mendips to Ebbor Gorge, and at times as far as Cheddar Gorge, and back. We played rugby on the top grounds of the Cedars, and cricket and hockey on Mundy's Meadow; we also had a tennis court on the lawn close to the Cedars.
>
> Alan Clements (1934–42)

I left Wells Cathedral School in 1949 having been head boy, captain of cricket and hockey, and vice-captain of rugby, if not a particularly effective scholar. I recall that the teaching of the time was suffering somewhat from the absence of young men who were largely still on active service. Two of my contemporaries were John and Christopher Waters, impressive because their aunts, Elsie and Doris Waters, were on the radio as 'Gert and Daisy' and their uncle was Jack Warner, the friendly TV bobby. My nickname at the time was 'microbe' and I can be seen in the team photographs as a thirteen-year-old mite of a scrum half at five foot nothing. The highlight of my time at Wells was games almost every afternoon, except Friday when we had cadet corps. Then there were matches most Wednesdays and Saturdays. I later trained as a PE teacher, and have always maintained my enthusiasm for the sport I developed at school, which has been the basis of my entire working life.

John Birch (1944–9)

education programme, which offers a range of activities, like dance, orienteering, water polo, and lacrosse. Every pupil is also taught to swim.

Facilities are excellent. The sports hall, built in the 1960s, has recently had a new floor, and the balcony above it houses the new well-equipped fitness centre. The swimming pool has also been completely renovated, and is now heated and has a retractable roof which means that it can be used all year round. When the school acquires a cricket pavilion on Cedars field and changing facilities at Tor Furlong, it will rival many other schools of comparable size in its provision for sports. As Martin Swarfield says, 'It is my ambition to be able to offer a sporting experience at Wells which the

pupils will enjoy while they are here and which will lead them to carry on wanting to participate in some sort of sporting activity after they have left.'

Overseas tours have been a feature of the sporting calendar for some years. Rugby teams have regularly organised fixtures in Europe and went as far as Australia in 2002, a boys' hockey team went to Barcelona in 2006, in the same year a cricket team went to Barbados, and in 2005 there was a girls' tour to play both hockey and netball in South Africa. Anniversary year, 2009, will see a mixed

team of boys and girls going to South Africa again, and also Namibia, to play rugby and netball.

Apart from the dedicated sports staff, many other staff members have had a major impact on sports and games at Wells. One of them is Alwyn Gillen, who joined the staff in 1972 to teach geography and history, and from 1975 until he retired from the role in 1996 was the coach and mentor of the first rugby XV. As Andrew Hignell recalled when he paid tribute to Gillen's twenty-one years of rugby at Wells, 'I became aware of the close link between Alwyn Gillen and Wells rugby even before I joined the school. When I told the master-in-charge of rugby at my then school where I was going, his response was immediate: "Andrew, you are in for a treat. That's Alwyn Gillen's school." During his years in charge, he has passed on to countless Wellensians his love for rugby football, which he first learnt in the beautiful Irish surroundings of his home in Ballymoney. A measure of his success is the fine playing record of the school's first XV and the fact that many want to carry on playing the game when they leave school and go on to university and college. We won't easily forget his fine booming voice which we have heard so many times on the touchline urging the boys to "stay on your feet".'

Malcolm Bradshaw, head of chemistry from 1967 to 1988, was a stalwart of the staff sporting teams and coached the second cricket XI. He was

given to analysing every match, win or lose, in Wisden-like fashion, and was fascinated by the curious rules and statistics of cricket. He is even said to have worked in the nets on his own version of Spedegue's Dropper (an exceptionally high full toss aimed so that it dropped from high in the clouds on to the batsman's stumps, and so-called after an Arthur Conan Doyle story about a village cricketer called Tom Spedegue who used it to bowl out the Australians). Nigel Walkey, newly arrived as head of maths in the early 1980s, remembers his first encounter with the cricket-mad Bradshaw at a pre-

Fundraising is something common to every school in the world. A device used at least twice during my time was an 'auction of promises'. It was not surprising that Philip Peabody should offer a visit to a Mansfield Town football match, with the promise of mushy peas at half-time; my offer was a visit to Lord's. A member of the chapter and a cricket-mad pupil joined me in watching Mark Ramprakash score a double century for Middlesex against his new county, Surrey.

John Baxter (headmaster, 1986–2000)

Danny Nightingale, who left Wells in 1972, won a gold medal in the team pentathlon at the Montreal Olympics in 1976. He came back to the school in the Lent term of 1977 to give a talk about his victory. As The Wellensian for the year recorded, 'One person listened keenly to the hero's story since he, Mark Wills, had only the week before beaten the previous school cross-country record (28.10), set by Danny Nightingale, by eighteen seconds (27.43).

Back in 1981 I rang my father to wish him happy birthday and he told me he'd seen an advert for a head of PE at Wells Cathedral School. I wanted to come back to the West Country, so I applied. During the interview Alan Quilter could not answer three of the questions I asked him, so I thought I might have a chance. The job was duly offered, and twenty-four years later I left!

I was always impressed by the great amount of good will of the staff in taking teams, which made my job much easier; and the pupils were so responsive and keen to play sport. Staff also gave up many Saturdays to take pupils to matches; I attended on over 700 Saturdays myself, and always enjoyed the thrill of seeing teams do well. For many years I used to make an award at the Monday staff meeting to a member of staff whose team had triumphed the week before; but this later changed, when I made the award to someone who had made some sort of sporting bloomer the previous week. I managed to embarrass most of the staff at some stage in this way, including head teachers.

I also ran the Willows staff cricket team, and arranged about twenty matches throughout the season. The object was to make sure everyone was involved in the game, and if we won it was a bonus. It was harder to skipper that way, but we were strong and won more often than not. Away matches were popular with the staff, though less so with their wives as detours were taken and curry houses visited. We once played against the Officers at Yeovilton, where the beer in their mess was only £1 a pint. We were in our element, but then after half an hour they announced that as it was now happy hour the price had halved. Ray Robbetts often drove the minibus, but I am sure that this was to cover up for him being a lightweight on the drinks front. And I also recall fining John Baxter, the headmaster, for 'showing off' after his first game for the Willows; he hit the first ball bowled to him for a six!

Mike Stringer (staff, 1981–2005)

In my time at Wells swimming was a sport assigned to the short summer term as the pool lacked the cover it boasts today. The boys had a swimming team but not, initially, the girls; but when I was in Remove I was picked, along with a sixth form girl, to swim in the boys' team. We had a gala away at Downside Abbey, where I did not do particularly well, but felt it was a great honour to be in the team. Happily, my father was posted to Malta at the end of year 7 and a summer spent principally in the sea helped me to develop my skills. I won several events in the school gala the following year and went on to be captain of girls' swimming in the sixth form.

I also experienced some success at cross-country, though I maintain to this day that this was because all the other girls preferred to walk and chat. One year Miss Blakemore took a group of us to the county trials. It was so cold that my hands locked solid and the pain as they defrosted was excruciating. I was selected to run in an inter-county meet, which was cancelled due to snow, and so I got through, by default, to the national finals in Windsor Great Park. As I was blissfully unaware of the term 'training programme' I found the going tough, but I completed the course albeit towards the tail of the field.

Kathryn Hill (1974–81)

term staff meeting: 'He was clearly anxious to test me out with an early googly. Who, I was asked, played at Lord's in the morning and Trent Bridge in the afternoon? The answer? The Royal Artillery Band – and it was maths bowled chemistry for a duck.'

Bradshaw himself remembered turning out for the last ever staff v boys soccer match on Tor field in 1968: 'It was an enthusiastic goalless draw during which our goalie got concussed and soon found a more peaceful existence as a noteworthy Mendip artist. Unfortunately, he was also 50% of the Willows XI (the staff cricket team) bowling strength, so he was a loss…'.

The Combined Cadet Force
Geoffrey Green

That there is a long history of military cadet training at Wells is shown by reference to old school magazines, old photographs, and the existence of the splendidly named but well worn, not to say well battered, Musketry Cup. Old boys such as John Barrett (1935–44; fifth from left, front row, above) remember being in the cadet corps during the final years of the war, under Mr Forman who was the captain. But by 1966 the school platoon of the Somerset ACF was petering out and the flight of the ATC was stuttering too. Having had experience as a cadet and a National Service Royal Marine, I agreed to try to take over these invaluable extra-curricular activities as contingent commander of a Combined Cadet Force unit. In the 1960s there were many sons of service parents in the school, so the application to establish a Wells contingent was duly processed and our first parade was in September 1968.

As part of the new start, the ancient wooden building next to the decrepit .22 range was removed, and a new hut with office, stores, and classroom was built in the laundry garden area. The range was refurbished, and the old fives court backing onto it was later roofed and decorated as a classroom. The

army section retained its Somerset Light Infantry beret, badge, and flannel shirt, and both sections retained the old battledress and Lee-Enfield rifles. Equipment was sparse.

I insisted that joining should be completely voluntary but, with a programme of serious hard work and fun, we always maintained our numbers and always received very pleasing annual inspection reports. I emphasised that we were wearing the queen's uniform and expected high standards of pride in turn-out, bearing, and drill, though in the 'flower-power' days of the 1960s long hair was a permanent problem. Nevertheless, in the contingent's first year, we were privileged to provide a guard of honour for the Queen Mother when she opened the new sports hall.

From the start the emphasis was on the educational contribution of character training and self-esteem, outdoor physical challenge, and leadership. Cadets were involved in the design and construction of a demanding assault course in the woodland surrounding Cedars field, and weekend camping on the Mendips became frequent and popular. I was keen to encourage the concept of

public service, and for many years much labour and some enthusiasm went into building steps in Ebbor Gorge, restoring the Caen Hill locks at Devizes, and repairing the First World War badges cut into the chalk hillside at Fovant. Cadets were not infrequently urged, 'The more you put into it, the more you get out of it.' Adventure training in the Lake District during the Easter holidays introduced many to the rigours and rewards of mountain walking, and was often over-subscribed, while the three-day 'yomp' across Exmoor towards the end of the summer term became an annual highlight. Later, the Ten Tors expedition considerably raised the physical demands. After 1984, when girls were first recruited (though I had been known to protest that such a move would be 'over my dead body'), their participation and contribution further increased the value of the contingent to the life of the school.

None of this would have been possible without the enthusiasm and commitment of many officers in both the army and the RAF sections, and my gratitude will be echoed by many hundreds of Wellensians. We can't name them all, but I would single out Paul Johnson for his unstinted dedication especially to the meticulous organisation of adventure training, Alwyn Gillen for his long service to the RAF section, and Sarah Hopkins (Laing) for becoming the first female officer. Long may the contingent flourish.

Ray Evans, the ATC commanding officer, had arranged for the squadron to go to RAF Colerne for a summer field day. A few days before, the air cadet liaison officer rang the school cancelling our visit as it was the station's annual sports day. Ray decided that we would go anyway: the coach was booked and there was no time to arrange an alternative visit – but the unit must not know of our presence! The cadets were told to wear 'mufti' (neither school nor cadet uniform) and if 'captured' by the RAF police not to disclose they were from Wells until 3pm – our rendezvous time at the coach which would wait on the road 100 yards from the main gate. All cadets were given a quiz sheet about the station as if they were spies, for example name and rank of the station commander, type of aircraft flown, when the NAAFI was open, times of chapel services, etc. The lads were told to go in small groups of not more than four, and on the day were dropped off the coach, eldest first, at intervals starting about two miles from the main gate.

Two cadets decided that a straight line was the shortest distance between two points and set off across country, heading for the control tower. When they came to a high wall they clambered over and landed in the arms of a nun! It was not a convent, but a home for wayward girls run by a religious order. Following instructions, and not wishing to jeopardise the day, they gave nothing away until the police were involved, when a call to the school resolved matters and the trespassers were released. At least the RAF was still very much in the dark.

The other boys all enjoyed the day, mingling with the families and even entering the races for the sons of airmen. Although we saw many boys wandering around, the surprise was to see Edward Hopkins in mac and trilby in the officers' tea tent. When Ray challenged him, he just said, 'Press, sir': typically original. It was a memorable day, and the RAF never knew that we were there. Of course in the 1950s security was more relaxed and it just could not happen today – pity.

Arthur Carter (staff, 1956–60)

I joined the CCF as soon as I came to Wells, as I was already an RAF officer at Campbell College, Belfast, making it a simple matter to transfer to another contingent. When Graham Crocker retired I took over the RAF section with the rank of flight lieutenant, and later, when Geoff Green retired, I became contingent commander with the rank of wing commander.

The CCF provided boys and girls with such stimulating experiences and so many challenging and rewarding opportunities, such as rifle shooting at Yoxter, canoeing on Emborough Pond, and air experience flying at Filton, as well as camping on Exmoor, in the Lake District, and in Snowdonia. And there were amusing incidents too, such as the time when I agreed to be a guinea pig when a navy helicopter pilot was demonstrating over Cedars field how to winch a man from the ground into an aircraft. All went well, and I was easily winched up almost to the door of the aircraft – but the pilot then slowly manoeuvred the helicopter until it was over the goldfish pond at the top of Cedars lawn, and then lowered me slowly, but inexorably, into the water and the green slime. This was, of course, much to the delight of the assembled cadets!

Alwyn Gillen (staff, 1972–99)

The main obstacle to the entry of girls into the CCF, apart from the honour of it being a boys' CCF, had been the lack of a female officer. Then Miss Hopkins volunteered for the job and, after attending a course and several Wednesday CCFs, she was given the rank of lieutenant and duly appeared in uniform. In September 1984, twenty girls started a basic section. This in itself was unusual, because boys always start in January. During the first few weeks a large number of people came to watch and laugh, but as we improved we were accepted as part of the scene. Uniforms were issued bit by bit, most of which fitted us even worse than the boys' uniforms. The jeans and trainers with our CCF jumpers and berets caused some comment during the field day at LI Tidworth. At Christmas several girls left, while the remainder of us split into RAF and army sections. We continued with orienteering, assault course, and .22 rifle shooting, against the boys.

Adventurous training at Easter was the first camp with both boys and girls. Despite the fact that it hardly stopped raining, we all enjoyed ourselves. The cooking rota proved that girls are not necessarily better cooks than boys, as the potato turned out as soup one day and a dry, powdery cake the next. Coming back to Temple Meads in our muddy boots, we weren't always appreciated by the other Easter Saturday rail travellers. Some of us, however, still managed to travel in the first class compartments on one train. In June we all set out again, this time for the annual trek across Exmoor. Several of us used this thirty-mile walk to contribute towards our Duke of Edinburgh Silver Award. The weather was hot and sunny, so we all came back very sunburnt, and we ended up wading through six-foot-high bracken. We all got back safely – and girls are now in the CCF to stay, whether certain commanding officers like it or not.

Katherine Clapham (née Hard, 1975–86)

CCF commanders, left to right: Geoffrey Green, Alwyn Gillen, Clive Mitchell, Jonathan Barnard

Shooting

There has always been a strong tradition of rifle shooting at Wells, particularly encouraged by John Murphy in the 1990s, who fostered a great deal of success in Commonwealth shooting competitions. With the recent arrival of Dave Lee, the new shooting master and a National Rifle Association coach, the shooting team has reached a very high level in an extremely short space of time. In July 2007 they competed for the first time in the national schools championships at Bisley, and finished in the top ten, with two year 10 pupils achieving outstanding results. The squad travelled to Germany in January 2008 to attend a masterclass with the German national team, and two months later put in an excellent performance at the national junior rifle and pistol championships at Bisley, with the rifle team coming second and the pistol team coming fifth. These results – again on their first ever entry in the competition – made them the top performing shooting school in this competition in Great Britain, and resulted in the selection of one of the rifle team, Martyn Prout, for the Great Britain junior squad.

Explorations and expeditions

Over the last thirty or so years the adventurous activities undertaken by various groups within Wells Cathedral School have embraced ever widening challenges, both in the UK and abroad, many of which have been lyrically described in the pages of *The Wellensian*. One CCF camp in the Cairngorms was enlivened by the appearance of 'Angus' one evening, as the campers relaxed after the rigours of the day, 'each content, each thinking grand thoughts of the grand mountains to be climbed the next day. Then Angus appeared. Our lives were never quite the same again. Angus could (and frequently did) eat everything in sight; Angus undid tents in the still of the night when all God's sensible creatures were asleep; Angus stole, broke, hassled, and made a

nuisance of himself whenever the opportunity to do so arose, and was a large, very tame, and very rude red stag.'

Adam Martin (1986–92) was robust about the Ten Tors challenge in *The Wellensian* for 1989–91: 'Don't believe anything you hear about Ten Tors, because nothing can describe the mental and physical agony that it entails. If you're a born masochist, fine, but for normal people the walk will be the most painful experience of their lives. Anyone who hasn't done it cannot begin to comprehend the physical and mental feelings and emotions that accompany walking fifty-five miles in twenty-five hours. It may not sound much – but add large packs, hills, and mist and some idea of its enormity will be

formed. If you're wondering what you talk about, you don't. You don't even think. The whole world revolves around the patch of grit or grass at your feet, with a vague idea of a tor somewhere ahead, and the finish a place where you will be able to sit without the need to stand again. The finish becomes the ultimate goal, a heaven of warm baths and cold drinks. Nothing matters until you get there and nothing matters but getting there. Until then you walk. But that said, the pain only heightens the feelings of success and accomplishment that accompany stepping over the finishing line. If it were easier, the feeling would not be the same. Ten Tors is impossible to forget, and for that we have to thank Mr Crane, who made it all possible and whose name is synonymous with having a good time, and Ian Allen who got our team round in one piece.'

Dick Crane came to the school to teach junior school maths, but was then appointed as an outdoor education teacher, specifically to lead, encourage, and cajole his pupils into such activities; as one of them wrote, 'Once again Mr Crane has succeeded in persuading half the school to force itself up cliffs, into deep dark holes in the ground, and even to brave the dank depths of Emborough Pond. We become embroiled in mysterious plots to encourage us to plunge out of an aeroplane or spend two weeks in the middle of winter with marines in Norway. Canoeists survive the rigours of white water or sea-canoeing – a gentler form of exercise, though nothing can beat the shame of feeling sea-sick in a canoe. And it came as a bit of a shock to some members of the upper fifth that rock-hopping is not climbing or scrambling among boulders but trying to beat the waves while weaving in and out of rocks on the shoreline.'

Wells is fortunate in its closeness to the Mendips, where both caves and crags abound. Troglodytes glory in the wide choice of caves open to them, including some that involve total immersion in freezing water before swimming through a short sump. Climbers immerse themselves in the golden silence on cliff tops within peaceful wooded valleys – until rocks crashing around accompanied by swearing from above bring them (not literally) back

to earth. One pupil paid tribute to Dick Crane and his attitude towards anything impossible – 'it's not!'

He was the guiding spirit behind the Andrew's Tandem weekends, and also the Children of Chernobyl initiative, whereby the cathedral school along with the Blue School welcomed thirty children from that devastated area of Russia to Wells and took them on camping and caving holidays for three weeks at a time. He also ran Duke of Edinburgh Award activities at all three levels, and took teams on testing walks such as the Ten Tors and the Lyke Wake walk in Yorkshire, which requires its participants to travel the forty-four miles from Ostmotherly to the coast on foot in twenty-four hours. He organised climbing trips to Snowdonia and the Lake District, winter skills courses in Scotland, canoeing on the Exe and Dart and on the sea at Charmouth, and took the post-GCSE pupils on camping trips in north Devon.

Some of the activities formed part of curriculum work, for example potholing as an element of the sixth form general studies course; and there was lots of extra-curricular activity at school, for example a canoe rolling clinic in the swimming pool and a project to build a climbing wall on the sports hall balcony (it has only recently been removed to make way for the fitness centre). Dick Crane took a robust view of hesitation or tears: 'I enjoyed generally making children's lives a misery.' But their memories of the challenges he persuaded them to overcome indicate just the opposite, as *The Wellensian* records; and he also recalls with amusement taking the blame when the school minibus was stopped by the police when one of its occupants threw an apple core out of the window.

The constraints of the curriculum and the pressures of league tables and constant monitoring have taken an inevitable toll on the breadth of such outdoor activities as are now possible; and health and safety legislation has also had its effect. Increasingly perhaps now, adventures are confined to the sporting field, at home and abroad, though there continue to be trips and expeditions arranged overseas, as the next chapter records.

THE WIDER WORLD

UNDER BOTH FRANK COMMINGS AND ALAN QUILTER Wells had started to spread its wings beyond the UK, by both welcoming students from countries all over the world and sending its musicians, both choristers and instrumentalists, to perform abroad. But it was under John Baxter that these overseas contacts really took off, and not just through music. As he writes, 'Initial international interest in the school arose from music, but this was not exclusive. Applications from music students in China, Hong Kong, Japan, Korea, Malaysia, and Taiwan, and less frequently from Singapore and Thailand, did indeed lead to closer contacts with schools in those countries. In 1993 I was awarded a Frank Fisher scholarship and a Korea Foundation fellowship to make a study of specialist music provision in Pacific Rim countries. From that experience came formal links with specialist schools in Seoul, Tokyo, Kuala Lumpur, and Ipoh, and with the Academy of Performing Arts in Hong Kong. A short tour of Moscow and Yaroslavl by a small cross-section of specialists led to contact with the world famous specialist schools in Moscow.

'But beyond music, an unusual opportunity arose from the school's association with ZERI (Zero Emissions Research Initiative). An enterprising UK company canvassed all HMC schools, and Wells was initially the only one to respond positively. A partnership was arranged with ICI in Shepton Mallet, and each week a group of sixth formers spent time with research scientists working to find an efficient means of using waste material at the factory. A viable solution was found, the school won two prestigious awards, and I was invited to deliver a paper at a distinguished international conference in Namibia. While there I met the British Council representative, who invited the school choir to spend a week in Windhoek making music with African children. Another spin-off from musical contacts was the opportunity for academic staff to enjoy fruitful exchanges. The head of science spent a month in Korea and the head of English, together with students, spent a similar period in Washington DC. More conventional staff exchanges also took place in Australia. In addition to scholarships in Johannesburg linked to the Bishop Simeon Trust, two students from world-famous Soweto Strings spent time at Wells. So too did two students from Svetlogorsk in Belarus, brought to the school through the work of Children of Chernobyl. All this and regular exchanges with Europe and exciting expeditions further afield helped students to become more aware of cultural differences. The universal language of music is, of course, a help.'

Several of the academic departments regularly lead school trips abroad. In addition to participating in rugby tours, Duncan Gowen, history teacher and houseparent of Shrewsbury, takes his GCSE history students every other year to Moscow and St Petersburg. There have also been history and English trips to the great Italian cities, German and French exchanges, and geology trips to Iceland led by David Rowley. From 1996 until 2007 the whole of year 9

Sporting teams regularly travel abroad, like the rugby team below, on a visit to Australia

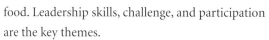

Musicians in Moscow

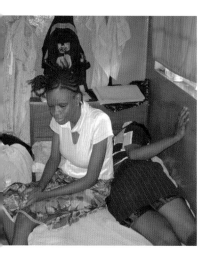

food. Leadership skills, challenge, and participation are the key themes.

As David Rowley wrote of the Himalayan trip, 'When we were fifteen hours from Islamabad any vestiges of western culture had long since disappeared. The humid monsoon deluge of the previous day had been replaced by a dry searing heat. We had a day in Chitral to buy food and equipment for the Tirich Mir trek, which meant that some of us had to learn the delights of haggling. This trek was a four-day acclimatisation for later rigours, and things went well: the porters were good, morale was high, altitude sickness mild, and diarrhoea didn't seem to last more than twenty-four hours. But things then went wrong, when we learned that a large landslide had destroyed the road to Gilgit, our next base; and one of us ended up in police cells with his passport confiscated as we had not reported our arrival in Chitral. We had tried, but the police station was closed for a holy day; but this apparently was not a good enough excuse.

'We negotiated both those blockages, and before long we were trekking in the shadow of Nanga Parbat, one of the truly great mountains of the world – it is a staggering five vertical kilometres from the Indus Valley to the top. We were due to attempt a lower peak, a mere 5100m high, to the south, called Shaigiri. This trek had a different feel: we were better prepared, the mountains were more precipitous, and the porters were a pain in the neck. And we didn't quite make it, because the sun's heat was loosening boulders on the cliffs above so we had to retreat. However, we were content to have reached 5000m, higher than any mountain in Europe. And we were also content to have coped well with the pressures of altitude, Pakistan's climatic extremes, the discipline of working to a budget, illness, and the perils of bureaucracy!'

Another fantastic – and highly unusual – experience was enjoyed a few years later by a team of ten year 11 pupils led by Paul Edmunds. As Matthew Truman (1991–2000) and Oliver Truman (1991–2000) described it, 'Mr Edmunds wanted the challenge of taking a group of young and

were taken on trips to the battlefields of Ypres and the Somme; these were usually in the summer, but on one memorable and fantastic occasion they went in February and got stuck in a snow drift deep in rural France. And in 2008 Roland Ladley hopes to forge a new link with a school in Freetown, Sierra Leone, with the possibility of Wells students visiting regularly to help with teaching, sport, and building work.

For many years also now, Wellensians have proved that the adventurous spirit they display at home is not constrained within UK borders. Dick Crane led climbing teams of sixth formers to conquer foreign peaks, like Mont Blanc in the Alps, and groups of CCF members to tackle the Arctic winter in Norway; and groups of boys and girls have undertaken expeditions to far-flung corners of the world, which offer experiences totally outside the norm. Some of these have been set up by World Challenge, an organisation that specialises in expeditions for young people. These have included trips to Borneo, and one in the early 1990s to the Hindu Kush and the Pakistan Himalaya. Although led by teachers, the ethos of these challenges is that the students are in charge of the everyday running of affairs, from the hiring of porters to the purchase of

inexperienced cavers to help explore the caves of a state in north-east India called Meghalaya. Because access to the area was until recently restricted for foreigners, and because the caves are so remote, it is thought that many of them may never have been set foot in by man. Mr Edmunds, however, is one of a group of European cavers who have begun to explore and map them.

'The expedition lasted three weeks, and started with eighteen hours of travelling to Calcutta followed by two further days on the road before arriving in this remote region. Our accommodation there had no running water and only a petrol generator, which was switched on for a few hours in the evening. We took turns at sleeping in one of the two beds, and otherwise slept on the concrete floor. But the villagers were so welcoming that we felt very at home and soon got used to this completely different way of life. Our days were spent exploring and surveying the caves, and our evenings entering the data onto our laptops, which had software that allowed us to see a three-dimensional map of the cave passages we had surveyed that day. It was very satisfying, particularly when we found that we had surveyed over 4k of new passages and had found several other new cave entrances. A few days in Shillong on the way home provided us with time to do some sightseeing and to visit schools, one of which put on a show for us of traditional songs and dances from north-east India. We feel very privileged to have had such an insight into a culture not many westerners, especially those of our age, have seen and experienced.'

Top and above: The chamber choir in Beijing, 2007

Young Enterprise

As Charlotte Thomas (1990–99) reported in *The Wellensian* for 1998, she and her fellow lower sixth formers were the recipients of mixed messages at the beginning of the year about Young Enterprise. On the one hand there were the upper sixth formers who forcibly warned her not to get involved at any price; and on the other was Mr Taylor whose advice was, 'Universities will love it. It'll look great on your UCAS form.'

However, forty members of the lower sixth did take the plunge and formed themselves into two companies, with mission statements that aimed 'to provide other members of the school and the local community with innovative and useful products of good quality at a reasonable price'. Charlotte was elected managing director of one of these, called Wham, and she and her board of directors set about agreeing a list of products and raising the capital to finance their production through the sale of shares. As she wrote: 'The first term progressed amazingly well, and we met all our expectations and made a profit. We were at an advantage with a fair proportion of the company's members being boarders. The second term started slowly, but the trade fair at Glastonbury restored our enthusiasm, particularly when we won the poster competition and the award for the best presented stand. We managed to survive the area board finals (though the other Wells company, Eclipse, was unfortunately knocked out at that stage), and we went on to represent Somerset at the South West England finals. No other Wells company had ever got so far, and though we failed to reach the national finals – being well beaten by other companies who were selling to America and making £6000 – we felt we had improved the reputation of the Young Enterprise scheme within the school community, as well as contributing several glittering trophies to the school's collection. As for myself, I felt extremely privileged to have been given the chance to run a company, and although it was a huge amount of work and at times very stressful, I honestly enjoyed the experience and feel very proud of Wham and all its successes.'

WELLS CATHEDRAL SCHOOL took the first step into modern governance practices when it became a limited company in 1956. However, its only directors (and governors) at that stage remained the members of the dean and chapter. But there was now a provision whereby they could appoint lay governors; and this option was taken up in the early years of Alan Quilter's headship, when David Tudway Quilter became the first lay governor. He was followed by many others; and meanwhile, successive Deans of Wells proved influential and supportive as chairmen of the board of governors: David Edwards, Patrick Mitchell, Richard Lewis, and now John Clarke have all been unstinting in their work for the school.

Alan Quilter was the first head to be elected a member of the Headmasters' Conference (HMC). When John Baxter arrived, he found that 'the complexity of Wells inevitably resulted in membership of a plethora of associations, at all of which it was impossible to be a regular and useful participant. However, chairmanship of the south-west division of HMC for two years, of the Choir Schools Association for three years, and of the newly formed National Association of Music and Ballet Schools provided sufficient opportunities for the school to play a full and effective part in all relevant areas.'

In the 1980s it was still the case that the *quinque* (the five members of the cathedral chapter) had to have a majority on the governing body; and thus there were then still only four lay governors. It was also important that the dean was prepared to take a close interest in the school; as Richard Lewis remarked when he became dean in 1990, 'Through all the fortunes of our school, and for more than a thousand years, the relationship of cathedral and school has been constant, although not always without controversy; and not always cordial. Such was not the state of affairs when I arrived. In my

David Tudway Quilter

'You are part of the history of this place.' Those words, spoken to David Tudway Quilter by John Clarke, Dean of Wells, are an undeniable truth. A banker by profession, DTQ, as he was known, inherited the Cedars estate from his uncle, Lionel Tudway, in 1962. He had already agreed to his uncle's suggestion that he add the name Tudway to his own, to preserve the 200-year-long connection of the Tudway family with their Wells estates. On coming to live in Wells he immediately became a strong supporter of the school, and when the decision was taken to appoint lay governors early in Alan Quilter's headship, he was the first.

He brought to the school both his financial expertise and his ability to take a broad view of what was needed. He supported the admission of girls, and was instrumental in the appointment of the first women governors. Successive heads found his unstinting efforts on their behalf an essential support; and even after he retired from the governing body and became the first ever life president, he continued to attend meetings and offer his help. As his wife, Elizabeth, recalls, he worried a little that he might be seen as interfering. 'Interfere all you like' was the unanimous response.

Put simply, he loved the school. A Wimbledon standard tennis player in his youth, he would play the game with the boys and give them the benefit of his expertise. He came to sports matches, plays, concerts, events in the cathedral… indeed, as is recorded elsewhere, the junior school Christmas Celebration was the last event he attended before his death in January 2007. He and his family particularly loved all the music, by which when he was at the school he felt constantly, and happily, surrounded; and to quote his wife again: 'He treated the children like his own.'

I first drove down The Liberty in Wells on a uniformly grey day in February 1990. The grey of the sky was well matched to the colour of the stone of the ancient houses that stand close to the road there. As I came towards the sharp right turn at the end, a board on the left said that this was Wells Cathedral School. More dramatically, on the right and opposite the house to which they gave their name, lay the remains of one of the great cedar trees, shattered and felled by the great storm that had blown the previous week. On that day, as I went secretly to meet the Bishop of Bath and Wells for the first time as the prospective Dean of Wells, I wondered if this was a portent. Reflecting now, eighteen years on, the 'new' cedar planted by David Tudway Quilter to replace the one blown down is a better parable. Already it stands tall; already it reaches for the light and spreads its shade in the heat of summer.

The physical and spiritual relationship between the school and the cathedral should not be underestimated. Down Vicars' Close and along St Andrew's Street in the late afternoon as darkness falls in November or on a warm May evening, the sound of music played by individual or ensemble fills the air. It is spine-tingling. Just across the road from the north porch of the cathedral you may hear the great sound of the Big Band or listen to a symphony orchestra in full voice. The cathedral itself is at present the concert hall and all who come stand amazed at the quality and the talent of the young musicians.

Young voices and hurrying feet bring life to hallowed paths and places. The eastern part of Wells comes alive when the school is in residence; something goes from it at holiday time. We laughed a great deal and wept only sometimes; to guide young people towards adulthood is an infinitely varied and fascinating experience. To have the responsibility of nurturing young minds and bringing them towards maturity is not without its difficulties, but at the same time it is a privilege beyond compare.

Richard Lewis, Dean Emeritus of Wells

early conversations with the headmaster, I found John Baxter's enthusiasm infectious and his vision clear. The excellent work in establishing the specialist music status of the school, already accomplished under Alan Quilter, was being consolidated and taken forward. But we knew that any development had to take place now against a changing society and this presented threats as well as opportunity.'

An urgent priority was building work. But medieval houses built on a grand scale and for more leisurely times do not easily accommodate themselves to thirty or forty young people living in them in the twenty-first century, and the Children Act of 1989 made pressingly necessary an urgent upgrading of facilities, not least the boarding provision. A programme of refurbishment was begun, and at the same time plans were laid for the building of a new science block and the provision of good IT facilities and a sixth form common room. To support this work an appeal was launched for both buildings and bursaries. The Children Act also meant that better provision had to be made in the cathedral for the choristers; and this became even more necessary when the decision was taken to start the new girl choristers' choir. Richard Lewis again: 'We judged that the time was right, and the will was certainly present, to introduce a new chorister foundation. But sustaining sufficient funds for both girls and boys was problematical. We also had to deal with the implications of construction in and around a building of such beauty and national importance; our problems will be better understood when it is realised that the project to care better for the choristers at the cathedral, begun in 1992, was only completed in 2008 with the opening of the music and education centre off the east cloister.'

With no endowment with which to finance change and expansion, the number of pupils in the school was crucial, and this was against a background of a nationwide decline in the demand for boarding. Political change removed the support assisted places had provided; the age of the information technology revolution was dawning; the

The board of governors

The Very Reverend John Clarke
(2004–present) Chair of Governing Body and Development Committee

The Reverend Canon Andrew Featherstone
(2005–present) Chancellor, Deputy Chair of Governing Body, Chair of Personnel and Remuneration Committee

The Reverend Canon Patrick Woodhouse
(2000–present) Precentor and Chair of Choristers' Committee

Prebendary Helen Ball
(2003–present) Chair of Education Committee

Prebendary Elsa van der Zee
(2005–present) Chair of Music Committee

Peter McIlwraith
(1996–present) Chair of Finance and Audit Committee

Stella Clarke
(1986–present)

Robert Sommers
(2003–present)

Jo Ballan-Whitfield
(2007–present)

Martin Smout
(2008–present)

Patrick Cook
(2008–present)

demand for world and electronic music was growing. And, as Richard Lewis commented, 'the demands of commitment, dedication, team working, and long hours devoted to rehearsal by music students, whether instrumental or choral, were running counter to the spirit of the age that seemed to place personal needs and fulfilment against the good of the whole. However, if money and space were in short supply, imagination and commitment were not. And then in the early years of the new millennium – the third of the school's existence – John Baxter retired and the baton was handed to Elizabeth Cairncross to hold the vision and to take it forward. The process of selection was thorough and the governors felt they had chosen well. The new head brings great talent and boundless enthusiasm to her new role. The school flourishes in the twenty-first century. What seems abundantly clear is that in

The geology building

Part of the sixth form centre

Wells Cathedral School we have a responsibility for something that is a precious resource and a hope for the future.'

The school bursar, Steven Webber, manages everything at the school which is not related to teaching or pastoral care, and is a member of the senior management team which, under the head as chair, includes the two deputy heads, the director of music, and the development director. He is also clerk to the board of governors, where his role is to manage the termly meetings of the whole board and its committees, which currently deal with finance, development, education, personnel and remuneration, music, the choristers, and communication. A large part of his job is managing the school estate, now much larger than it used to be. While the cathedral continues to own the parts of Vicars' Close that are in school use, as well as St Andrew's Lodge and all the ex-canons' houses on The Liberty, the school now owns the Cedars estate, the buildings on New Street and at the west end of The Liberty, and the outlying sports fields. For the rest, it pays a commercial rent to the cathedral.

Under John Baxter and Elizabeth Cairncross, the composition of the governing body has changed and evolved, not only with movements within the chapter, but also with the appointment of non-voting lay consultants and with the chapter having the option to elect substitutes. David Tudway Quilter's place as treasurer was taken on his retirement by Peter McIlwraith, whose sharp financial mind helped steer the governors through the choppy financial waters of the late 1990s, and the board of governors has been regularly and continually enhanced by the appointment of people who could bring high levels of expertise to the task. The first woman on the board was Lord Waldegrave's sister, Sarah Wright, and she was joined in 1986 by Stella Clarke, who brings to the role huge experience of managing complex organisations through her position as chair of Bristol University Council. She remembers that when she joined there were still issues that had to be addressed about the interface between both cathedral and lay governance

Parents' Association

The Parents' Association at Wells, which started during John Baxter's headship, is still thriving and continues to support the school. Its current (summer 2008) chairman is David Corp, himself an Old Wellensian, but he is due to stand down in September and hand over to Deborah Orrett.

The association organises and supports a number of social and fundraising activities each year, all indicative in different ways of the inclusiveness of the school and the links the association can help to forge between its various parts. Deborah Orrett considers the summer ball to be one of the most significant events: 'We rely on this occasion to mark not just the completion of the education of some of our pupils, but the poignancy of another year passing.' For David Corp it is a wonderful opportunity for the parents whose children are leaving to celebrate the end of an era, and an opportunity for parents of younger children to realise what a special place Wells is.

As a parent of 'sporty' children, David Corp did not initially view the jazz picnic as 'our thing' until he became involved with the PA, 'when I realised what an incredibly inclusive event it is'. It celebrates both the musical focus of the school and the union between that part of the school and those who simply enjoy great jazz. Other events include the family quiz, which brings together all year groups in an atmosphere of friendliness and informality, and helps parents of children of different ages to get to know each other; and 'the brightest team always wins!' For new parents, there is a drinks party which 'offers new parents and pupils the opportunity to get to know each other and to find out how Wells works at a time that can be full of uncertainty and stress; the aim is to enable everyone to leave in a more relaxed state than when they arrived, and to be a celebration that marks the start of the children's academic careers.' Parents are also invited to drinks after the Advent Carol Service in the cathedral, which provides an enjoyable social and festive occasion for members of the school and wider community.

In conclusion, as David Corp says, 'The Parents' Association evolves as the school changes from year to year and reflects the different people who make up Wells Cathedral School. It comprises a lively, fun-loving group of people who support the parents and the school as a whole.

The Wellensian Association

All former members of Wells Cathedral School, pupils and staff, automatically belong to the Wellensian Association. Since the 1980s, a small amount added to the pupils' accounts for six terms has made this arrangement possible, and as a result the membership database now contains well over 3500 names.

The association is very fortunate to have had the support and hands-on help of many of its members; two in particular must be mentioned, who have been crucial to its development and ongoing strength over the last several years. Alwyn Gillen, its president, was a stalwart of the staff from his arrival at the school in 1972 to teach history and geography until his retirement in 1999. He now regularly spends hours on his computer, writing to OWs and keeping in touch; and this former housemaster and rugby supremo is the fulcrum of all Wellensian functions, the teacher and mentor whom returning Wellensians come to see and reconnect with; as Elizabeth Cairncross says, 'He has his arms around the whole school.'

Chris Neave, who attended Wells between 1969 and 1977 and was head boy in his final year, is the other: in spite of being a very busy captain in the Royal Navy, he has been a hugely active, hands-on chairman for the last eleven years, and it is difficult to envisage the association maintaining its high profile without his tremendous input. He has single-handedly produced two newsletters each year, in both paper and electronic formats, which are keenly awaited by thousands of Wellensians all over the world; full of information about the school, the association, and OW functions, they enable members everywhere to keep in touch and read about the exploits of their school friends.

The association arranges two dinners each year, one in January or February at the Royal Air Force Club, Piccadilly, London, and one in Wells in late June, usually in a marquee on Cedars lawn, and often followed the next morning by numbers of Wellensians taking the opportunity to have a nostalgic walk around the school. The OW rugby matches against the school XV have had to cease for health and safety reasons, but cricket and tennis matches still take

Above: Alwyn Gillen with the chaplain, Juliette Hulme

Left: Chris Neave

place, normally on the Wellensian weekend in June/July. The association also raises funds to improve the facilities in and around the school, for example the design and implementation of the Cedars lawn gardens, as well as improvements in the play area where the old school shop used to stand. Working from its well equipped committee room in the stable yard, the Wellensian Association is a vibrant organisation which not only has a positive and effective influence on the school today but also enables thousands of former pupils to retain contact with their alma mater and each other.

on the board and between men and women; but the vastly increased breadth of expertise that the board can now boast – much of it coming from highly qualified parents – and the more equal gender balance have made it effective and powerful. Moreover, she relishes the task: 'There's little point in doing it unless you are interested and involved.'

Helen Ball is one of the new breed of lay chapter members who, along with Elsa van der Zee, has been appointed to the board of governors as a cathedral representative. She brings to the job the experience of having served nearly thirty years as a head teacher, and is clear that over the five years that she has been a governor the efficiency and involvement of the governing body have greatly moved on. The committee structure is powerful, the current dean, as chair, is strong and effective, and the membership brings to the task all the requisite skills. Both she and the other governors recognise that consolidation on the one hand and change on the other are necessary elements of how the school is governed now and how it needs to be managed in the future. And she too enjoys the work: 'The governors are in good heart, very buoyant and excited about the future, if a little apprehensive; but the climate is right, and we and the school are in confident mode.'

The Wells Cathedral School Foundation
Tony Bretherton

The history of Wells Cathedral School reflects both instances of generous benefaction and periods during which there was little in the way of philanthropic support. Named buildings reflect our history and the generosity of individuals, and in the concert hall the Calouste Gulbenkian Foundation is thanked and honoured for their help in enabling the school to secure the old Wells Theological College as our music facility.

The first Foundation Fellow, Michael Eavis, with his wife, Liz

Committed individuals have worked hard to raise funds for the school – most recently to enable the upgrading and covering of the swimming pool – but despite centuries of history, less than £500,000 exists as an endowment fund in support of the school, and all this is committed to support bursaries.

Trusts including the Dulverton Trust, Carnegie UK Trust, the Leverhulme Trust, and the Vandervell Trust have supported the school. Lord Hussey, Lord Rees-Mogg, Lord Armstrong, and Sir Roger Young as trustees of the Wells Cathedral School Development Trust did much to secure the future of the school, both by working for Campaign 2000 (which raised £666,000) and by ensuring that the assets of the trust were safely in the possession of the school when it was wound up.

In 2006 I arrived as the new director of development and set about the long-term task of embedding philanthropic giving in the life of the school. The Wells Cathedral School Foundation has been established with Lord Armstrong continuing his service to the school as a trustee, and a parent of three pupils, Gary Brown, becoming inaugural chairman.

The annual Foundation Dinner has been established, and the Annual Giving programme launched. By the time this book is published the Wells 909 Legacy Society will have been born, reminding Old Wellensians and all others associated with the school that part of our legacy as we leave this world can be to provide for an enhanced learning experience for the children who will follow us here at Wells Cathedral School.

In a far-sighted move, the new foundation has established the Wells Cathedral School Foundation Fellowships, which are the most significant honour the school can offer to Old Wellensians who have excelled in their chosen careers. At the inaugural Foundation Dinner in 2007, Michael Eavis received the first Foundation Fellowship, and in 2008 Terence Mordaunt and Josephine Knight are being similarly honoured. The fellowship can also be offered to non-Wellensians who have, in the view of the nominating committee, provided the kind of leadership in association with the school that our present and future pupils may find inspiring.

My view of philanthropy is that it provides pathways whereby those who seek to see Wells excel may be enabled to support and resource its future. As the school marks 1100 years of music and education, we will be seeking to establish new classrooms, bursaries, a sports pavilion, and a new music facility presently known by the working title Cedars Hall. You may be reading this volume while these projects are still part of our challenge to become 'a school everyone would want to come to' and 'the most outstanding music school in Europe'; or perhaps, as you read, we may have completed these projects and have moved on to new challenges.

Wells Cathedral School seeks to provide an inspiring education set in a musically alive and beautiful environment as a brilliant foundation for life. The foundation seeks to ensure that this dream is financially possible now, and is sustained into the future.

Gary Brown, chairman of the foundation

A BRILLIANT FOUNDATION FOR LIFE *Elizabeth Cairncross*

THERE ARE TWO SENTENCES that sum up the fundamental attitudes that I found at Wells Cathedral School when I arrived, and which I am determined to foster today and into the future. The first is 'We'll find ways of making this happen', and the second is 'No one told us that it's supposed to be difficult.'

And there is of course a third: our school motto *Esto quod es*, Be what you are.

Those three sentiments were completely appropriate for the school which I inherited in 2000. I have already spoken of the buzz I felt when I arrived here, of the 'can do' ethos, of the very special values which were and are so evident. It has been my role over the last eight years to retain all those values and that atmosphere while recognising that we can never

stand still, we can never justify hanging on to something whose time has gone, and that change has to happen – but change that enhances what we already have.

A useful and familiar metaphor for school heads is that of the gardener, nurturing and caring for the young growing plants so that they blossom into vigour and strength. I see my role somewhat differently: as the one who is responsible for looking after the climate of the school, for creating and maintaining an environment within which others can plant and tend and gather, and which makes it easy for the young shoots to thrive and flourish. At Wells, too, I am aware every day that I am walking in the footsteps of centuries of predecessors – literally, in my office in Cedars, which is built on the site of the school in the early thirteenth century, nearly 800 years ago. I am humbled by the weight of those centuries, and look around in wonder at the extraordinary beauty of the place where we are lucky enough to live and work. And I feel privileged to be the one who has been charged with looking after the school now and ensuring its future.

Standard management tools related to strategy and development tend not to be easily adaptable to the specific needs of a school – particularly a school like Wells which is both small and complex. One that does work is 'Peak Performance' – the one Sir Edmund Hillary adopted for his charitable foundations in Nepal, and which has also worked well with successful sporting teams. It is based on in-depth thinking about what you are and what you believe in, and it embraces positive change while insisting that such change has to be organic and that nothing is suddenly newly imposed.

I used that model to work with governors, staff, and pupils to produce the strategy we call 'Purpose', which sets out our character, our beliefs, and our focus, and dares to allow us to dream. It adds to the words which could be used to describe the school when I arrived, by talking of us being 'bold', 'competitive', and 'inspiring' – and it also uses the word 'loving', not in a mushy sense but in the hope that the spirit of the school will create a passion for learning and life within a caring environment. Of course we are aware of league tables, and we value high academic standards and good sporting results – and I have to say that, at Wells, the tradition of deep commitment to excellence makes it easy to nurture a culture of achievement. But we also want our pupils and staff to feel supported and encouraged, rather than driven.

We are also aware of our perhaps unique position, as a small school within a small city playing a central part in our community. Those who live and visit Wells can't miss us – not just because we inhabit so many of the fine buildings that surround the cathedral, but also because our music wafts out of the music school and our music department in Vicars' Close and our choristers are there in the cathedral so often contributing their splendid young voices to the services. And it is this spirit of community that we want to foster; our stated beliefs as expressed in 'Purpose' draw on the need to celebrate and communicate personal and community achievement, while upholding our Christian tradition and living and learning within the heritage, mystery, and wonder of the magnificent city around us. Yet we welcome other faiths too, and recognise the value that different traditions and cultures can add to life at school; and while seeking the heights for our pupils, whether in music, academic life, sport, or simply a personal sense of achievement, we also recognise that some things we do can just be fun!

Yes, we aim high. We want our pupils to achieve at the top of what they are capable of, in whatever field. We want them to be both team players and leaders, and we seek to achieve this through encouraging a rigorous, competitive, yet supportive and accepting climate throughout the school. To return to my three maxims: we are not here to say no, that's impossible, or no, that's too hard for you. And most of all, we recognise differences, and celebrate the diversity that is implicit in our motto.

Wells Cathedral School has had a particular, challenging focus for the last forty years since Alan Quilter set it on its current path. What 'Purpose' calls our 'greatest imaginable challenge' is to 'become an oversubscribed school at every level AND the most outstanding musical school in Europe'. But at the same time, my eyes are focused, on our pupils' behalf, on ten years' time, when parents and school have lost their influence and when they will need to stand on their own feet and make their own choices and mistakes. Above all, I want them to be decent people, equipped to deal with what life will throw at them, after enjoying and benefiting here from – to quote 'Purpose' again – 'an inspiring education set in a musically alive and beautiful environment as a brilliant foundation for life'.

Current staff – July 2008

Lynn Acreman
Suzanne Anderson
Robert Anderton
Gillian Andrews
Alison Armstrong
Diana Armstrong
Claire Arrowsmith
Rosalie Ashton Butler
Martin Ashton
Claire Barker
Sylvie Barham
Jonathan Barnard
Paul Barnett
Simonetta Barone
David Barnes
Peter Baron
Andrew Barrett
Julie Barrow
Maureen Batson
Diana Bellamy
Helen Bennett
Janet Bennett
John Berry
Sarah Berry
Jacquelyn Bevan
Georgina Bird
Jeremy Boot
Katriina Boosey
Neil Bowen
Wayne Bradshaw
Tony Bretherton
Chris Bridson
Alison Brock
Angela Brock
Nicola Brookes
Harriet Brown
Ross Brown
Mary Browning
Ed Burns
Judith Burns
Denise Bush
Gail Button
John Byrne
Charles Cain
Hilary Cain
Elizabeth Cairncross
Tina Caswell
Richard Causton
Katy Chantrey
Angela Churches
Amanda Clark
Isabella Clark
Veronica Clarke
Stephen Clay
Hilary Coates
Nicola Connock
Russell Collins
Clare Coppen
Claire Corum
Victoria Currell
Carla Dabinett
Susan Davey

Diana Davies
Susan Davies
Alan Davis
Laurence Dawson
Christopher Day
Ashley Deacon
Antonia del Mar
Paul Denegri
Ruth Denegri
Simon de Souza
Ryan Dickinson
Cathy Dimaline
Tina Dors
Debbie Downton
Jan Doyle
Penny Driver
Jill Edmonds
Christine Edwards
Rebecca Edwards
Pauline Evans
Sylvia Evans
Ruth Faber
Kelly Fairey
Jan Faulkener
Michelle Field
Mandy Fielding
Christopher Finch
Yvonne Fleming
Marta Fontanals-Simmons
Elizabeth Fyfe
Zoe Gallacher
Philippa Garty
Janice Gearon
Jayne Girling
Alele Golding
Duncan Gowen
Jane Graham
Ann Grayburn
Sally Greenhalgh
John Gregson
Geraldine Griffin
Michael Grogan
Christine Hael
Penelope Hall
Emma Hamilton
Dominic Hansom
Peter Harrison
Iona Hassan
Abigail Heckstall-Smith
Rob Henson
Kim Heppinstall
Caroline Hessian
David Heyes
Pauline Hole
Karan House
Diana Hudson
Sam Hudson
Juliette Hulme
Christine Humphreys
Ken Humphreys
Margaret Humphreys
Debbie Hunt

Vivienne Hurman
Alan Hutt
Alex Huxham
Sylvia Ingham
Richard Ireland
Susan James
Susie Jameson
Teresa Jarman
Jane Jay
Lavinia Jenkins
David Jones
Raymond Jones
Simon Jones
Molly Joy
Craig Keast
Caroline Kelly
Abygail Kench
Annette Kenniston
John King
Sally King
Nancy Kingham
Brigid Kirkland-Wilson
Gary Knights
Xunyi Kong
Claire Ladley
Roland Ladley
Marcus Laing
Sarah Laing
Daniel Lane
Rosemary Lansdown
Katy Latham
Edward Leaker
David Lee
Abigail Leigh
Emma Lewis
James Lewis
Julia Leyton
Shi Tian Lim
Catherine Lord
Caroline Lowe
Alastair Lyle
John Machling
May Madden
Doreen Mahy
Alison Maidment
Hilary Marks
Lara Marks
Marisa Marks
Denise Marshman
Martyn Masters
Richard May
Christine Maynard
Stephen McCarthy
Brian McGee
Penny McGee
Sophia McKett
Carolyn Meade
Sarah Meek
Josephine Melmoth
Adrian Mickleburgh
Martyn Miller
Iain Milne

Jennifer Mitchell
Moyra Montague
Mary Morgan
Emma Morley
Michele Muir
Kevin Murphy
Barbara Murray
Dhevdhas Nair
Dorothy Nancekievill
Cressida Nash
Lisa Nelsen
Judith Newberry
Robert Newman
Andrew Nowak
Jayne Obradovic
Filiz Oncel
Keith Orchard
Richard Ormrod
Timothy Orpen
Matthew Owens
Kenneth Padgett
Anastasia Page
Elizabeth Parfitt
Tanya Parbury
Claire Pattemore
Elaine Paul
Anne Payne
Peter Penfold
David Perrin
Edward Phillips
Lawrence Plum
David Ponsford
Molly Porter
Sarah Powell
Diane Price
Gemma Pritchard
Jennifer Rabbitts
Luke Raikes
Lisa Reakes
Rebecca Redman
Rosemary Reidy
Hazel Rigby
Clare Rippingham
Ray Robbetts
David Rowley
Sally Rowley
Stella Rowlinson
Maria Rumley
Alison Sackett
Bradley Salisbury
Kate Saunders
Menna Searle
Elizabeth Seller
Diane Shepherd
Dan Shorland Ball
Olena Shvetsova
Deirdre Sisson
Paul Skelton
Gemma Slight
Katharine Small
Tricia Smart
Jenny Smith

Sarah Smith
Steven Smyth
Matthew Souter
Sylvia Spirrell
Gesine Stegmann-Gordon
Nicola Stenning
Rodney Stephens
Ruth Stephens
Joanna Stitch
Linzi-Jane Stockdale-Bridson
Lisa Stockley
Rebecca Stott
Julie Stratton
Mark Sully
Martin Swarfield
Claire Talbot
Kathy Tang
Jan Tapner
Stephen Tapner
Ben Taylor
Andy Thomas
Keri Thompson
Joe Tong
Karen Trego
Jane Tucker
Tracey Tully
Rachel Tunley
Andrew Tweed
Andrew Tween
Amanda Upshall
Victoria Upshall
Sarah Vesty
Kim Vincent
Simon Vlies
Lynn Walkey
Nigel Walkey
Jill Walsh
Shelley Ware
Rosie Warner
Mervyn Watch
Susan Weare
Rebecca Weaver
Frances Webb
Steven Webber
Camilla Wehmeyer
Laurence Whitehead
Jon Whitfield
Jane Whittaker
Simon Whittaker
John Williams
Raymond Willis
Anna Kuzminska Wilson
Jane Wilson
Nick Wilson
Jean Windridge
Louise Wiscombe
Nola Woods
Patricia Woods
Hilary Wynne Murphy
Paul Yates

Index of names

Bold denotes authorial contributions; italic denotes illustrations

Index of subscribers

This book has been made possible through the generosity of the following:

Peter Adams
Phyllis Andrews
Edward Anstee
Robert Armstrong
Dr Adrian Arnold-Smith
Esther, Ruth and Joseph Arnold
Roger Askew
Amanda Ayliffe (née Fearon)
Mr and Mrs M. Bacon
Simon R. Baggs
Jonathan Bailey
Guy Baird
David W. Ball
Prebendary Helen Ball OBE
Sylvie Barham
Professor Michael R. Barnes
Andrew and Katie Barr-Sim
John V. Barrett
Bryan Bass
Adrian and Mandy Bateman
Fiona Bates
Richard J.S. Bates
Lewis Batten
John Baxter
Andrew Beach
Tim Bell
Michael F. Bennett
Pete and Sue Betley
Rory Black
Thaddeus W.B. Bligh
Rebecca Boston (née Shallish)
The Bowker Family
Jeremy Brade
Diane Bretherton
Robert Bretherton
Tony Bretherton
Dr C. Bridson
Andrew Bright
Angela Broad
Simon Broad

John R. Brookes
Kate Brown
Mrs L.P. Brown
R. Mark E. Brown
William, Lauren and Eleanor Brown
Clive and Mary Browning
Mr Carmine Bruno
James Buckle
Jonathan Buckley
Lorna Buckley
Oliver Buckley
George Bunting
James Bunting
John Burbridge
Thomas Burns
Alan Bush
Alison Bush
Glenn and Courtney Button
Katie Cade
Charles and Hilary Cain
Mrs Helen Cain
Nick Cain
Elizabeth Cairncross
Dr Ian Capstick
Mr and Mrs Frederick Carson
Andrew Mark Carter
David M.B. Carter
Helen R.B. Carter
Nick Cary
Nigel A. Cavey
D.W. Chapman
David Chapman
Cheng Wai King
J. Geoffrey Chick
Tony Chivers
David Chubb
Jamie Chubb
Joanna Chubb
Amanda Clark
Professor John Clarkson
Ms Jane Clisby
Richard Clissold-Vasey
Michael Cole

John A.B. Cook
Norman Cook
Peter Cook
Michael J. Cooke
Sally Ann Copeland
D.S. Corp
Mr and Mrs J. Corr
Alex Corum
Miles Corum
Max Costantini
Caroline Cowan
Joanna Craddock (née Smith)
Rupert Critchley
William Critchley
Jill Croft-Murray
D.R. Cromwell
Alex and Charlie Crooks
Alison Crooks
Kate Cropper (née Gladwin)
Ben Croxford
Michael Csanyi-Wills
Rebecca Curtis
Jason A.D. Dalby
Mr and Mrs Berian M. Davies
Ceri Davies
David and Helle de Chazal
Ashley, Harriet and Edward Deacon
Pushka Deiana
Major T.M. Denning
John Dennis
Barbara Dickinson
Alex Dodd
Mark Dodd
The Donoghue Family
Rodney and Teresa Drew
Paul Duck
Karen Dyson
Kirsty Ebenezer
Miss Judith Edmondson
J.K. Edwards
Daniel Evans
Jonathan Exten-Wright
Rebecca Fairley

Mrs M. Farrell

Joe Fearon

John Fennell

Victoria Fielden

Mrs Yvonne Fleming

Emma Fogden

Polly Fogden

Tom Fogden

Derek G.D. Ford

Elaina and Adriana Ford

Hannah C.M. Ford

James W.T. Ford

Peter and Angela Fordham

Julian Forsey

Dr Ian Foster

Linda Francis

Stephen Paul Freke

Claire Fripp

Graham Fudge

Sarah Fryer

Jennifer Gallagher

Tony Garcia

Michael Garrod

Douglas and Hannah German

Nicola Gibson

Alwyn Gillen

Drs Hugh and Dorothy Goddard

Revd Preb. and Mrs D.C. Goodman

Lydia Grace Gosnell

Andrew Gray

Mr and Mrs R.A. Green

Mrs Sally A. Greenhalgh

Zoe Greenhalgh (née Smith)

Elizabeth Jane Grey

James Grey

Sarah Grey

Ruth Griffiths

Rachel and Kieran Griggs

Victoria Gumbley

Nicholas Hale

Mark Hammersley

David Hard

Jules and Amy Harding

Rachel, Matthew and Mark Hardyman

Catherine Hart

Toby A.C. Hart

Simon Haynes

Carol A. Hazelden

Revd Dr Benson Headley

The Heath Family

Robert Hector

Alexandra Heeley

Oliver Heinz

Frances Henderson

Rosy Henderson

William Henderson

Dr Wolfgang Hengstebeck

Dr Rob Henson

John, Julian (Aubrey) and Jane Hewson

Heledd S. Highnam

Elizabeth S.J. Hill

Kathryn Hill

Toby Hiscock

Mr Stewart R. Hobbs

Emily and James Hogarth

John Hole

Dr Charles Holme

Katy Howell

Revd Juliette Hulme

Louise Hunt

Miss Rosie Hutchison

Kit and Margaret Jackson

Gordon L. Jacobs

Michael James

Roger A. Jameson

Mr C. and Mrs L. Jarman

Rosalind Jeal (Townsend)

Kristin Jeffs

C.I. Johnson

Annabel Jones

Nicola Lloyd Jones

Mrs Sue Jones

Molly Joy

Craig Keast

Mrs Edith Kenney

David Keysell

The Khoo Family

Charles Alexander Anton Kooij

A.M. Laing

Catherine, Anna and Victoria Lake

Alexander G.F. Lamb

Richard Lambert

The Larcombe Family

Veronica Launn

Peter and Jackie Laws

Captain Nairn Lawson

Michael and Jessica Leach

Lee Jae Phang

Mrs Sue Lee

Harry and Rosie Leng

Lawrence Lewington

Daniel Lewis

Daniel, Edward, William and Jessica Lewis

David Lewis

Joseph Lewis

The Very Revd Richard Lewis

Tim Lewis

Pierre-Charles Lihou

Liew Se Yeoh

James Lill

Caroline and Robin Lim

Clive Lindley-Jones

Colin N. Linford

Andrew Livsey

Edward Lloyd

Mark and Nicole Lynch-Staunton

Ann Macleod

Bridget Macrae (née Adams)

Susanna Macrae

Andrew P. Manners

Mr and Mrs R.R. Marsden

Frank Martin

Stephen Masters

Helen Elizabeth Matthews

Mr and Mrs Maxwell

Mr and Mrs G.P. McCann

Mrs Clare McCarter

Sophie McIlwraith

Michael S. McNeill

Bernard K. Mealing

Katherine J. Medway

Jane, Alastair, Joshua and Harry Middleton

Michael and Geraldine Mills

Sqn Ldr and Mrs C. Mitchell

Mrs E. Moody

Bryan Moon

Terence Mordaunt

Justine Morris

Harry Morton

Simon Moss

John Moxon

Kiyomi Murayama

Sophie Murray

Andreas Naarmann

Robert Neal-Smith

Carole Newman

James Newman

Ng Yee Why

Dr Edward Nicol

Christopher Norman

Henry Jack O'Sullivan-Page

Dawn Osborn

Charles Osborne

George and Lois Osborne

Carol Outerbridge

Tom Oyston

Mrs Rachael Pankhurst

Andrew Parker

David M. Parnell

Mr Barry George Paynter

Philip, Daphne, Jane, Roger and Jeffery
    Peabody

N.A. Pell

David Penwarden

John Penwarden

Kevin Penwarden

Athelstan Perch

Ann Perreau

Peter Petheram

Ben Phillips

James Phillips

Richard Phillips

S.J. Phillips (Sue Boddy)

Mr C.S. Pickles

Nick Pickles

Ping Lin Law

Ann Poore

Mrs S.C. Powell

Bruno Price

Sam Price

Paul David Pross

Richard George Pullen

Deepa Raval

Meeta Raval

Nicky Reading

John H. Reed

Jon Rolls

James Charles Ross

Georgina Routen

David and Sally Rowley

Jonathan Sackett

Stephen Sanders

In Memoriam Trevor Saunders and
    Frank Commings

Rasmus Schroeder

Menna Searle

Christopher Seaton

Jeremy Sellick

Miss Alexandra Shallish

The Shercliff Family

Nicola Jane Sheringham-Smith

Mr and Mrs M.J. Shiner

T.D. Shorland Ball

Mrs Beryl Siddons

Phillip Simpson

Michael Sinden

Peter Slocombe

Kate Small

Patricia J. Smart

C. and J. Smith

Max Smith

Saphora Smith

Shirley Smith

Tony Smith

Merlin Southwell

Merle Spangenberg

Henry Spencer

Gesine Stegmann

Elizabeth Sternberg (née Fearon)

Michael J. Stirling

Mike Stringer

Kate Suthers

Patrick Suthers

Richard Talbott

William Tamblyn

A. Brian Taylor

Ben Taylor

E. Donald Taylor

Ray Taylor

Wenna Thompson (née Hughes)

Giles Thorman

Rupert R. Thorogood

Rebecca Townsend

Matthew L. Train

Nadia Howard Tripp

Mrs Tudway Quilter

Harriet Tully

Neil Tully

Patrick Tully

Rollo Tully

Rachel Tunley

Joe Urch, Lord of Stowey

Laurens F.H. van der Graaf

Maurits W.R. van der Graaf

Alice Venner

Miss Anna Voisey

Simon Vowles

Peter W. Wade

C. and S. Waelchli

Jo (Besgrove) Walker

Miss Sarah Walker

Lynn and Nigel Walkey

Doug Ward

J.P. Warren

Nigel Warwick-Brown

Daniel Peter Watts

Commander Steven Webber RNR

Mr T.R. Weeks

Dr Claudia Weise

Hannah Wheeler

Mr and Mrs K.J. Wheeler

William Whittle

M.F.W. Willey

Revd A.F Williams

Mr and Mrs M. Willliams

Ann Willis

Mark Wills

Clare Wilson

David Wilson

Michael and Faye Wilson

Nick Wilson

Elaine Winfield

Verity Wingate

Wyndham I.D. Woodburn

Alice Jane Woods

Pat Woods

R.D.J. Orrett and D.J. Woolven-Orrett

Charlotte Wright

D.J. Wright

Jeremy Dixon-Wright

T.G. Wright

Will Wright

Marie Wuerttemberg

Dr Peter Wykes

Jennifer Wylie

Wallace Yip

David A. Young

Iona Zuiderwijk